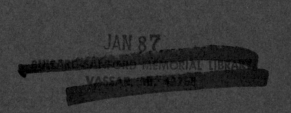

THE AKC'S WORLD OF THE PURE-BRED DOG

The AKC's World of the Pure-Bred Dog

Edited by Duncan Barnes

and the

Staff of The American Kennel Club

HOWELL BOOK HOUSE INC.
230 Park Avenue, New York, N.Y. 10169

ACKNOWLEDGMENTS

To produce a book of this complexity and magnitude has taken more than four years of hard work and exceptional dedication by many people deeply involved with the world of the pure-bred dog in America. Many of those who have contributed to the book have byline chapters; others—who have been equally important in a variety of ways—did essential work behind the scenes and should be singled out for their unstinting help. I welcome the chance to acknowledge and thank warmly those who served this project with special distinction.

WILLIAM F. STIFEL, President of The American Kennel Club, showed unflagging interest in this project. He was central to its original conception, he provided a wealth of valuable ideas, and he always insisted upon the accuracy of even the smallest details. His fine sense of taste and sure judgment, and his abiding love for the pure-bred dog in America, are at the heart of this book.

A. HAMILTON ROWAN, JR., Chairman of AKC's Editorial Committee, has been of inestimable importance to this project. He put his heart and soul into making this book happen, while somehow managing to conduct his regular duties as Director of Field Trials for AKC. Along with acute editorial supervision of every detail in this book—from solicitation of chapters to editing to final layout—Ham also took many of the best photographs. In particular, he photographed all the art in the extensive color section (except as otherwise noted), and he took most of the photographs in the Field Trial and Inside AKC chapters.

PAT BERESFORD, Vice-Chairman of AKC's Editorial Committee, and Editor-in-Chief of the *AKC Gazette*, brought sound counsel to a host of editorial and production matters; her contributions to the special field of Dog Shows, and to questions about the Breeds, were valuable.

ROBERTA VESLEY, Director of AKC's Library, brought keen expertise to all research questions, including (but not limited to) use of the immense resources of the Library. She was crucial to the collection of all photographic and illustrative material used in this book, and gave cheerful help and tasteful advice on all aspects of the book.

ROBERT G. MAXWELL, AKC Controller, served as our firm guide and adviser for all the many financial matters.

CHET FISH, Photographic Editor for this book, brought his many years of magazine and book experience to the task of researching, obtaining, culling, and finally selecting the illustrations that give this book its strong visual presence. His integrity and persistence are everywhere in evidence.

PAT SKUZINSKAS, Ham Rowan's secretary, cheerfully typed (and often retyped) much of the editorial content in this book. In all major projects, there is always a special person who works behind the scene to get the details in order; Pat has been that special person this time.

MARIAN LANE, Administrative Assistant to James Dearinger at AKC, was especially helpful with a variety of issues connected to the important Obedience and Tracking chapter.

TASHA HALL, Production Editor at Nick Lyons Books, provided much help on production matters during the last (often pressured) months before the book came off press.

PETER BURFORD, Editor of Nick Lyons Books, proved perfectly masterful in pulling together all the diverse and often highly complicated elements of this book. He worked closely with AKC's staff at every turn, met key deadlines, and coordinated every aspect of the editing and production of *The AKC's World of the Pure-Bred Dog*.

For permission to reprint selections in "The Dog in Prose" section:

"Lost!"—from *Lad, A Dog* by Albert Payson Terhune. Copyright 1919, 1926, 1947, 1959 by E.P. Dutton & Co. Reprinted by permission of the publisher, E.P. Dutton, Inc. "The Last Will and Testament of an Extremely Distinguished Dog" by Eugene O'Neill—Collection of American Literature, Beinecke Rare Book and Manuscript Library, Yale University. "Every Dog Should Own a Man"—© 1952 by Corey Ford. Reprinted by permission of Harold Ober Associates Incorporated. "Fred"—reprinted by permission of *Field & Stream* and the author. "The Dog That Bit People" by James Thurber—© 1933, 1961 by James Thurber. From *My Life and Hard Times*, published by Harper & Row. "Charley and the Bear"—from *Travels with Charley* by John Steinbeck. © 1961, 1962 by The Curtis Publishing Co., Inc. Copyright © 1962 by John Steinbeck. Reprinted by permission of Viking Penguin Inc. "The Watermen"—from *Chesapeake* by James Michener. Copyright © 1978 by Random House, Inc. Reprinted by permission of Random House, Inc. "Blue and Some other Dogs"—Copyright © 1977 by John Graves. Reprinted from *From a Limestone Ledge* by John Graves by permission of Alfred A. Knopf, Inc., and the author.

—DUNCAN BARNES

Photographs taken by A. Hamilton Rowan, Jr., unless otherwise credited, appear on pages 5 (upper left), 6 (lower left), 11, 23, 30, 35, 52 (lower left), 57, 63, 65 (lower right), 67 (lower right), 75 (lower right), 96 (lower left), 101, 102 (lower left and right), 103 (bottom), 110, 114, 128, 132, 133, 134, 135, 136, 148 (top right and left), 151, 153, 157, 158, 160, 164, 166, 167, 169 (upper right), 170, 171, 172, 173, 175 (lower), 182, 184 (upper left), 185 (lower right and left), 187, 188, 189, 190, 191, 219 (lower left), 330, 333, 334, 335 (lower left and right), 337 (lower left), 339 (upper right); and all color photographs except as credited.

Library of Congress Cataloging in Publication Data
Main entry under title:

The AKC's world of the pure-bred dog.

"Nick Lyons books."
Includes index.
1. Dogs. 2. Dog breeds. 3. Dog shows. 4. Dogs—
United States. 5. Dogs in literature. I. Barnes,
Duncan. II. American Kennel Club. III. Title: A.K.C.'s
world of the pure-bred dog. IV. Title: World of the
pure-bred dog. V. Title: Pure-bred dog.
SF426.A43   1983   636.7   83-6117
ISBN 0-87605-406-8

This book was produced by: Nick Lyons Books,
212 Fifth Avenue, New York, NY 10010

Preface

Welcome to the rich and diverse world of the pure-bred dog! It is a world that includes 125 registrable breeds, the fascinating sport of pure-bred dogs, and the dog in daily life, art, and literature. The American Kennel Club is proud to present this book as part of its One Hundredth Anniversary celebration, and we are hopeful that in its wealth of interesting text and illustrative material you will gain a fuller sense of how wonderful this special world can be.

There are overviews of the seven Groups, a long and colorful depiction of the excitement and drama of dog shows, and a close look at Obedience and Field Trial competitions. For thousands of years, many superb artists have taken the dog as their subject, and you will find in this book a useful survey of the highlights of art that focuses on the dog, along with a full-color section, including items from AKC's own collection of important paintings and sculpture. The dog has also been the principal character in some engaging literature and you're bound to find a new favorite or two among the moving stories in the sampler included here. Finally, there's a vivid glimpse of the inner workings of The American Kennel Club itself, which has seen astonishing growth over the past century yet still strives as its principal objective to preserve and promote the integrity of the pure-bred dog.

Chiefly, we want to share with you—in word and picture—our celebration of the pure-bred dog in America. We think it's an exciting celebration . . . and we hope you do, too.

WILLIAM F. STIFEL
President, The American Kennel Club

CONTENTS

Pointer, English Setter, and Gordon Setter.
Oil on canvas. G. Muss-Arnolt. *AKC Collection*

The Pure-Bred Dog In America

William F. Stifel

If the dog is man's best friend, it is also true that, as the first domestic animal, the dog is man's oldest friend. Remains of the dog have been found together with human artifacts in Iraq, dating back fourteen thousand years, and in the United States traces of a domesticated dog that lived 10,500 years ago have been found in Idaho. In that context, the birth of the American Kennel Club was only a small formal step of recognition for one of mankind's oldest associations. But it was an important step.

Inherent in the concept of domestication is the selection of dogs by traits of appearance and behavior—and the selective breeding of such dogs. From the earliest times, travelers not only took their own dogs with them on trips, but also brought back with them from far-off places new breeds and varieties. The first Europeans brought dogs with them to North America—and they found that Indian tribes on this continent already had dogs of their own.

Probably no one did more than the English to cultivate the domestic dog consciously. John Caius, an English physician, wrote a book in Latin about English dogs in the sixteenth century and described six varieties: sight hounds; scent hounds; water and land Spaniels and Setters; working Terriers and Terriers that were bred for fighting or animal baiting; Mastiffs (which, along with other big breeds, were bred for ferocity and used for protection); and Shepherds (represented today by the various Sheep and Cattle Herding dogs). The only basic group of dogs that Caius did not mention are the sled dogs that were, and still are, used in the far northern countries around the world.

It was not until the mid-nineteenth century, however, that the first recorded dog show was held. This was in Newcastle, England, in 1859. At the same time the showing of dogs in the United States was becoming more and more popular, and at the first Westminster Kennel Club show, in 1877, more than 35 breeds were represented.

As dog shows grew in number, a need was felt for a governing body and, in 1873, the Kennel Club of England was founded. Then, on September 17, 1884, the American Kennel Club was formed. The AKC is the second oldest amateur sport-governing body in the United States, having been started three years after the United States Lawn Tennis Association. At its first meeting, in Philadelphia, a dozen or so men attended, representing dog clubs mainly in the eastern part of America. Their first aim was to set up a uniform code of rules and regulations so that anyone entering a dog in any of their events anywhere in the country would know that he would be competing under equal conditions. In a very real sense, from that moment on, to trace the history of the American Kennel Club is to follow the formal sport of pure-bred dogs in America.

The first President, Major James A. Taylor, described the organization as a "Club of Clubs." It is a good description that still applies today. There is no provision under which individuals can join the AKC—it is an association of clubs. And its structure is quite simple. The voting power of each club is exercised through its elected delegates. The delegates, who meet at regular quarterly meetings, elect a Board of Directors. The Board of Directors in turn elects the officers, and the officers and their executive staff conduct the Club's daily business.

Page one of the minutes of the first meeting of the AKC, September 17, 1884.

Major James A. Taylor,
AKC's first president.

Interior and exterior views of the original Madison Square
Garden on Madison Avenue, site of the first New York dog
show in 1884.

Basic to the entire structure—one of its most vital aspects—is the specification in the by-laws that all delegates must be amateurs. Professional judges of dog events; professional trainers and handlers; a person directly engaged in selling dog food, dog remedies, dog supplies; a person owning a pet store that sells dogs; a person who buys dogs (or litters of dogs) for resale—none of these people is eligible to become or remain an AKC delegate. By definition, the AKC is of, by, and for the amateur.

During its first few years, the AKC did not register dogs or publish a stud book. But it was always clear that such historical and statistical data would be essential to anyone interested in improving a breed. At the time there were two canine registers in the country and, in its third year, the AKC started negotiations to acquire one of them. When the owner of one turned down a reasonable offer, Dr. Nicholas Rowe—who had been publishing the other one out in Chicago—offered to give his stud book to the AKC as a gift. Though Rowe used the name "National American Kennel Club," his venture was purely private. He had published three volumes (starting in 1878), but he understood the importance of such records being in other than private hands.

Shortly after accepting Dr. Rowe's gift, the AKC published Volume IV of the set, and this is the stud book that we still keep today, more than 25 million registration entries after Dog #1 in Volume I, an English Setter named Adonis.

A stud book is the basic reference book of any animal-breeding program. In its original form, the stud book included every dog registered by the AKC. But

"Adonis," an English Setter, the first dog registered in the AKC Stud Book. *New Bedford Standard-Times*

August Belmont, Jr.,
AKC's fourth President.

The New York Life
Building at
51 Madison Avenue,
site of the
present AKC offices.

The original
Madison Square
Garden.

in the late 1940s, because only some of the registered dogs were subsequently used for breeding, it was decided not to publish any dog until it had produced a litter and that litter had been registered. At that point the dog would be published in what is now called the *Stud Book Register*. Publication basically means publication of the dog's name, followed by the names of its sire and dam, together with a reference to the earlier volume of the stud book in which a comparable listing had been published for each of them.

It is thus possible to trace back through any number of generations the background of any dog in our files.

In 1889 the AKC took on a third basic function: publication of the *Gazette*. August Belmont, Jr., had been elected AKC President the year before; it was under his guidance that the magazine (now the oldest dog magazine in the country) first appeared. As originally conceived, it was to be the official organ for disseminating AKC business and communications to clubs and their delegates.

The first issue was 20 pages long, and carried a dog food ad on the cover. The list of new champions of record included 94 dogs of 15 different breeds. Eleven coming events appeared under "Fixtures". The issue contained the minutes of the previous meeting of the delegates, some new Dog Show rules, and a new breed standard for the Gordon Setter. It also included the results of one dog show. The price was 20 cents.

By the end of 1980, the sport of showing dogs had grown to such an extent that the results of 506 events were given in Show Awards. In January of 1981, the show Award section was taken out of the *Gazette*, and it is now issued as a separate publication.

In the *Gazette* itself, the Secretary's Page is still of basic importance. It carries names of clubs applying for membership, names of delegate candidates, notices of disciplinary action, board policies, proposed rule changes and amendments to breed standards, the names of persons seeking approval to become dog show judges, and the names of dogs that have acquired Championship or other titles.

The editorial content has been greatly broadened to reach new people coming into the sport—without neglecting the interests of those who are already well established. Articles about Junior Showmanship are written by juniors and former juniors themselves. Canine legislation across the country, as well as dog health and research on canine medical problems, is covered regularly. There are articles on guide dogs, hearing dogs, dogs that are of service to man and the community—and articles on what man can do for the dog, to serve this animal that serves him so well. Features and articles cover the whole spectrum of activities that make the local dog club a true service organization of the community in which it functions.

FIRST CHAMPION OF RECORD

On November 21, 1910, Championship Certificate No. 1 was issued to a Beagle named Sir Novice.

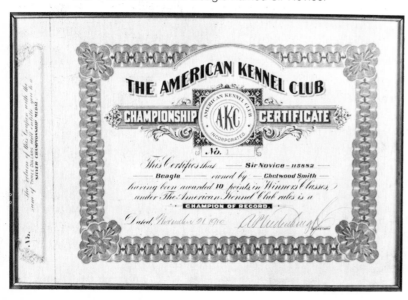

Note that the Championship Certificate bore a coupon, which, when returned to the AKC with the sum of three dollars, entitled the dog's owner to a Silver Championship Medal.

The Pure-Bred Dog in America

In 1908, at the age of 24, the AKC decided to incorporate. Its official purposes were (as they still appear in the forewords of our various rule books):

To adopt and enforce rules for dog events;

To regulate the conduct of persons who take part in these events or who breed or register or buy or sell dogs;

To detect, prevent, and punish fraud in connection with such activities;

To publish a Stud Book;

To publish a *Gazette*; and

Generally to do everything to advance the study, breeding, exhibiting, running, and maintenance of the purity of thoroughbred dogs.

After the first meeting in Philadelphia, meetings were held in other cities (Cincinnati, Boston, Newark, and New York), but the AKC had no permanent headquarters until 1887 when the organization moved to 44 Broadway in the Wall Street district of Manhattan. The first AKC residence was a single room. It was a very small room, only 15 by 20 feet.

The second and third offices at 55 Liberty Street and 1 Liberty Street were also in the Wall Street area—and they were not a great deal bigger than the first.

These three addresses (which take us to 1919) saw the organization through its formative years. The AKC took on functions that seem so basic now that we usually think of them as never having had a true beginning.

We started to register dogs imported to the United States from other countries. We started to explore relationships with registry bodies in such other countries as Canada and England. We set down a list of breeds that were eligible for registration in the Stud Book and decreed that the list could only be changed by formal action of the Club. The West Coast was not hours but days away then, so we set up a West Coast Advisory Committee that worked to improve our relationship with the then-remote part of the country. In 1898 we hired an editor whose job it was to make the *Gazette* more readable, with a broader educational base. In 1902 we installed our first telephone. That, some members of the staff still say, may be the worst mistake we ever made—but in fact our telephone-inquiry department is now one of the most important and useful links with the dog public.

Meanwhile, the rules were evolving—to the extent that as early as 1898 an editorial in the *Gazette* began: "From time to time one hears it said that AKC has never done tinkering at the rules and that it is impossible to keep track of the many changes."

The changes were not all that numerous, but one of them called for championships to be awarded on the basis of accumulated championship points, with the number of points to be awarded in any particular competition to depend on the number of dogs in competition. This was the beginning of Winners Class judging as we now know it.

In 1919, with 116 member clubs, eight paid employees, and 17,000 registrations for the year, the AKC moved to its fourth address; we were to stay on Fourth Avenue for over 44 years—so long that eventually the street number, 221, became virtually synonymous with the letters *AKC*.

MAN'S OLDEST FRIEND

A canine jaw and teeth that were dug from a cave site in Iraq in 1975 have now established that man's relation with a domesticated dog began at least 14,000 years ago. Until then, the oldest known example of a domesticated dog came from jaw fragments (*shown*) found in an Idaho excavation site, which, from radiocarbon dating techniques by the Idaho State University Museum, were determined to be some 10,500 years old.

Most authorities agree that dogs (*Canis familiaris*) were domesticated from wolves (*Canis lupus*). From the comparatively softer life given to domesticated wolves by early man evolved a dog/wolf possessing a uniquely refined facial expression. Scientists have determined that the earliest fossilized jaw specimens of domestic dogs, when compared to those of pre-historic wolves, show smaller over-all teeth with weaker root development, and a smaller distance between the alveolar border (gum line) and the zygomatic arch (cheek bone). That the skeletal remains of this ancient, doglike animal were often found alongside those of his human masters, to the complete exclusion of wolf remains in any era, hypothecated a dog/man relationship and the scientific dawn of *Canis familiaris*.

Then, as now, *Canis lupus* remained the "big, bad wolf."

IDAHO MUSEUM OF NATURAL HISTORY

Cover of the first *American Kennel Gazette*,
January 1889.

PURE-BRED DOGS
AMERICAN KENNEL
GAZETTE

DECEMBER, 1979/$2.50

1979

1941

The AMERICAN
KENNEL GAZETTE

Vol. 58, No. 10
Per Year $4

October 1941
Per Copy 50 Cents

1957

THE AMERICAN
KENNEL CLUB
Registration Dep't.

PURE-BRED
DOGS

AMERICAN KENNEL GAZETTE

"PEACE ON EARTH"

SCIENCE
HAS A NEW LOOK
AT BEHAVIOR

"CHRISTMAS PUP"

OLDSTERS
ALSO HAVE NEED
FOR DOGS

CHRISTMAS
PUPPIES' CARE
IS A MUST

DON'T
NEGLECT TO CURB
YOUR DOG

CH. HELKA ELLENBERT
(Dachshund)
Owned by
ELLENBERT FARM
Mr. and Mrs. Herbert Bertrand
Greenwich, Connecticut

Y by the AMERICAN KENNEL CLUB

THE AMERICAN
KENNEL
GAZETTE

GOLDEN
JUBILEE
NUMBER

1939

PURE-BRED DOGS
AMERICAN KENNEL
GAZETTE

PURE-BRED DOGS
AMERICAN KENNEL
GAZETTE

SEPTEMBER, 1973

ONE DOLLAR

1981

Gazette cover designs,
1939–1981.

1973

Mr. and Mrs. S. S. Van Dine with their Scottish Terrier, "Jocko."

S. S. Van Dine's "Miss Mac Tavish" drawn by Marguerite Kirmse.

This was the beginning of an era of unprecedented growth and expansion in the sport of pure-bred dogs. One of the most dramatic signs of this at the Club was a completely unforeseen increase in the registration of German Shepherd Dogs, probably because of the publicity that the breed received following World War I. By 1933 the sport in general and our reputation as a registration body in particular were such that S. S. Van Dine could write a murder-mystery book in which the principal clues were provided by a runaway Scottish Terrier.

The book is the famous *The Kennel Murder Case.*

Although the Scottish Terrier wore no collar or identification, the great Philo Vance immediately recognized the dog as a show dog, of good quality and in top show condition. Where else should Vance go but to the offices of the AKC at 221? There, among the meticulous records that the AKC keeps for shows and registration, Vance identified the Scottie as "Miss MacTavish"—and was thus able to get the first clue that led to his identification of the killer. The *Gazette* carried a picture of Miss MacTavish drawn by Marguerite Kirmse, the noted artist who illustrated many articles for the *Gazette.*

S. S. Van Dine was himself an active breeder and exhibitor of Scotties; he had his Philo Vance say that the AKC was "an entire institution based on the ideal of accuracy. It has no commodity to sell—it sells only accuracy and protection to the many thousands of sportsmen and dog lovers throughout the country."

In 1929 the first edition of what we now call *The Complete Dog Book* appeared. Under AKC by-laws, one of the duties of each national parent specialty club is to write the standard for its breed: a description of an ideal specimen of the breed, a "word pattern" against which the dog is to be judged in the ring. Our new publication brought all of these standards together for the first time into a single book.

In 1934 the AKC Library was officially begun. Three sections of bookshelves were built into a wall at one end of what was then called the "Club Room," and the books that had been in a bookcase in the *Gazette* office were transferred to these shelves. A modest beginning. Today, the AKC Library has grown into a collection of over 15,000 volumes. Its cornerstone is the AKC Stud Books and the complete set of AKC *Gazettes*. But the library includes the stud books and publications of other registry bodies all over the world; general books on dogs; books on individual breeds; books on hunting, on the care of dogs, on breeding, kennel management, canine medicine, anatomy and gait, training, dogs as pets and companions, dog law, and dogs in art. There is a particularly large literary section that contains books of anecdotes about dogs, true stories of dogs, fiction, poetry, essays, tributes and eulogies, and children's books.

There are other important dates.

-In 1936 the first obedience trial was held, an activity that introduced thousands of new people to the sport of dogs—and promoted the concept that dogs ought to become "good citizens."

In 1945 the position of Dog Show Field Representative was established. The Field Reps attend AKC events as observers. Since the 1970s, there have been as many as 15 or 20 on the staff at one time.

In 1953 the AKC produced a movie entitled *221*, which was the story of "What happens—and why it happens—at the headquarters of AKC." This was followed by a second movie, *Dog Shows and You*, the story of what happens at a dog show and why. It even included a full-fledged Bench Show Committee hearing at which a disgruntled exhibitor is suspended from all privileges after verbally abusing a judge. The disgruntled exhibitor is played by the only professional actor in the cast.

Ram's head over the entrance of 221 Park Avenue South, New York City.

First published in 1929 with the title *Pure-Bred Dogs*, *The Complete Dog Book* has gone through sixteen editions.

In 1954 *The New Yorker* published a two-part profile of the AKC by E. J. Kahn. The building at 221 was the American Woolen Building and, as Kahn said, it was "festooned inside and out with sculptured rams' heads"—the symbol of the woolen industry. The description of the AKC foyer, into which one stepped directly from the elevators, was strikingly accurate: There were high ceilings, dark walls, heavy carpets, and "it was lined with so many dozens of individually lighted portraits of dogs that the room resembles an art gallery."

The only jarring note, according to Kahn, was the drinking fountain: another sculptured ram's head "with water spewing from the ram's mouth." It wasn't a dog. That seemed to bother him. Something else might have troubled him, too, because one senses his vague feeling of frustration. He was writing about a sport in which thousands and thousands of people were competing each year. He could give facts and figures that were absolutely astounding. He deftly told stories that were funny at the expense of the dog lover. But he confessed to members of the AKC staff that there was one thing he had not found; he had not found a good scandal. A good scandal would have given his story a nice sense of unity. In a grudging way, Kahn was paying the sport of pure-bred dogs one of its finest compliments.

In 1964 we ran out of space. When we moved into 221 in 1919, the bound volumes of the show catalogs for that year took up exactly one foot of shelf space. In 1964, when we moved out, the show catalogs for the final year occupied 16 feet. During that time our staff had grown from eight paid employees to over 300.

We moved to 51 Madison Avenue, our present address, the New York Life Building. We are on the site of the original Madison Square Garden, when Madison Square Garden was actually on Madison Square. And that, by pure and happy coincidence, was the site of the first New York dog show held in 1884 after the founding of the American Kennel Club.

AKC's one-millionth registered dog, a Shetland Sheepdog, "Sheltieland Alice Grey Gown," registered in 1935. AKC President Russell Johnson, Jr. and Miss Caroline Edwards Coleman hold the registration certificate.

The ten-millionth registered dog,
"Eddie's Ginger," a Golden Retriever,
registered in 1966,
with its owner and
AKC President William Buckley.
Edward Ozern

The twenty-fifth-millionth registered dog, "Belair's Duke of Rock
Hills," a Scottish Terrier, registered 1981. *Richmond Newspapers,
Inc., Gary Burns*

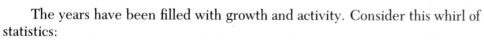

The years have been filled with growth and activity. Consider this whirl of
statistics:

In 1935, at the end of the first 57 years after publication of Volume 1 of our
Stud Book, we registered our one millionth dog; it had taken 57 years to register
a million dogs.

At the end of the next decade, 1945, we registered our two millionth dog.

At the end of the next decade, 1956, we registered our five millionth dog,
and ten years later we registered our ten millionth. 1981 saw the registration of
our 25 millionth dog.

So the time of our centennial celebration is also a time of unprecedented
activity in the world of the pure-bred dog. The American Kennel Club has
successfully supervised serious American interest in dogs from the day when
few people had dogs and almost no one showed them until today when there are
pure-bred dogs in perhaps 15 million homes, and hundreds of thousands of
people participate in the sport. There are nearly 10,000 licensed and sanctioned
dog shows, obedience trials, and field trials held under American Kennel Club
Rules each year—more than two dozen for every day of the year, with more
than two million entries.

This book is our attempt to share the diversity and richness of the world of
the pure-bred dog—the groups, the sport of dogs, the dog in art and literature.
We hope you enjoy this celebration of the pure-bred dog in America.

Five-millionth registered dog, a
Collie, "Lassie The Golden
Glory," registered in 1956.

PART ONE

The Groups

SPORTING GROUP   2   1

Previous page: The seven Group winners compete for Best in Show. *Callea Photo*

Sporting Group finalists at a California show.

1
The Sporting Group

C. Bede Maxwell

The American Kennel Club's Stud Book was born with listings of Sporting dogs in 1878, and the Sporting breeds have been batting leadoff in show catalogs and stud registers ever since. ¶ The Sporting Group includes 24 breeds, all of them developed for hunting feathered game. Sporting dogs are grouped by function—that is, how they hunt. There are Spaniels, Pointers, Setters, Retrievers, and the European Sporting Utility breeds. But in truth, each of the Sporting breeds is well equipped to perform all the functions of a good bird hunter.

Spaniels

Although his shape and size were subject to happenstance and fashion down through the centuries, the Field Spaniel is the basis for modern Spaniels. He was the jack-of-all-trades Spaniel, the very embodiment of true Spaniel working characteristics. He was a flushing, not a setting, Spaniel and has remained so through the years. At any reasonable guess he is the heir to the British as opposed to the European type of Spaniel—sturdy, compact, and a font of energy. His influence was imposed on most other Spaniels, and his most important spinoff was the Cocking or Cocker Spaniel, built up from those Field Spaniels that tended toward the diminutive.

In the dog show classifications of the nineteenth century, the rule of thumb that divided Field and Cocker Spaniels was weight. A Land Spaniel over a

17

18

One of the most popular breeds for many years, the Cocker Spaniel has gone through changes in type and coat in the past fifty years. Note the taller appearance and sparse coat of the early Cocker *(left)* as compared with this 1980 particolor. His coat alone would hinder him in the field.

certain weight was a Field; under that weight, a Cocker. Many a Cocker puppy in maturity had to be named a Field. Many Field Spaniels came to America; they have been on the AKC registry rolls since 1894. But this plain Spaniel, with no exaggerations and a head described as noble, has remained at zero in popularity.

That breed popularity *can* be recaptured has a strong witness in the American Cocker Spaniel. ("American" is not part of his official AKC title, but he has become as American as apple pie and is so identified throughout the world.) The Cocker today is second only to the Poodle in breed popularity in the United States and seems well on the way to regaining the number one position he held for over a decade until 1955.

Cocker Spaniels are said to have come to America on the *Mayflower*. True or not, Spaniels were crossing the Atlantic for centuries, representing all the breeds that Britain had in supply, from Toys through Fields, from Cockers to Welsh Springers. Not till the present century did there come to be a fostering of the type designed to be wholly American, and decades had to pass before it became stabilized. As in the case of all newly formed breeds, the ingredients came from the various Spaniels that were available.

It is obvious that the breeds we know today as the Cocker Spaniel and the English Cocker Spaniel were one and the same until after World War I when breeders increasingly selected for differing types. The Cocker became smaller, with a more profuse coat, a much shorter head, and a more domed skull. Both breeds come in a profusion of colors. Cocker Spaniels, perhaps in part because of the choice of colors but certainly because of their personalities (they are happy, alert, and willing family companions), became one of the most popular breeds in the United States, both as pets and show dogs.

Cockers were being shown in such numbers at the time of World War II that it was decided to divide them into three varieties by coat color for show purposes. The three varieties are *Black* (including Black and Tan), *ASCOB* (any solid color other than black), and *Parti-Color*. Cocker popularity declined significantly from 1955 until the 1970s, when the breed's natural attributes (except for hunting) again took it to the top of the popularity chart.

The English Cocker Spaniel Club of America was founded in 1935, largely through the support of Mrs. M. Hartley Dodge of Morris and Essex fame. In 1946 the AKC recognized the breed for show purposes, and the first separate English Cocker Spaniel registrations were recorded in the January 1947 Stud Book. Although the English Cocker Spaniel has not had the mass popularity of the American, the breed has enjoyed a steady growth in the United States. English Cockers possess the attributes of their American cousins—they are personable, alert, outgoing, easily maintained, and great companion animals.

Spaniels recognizable as Clumbers have been in the United States since before the AKC was founded; indeed, the American Spaniel Club actually predates the AKC. Clumbers were among the breeds recorded in Dr. Nicholas Rowe's 1878 stud book, which subsequently became volume one of AKC's Stud Book. At the turn of the century, the Clumber was the dog to beat in Spaniel field trials in England. This long, low, heavy-boned, massively headed dog—the largest Spaniel—was a favorite of British royalty, including King Edward

Clumber Spaniel. *Missy Yuhl*

English Cocker Spaniel.
John Ashbey

VII and King George V. His distinctive lemon- or orange-ticked white coat and easygoing manner would seem to mark him for greater popularity than he has enjoyed, and interest in the breed has increased significantly in recent years.

One has to be in England to see the Sussex Spaniel, and no one with interest in Sporting breeds should be in England and not budget time to see him. The best specimens still conform to the summing-up of Vero Shaw in his *Illustrated Book of the Dog, 1890:* "Sussex have earned a place of honor in any book of dogs; never common, but always held in great esteem, with a beauty of outline and the golden color that is so exceptional and of such value in covert shooting."

In Britain the Sussex was never favored for use on driven game but rather as a dog to beat out game where pace is less important. Which may help explain why, although he has been in America since the very first AKC registrations, he has not caught on in this country until recently.

In the early days (the nineteenth century) of dog showing, the Springers, known then as Norfolks, made the most trouble for those attempting to classify Spaniels. They were taller than other Land Spaniels, with a multiplicity of jacketings from close to curly. In 1902, when English and Welsh Springers were first given recognition as separate breeds by the Kennel Club (England), registration was on the basis of appearance. If a dog was red and white, generally he was Welsh; if liver and white, he was English.

Though English Springer Spaniels were registered by the AKC as early as 1910, it was during the 1920s that real interest in the breed began. The first conformation Specialty was held in 1922 and, soon after, the English Springer Field Trial Association of America became a member club of the AKC. This parent club for the breed was formed by sportsmen who ran their dogs in a field trial one day and then combed out the burrs and showed them in conformation the next day.

Fanciers continued to run and show their dogs successfully into the 1930s. But then show and field interests divided, and the dual pursuit became a thing of the past. Despite the division, the Springer remains a breed fully capable of hunting, and while a beautiful coat is desirable in the show ring, over-exaggeration of feather is not. The show English Springer has become one of the world's most attractive dog breeds.

If ancient status can be claimed for a Land Spaniel working the "springing" or flushing pattern, it might possibly be more accurately claimed for the Welsh Springer rather than the English Springer. Caius (1550) recorded that most of the Land Spaniels of his time were patterned in red-and-white patchings, and the association of red-and-white Spaniels with the ancient Celtic migratory people has been historically established. To this day, the Welshie, or Starter as he is also known, breeds 100 percent true to his Celtic color inheritance and is accepted in no other.

A hard, useful hunting dog, there is no discernible type gap between the show and the working Welshie. As a lower-stationed dog, he is often superficially described as "long-bodied." This is optical illusion and poor judgment and lacks the support of the standard. Although his original endowment of hazel eyes and flesh-colored nose have been darkened by modern crossings used to "pretty" him up for the shows, his distinctive shallow-flewed head has been preserved in the seclusion of the Welsh valleys.

English Springer Spaniel.
William Gilbert

Irish Water Spaniel Puppies. *Ludwig*

The increasing popularity of the little American Water Spaniel may astonish show-oriented folk, many of whom have never set eyes on one. As American-made as the Boston Terrier, the American Cocker, or the Chesapeake Bay Retriever, superficially he will remind some of an Irish Water Spaniel, but he is poles apart from the bigger fellow in all but color and a curled coat. His main sponsorship has always been in the Midwest where so many Sporting breeds received their early bolsterings. His type was not always exactly constant, but the predominant features survived the generations. His size has sometimes varied, but he was never a big dog. His useful versatility has been greatly valued, and the tight marcel effect of his brownish liver jacketing is recognized as his badge.

He is all Spaniel and has no oddities of build or coat pattern. The breed character is fully Spaniel in its charm, and he is easy to train. Importantly, such a pocket-size dog, whose earliest value included the minimal space he took up in a skiff and the minimal commotion he caused when he dove from the skiff after a downed duck, could win much favor in our ever-shrinking world.

The Pointer

The Pointer is the towering giant of modern Sporting breed history. He has been used in his own person and to help in the formation or improvement of many breeds. He has been siphoned into Setter strains and into retrieving breeds, and he strongly influenced the development of the German Shorthair and the Hungarian Vizsla.

"Spanish Pointer" came into England as a name for a dog that seems to have been introduced in the eighteenth century, but there is no documentation of the long-held belief he originated in Spain. He came with two great gifts—patience to stand to game and a magnificent nose.

Despite his present classification in the Sporting Group, the Pointer is a hound. However, he is within hound classification entirely unique in his classical endowments of work pattern and the duetted signature: his head and tail. The Pointer head is all roundnesses of Norman arch plus a prominent stop. The classic breed tail is thick at base, short, and bee-sting tipped.

It is unfortunate that even distinguished breeders have never bestirred themselves to make Dual Champions. AKC registrations in show stock have plummeted, although field trial breeding is prolific. It seems reasonable to believe that the world will never lack Pointers, and while not all countries agree as to type, the ancient heritage remains: A Pointer is a Pointer.

The Brittany

Few breeds have vaulted into popularity at such an astonishing rate as the Brittany. As late as 1927, the writings of even so distinguished a bird dog journalist as A. F. Hochwald made no reference to this small pointing breed out of France. His mention of the man eventually responsible for the introduction

Eighteenth-century painting illustrates a pointer in setting posture in foreground, while the other dogs stand high to honor the point.

and promotion of the Brittany here, Louis A. Thebaud, was merely in connection with Wirehaired Pointing Griffons—an earlier enthusiasm of Mr. Thebaud's. The Brittany was accepted for AKC registration in 1934. In 1982, it stood twentieth in popularity of all breeds, with more than 17,000 registrations each year.

The 1982 decision to drop the Spaniel designation from the Brittany's name was a sensible one. The parent club has long recognized that the Brittany is more a pointing breed than a flushing breed and identifies itself simply as the American Brittany Club.

The Brittany has been targeted as the dog for the modest, but keen, sportsman whose one dog will hunt grouse, woodcock, pheasants, quail, and chukars for him all day, every day. The American Brittany Club sponsors such an aim, as well as the ideal of the Dual Champion, and is proud of the more than 200 Dual Championships that owners have earned, more than any other breed.

The Brittany is celebrated for his good disposition. Though his standard describes him as leggy, his basic shaping is square, with body length matching a height of 17½ inches to 20½ inches. Of ancient Celtic fostering, his coat is orange or liver patched. Some are born tailless and those born with tails are docked. If more than four inches are left, the dog is disqualified from the show ring.

The Setters

Anatomical "experts" who provide a single skeletal drawing to cover all three of the varieties of Setters—English, Irish, and Gordon—do no one a service. Each is, in its own right, a distinctive breed, differing in heritage, habit, and anatomy.

Ancient writings and medieval tapestries establish the long existence of the dog the French knew as a Coucher and that Johannes Caius, the Elizabethan, identified as Index, the Setter. We know it specifically as the English Setter. The distinctive work pattern that gave the breed its name has been described as far back as the time of de Foix, in the fourteenth century.

The English Setter as we know it today in America was developed out of the kennels of two nineteenth-century English breeders—Edward Laverack and R. L. Purcell Llewellin. The earlier imported Laveracks possessed in full measure the beauty that Laverack valued highly. They were useful hunters, but they lacked the speed of the later-introduced Llewellin strain. Although founded on Laverack bitches, the Llewellin type was radically different. They became a great success in field trials on into the early decades of this century.

As with the Pointer, show and field trial English Setters march to different drums. The show English Setter has enjoyed considerable success in the ring, but there is no call for the making of Dual Champions.

The origin of the Irish Setter is virtually undocumented. Some prefer to believe that the breed was sprung fully formed from among the shamrocks, but history yields no such proof. Inevitably, researchers grasp after the red-and-white Celtic Spaniels, of which the Welsh Springer Spaniel is the modern example. Red-and-white Irish Setters predominated before the tide of fashion

Opposite: Brittanys. *Evelyn Shafer*

English Setter.

declared for solid reds. In his construction and working character the Irish Setter is also a hound, but he has the red-and-white Spaniel's shallower-flewed muzzle and he has a handsome coat that is more Spaniel than hound.

The Irisher was the most popular nineteenth-century hunting dog and did well in field trials when these were judged on field and bird work. He pleased the ordinary hunter, was pictorially pretty at stance, lofty and merrily lashing his tail, a sight much enjoyed in those days. What happened was the coming of the Llewellin English Setters, whose speed he could not match.

But while the field trial people discarded him, the show people set high store by the Irish Setter's beauty and waving tail. They sheltered, fed, bred, and showed him. More important, they preserved him as a recognized breed that is today by far the most popular of the Setters. At home he plays with the kids. On the weekend he goes off to the field trial or fun match or alternately to the show ring. In cultivating all aspects of dog excellence, performance, companionability, good looks, and prepotency, fanciers are doing very well indeed by the Irish Setter.

The fourth Duke of Gordon, now more than a century and a half gone to his rest, gave the handsome black-and-tan Gordon Setter the name by which it is everywhere known. However, that is not to say that the Duke actually originated a race of Setters. Black-and-tans had been known for centuries before his time. The Duke favored the color because he could see it easily on his Scottish hillsides.

A brace of the Duke's Gordons was imported to America by Daniel Webster and George Blunt in 1842, and the breed won early popularity here as a pet and gundog. He has been in the AKC Stud Books from the beginning. With the coming of field trial competition and its emphasis on "horizon runners," Gordon popularity waned. As his standard frankly states, "He suggests strength and stamina rather than extreme speed." The Gordon does not have a vast following in the United States, but his devotees are dedicated.

Laverack-type English Setter.

Irish Setters,
1938.

The Retrievers

As far back as Elizabethan times, Johannes Caius was identifying curly coated "Water Dogges" by the name of *Aquaticus feu inquisitor*, the Water Spaniel or "Fynder." The "Dogge" was efficient, playful, "bringing our Boultes and Arrowes out of the Water, which otherwise we could hardly recover, and often they restore to us our Shaftes which we thought never to see, touch or handle again."

One cannot but be impressed by the ever-growing popularity of the Labrador and Golden Retrievers. This public acceptance reflects far more than the fact that they are both superb practical working retrievers. For every Lab or Golden that competes, there are thousands that have never set foot in a trial area. Even those that are actually acquired for practical hunting can be more than matched by those whose owners merely want to have a nice dog around.

Most dog people believe the Labrador Retriever had its origins on this continent and was shaped in England. It is the type as crystalized in England that world (including present-day America) standards have accepted. The Labrador was first recognized by the Kennel Club (England) in 1903 and by the AKC in 1917.

Labradors are accepted in three colors: black, yellow (from Fox red to light cream), and chocolate. (In other breeds chocolate might be called liver.) Both English and American standards ask for a coat that is short, dense, and without wave and gives a hard feeling to the hand. The American standard does not include the important requirement made by the English for a "weather-resisting undercoat."

Apart from his superb retrieving abilities, the Labrador is one of the most versatile of dogs. He is today the favored guide dog for the blind. He also serves the army, and he is being used worldwide for sniffing out drugs and explosives.

The Golden is one of the breeds shaped in the last half of the nineteenth century, a period rich in dog yield. He was developed in the kennels of Lord Tweedmouth in Scotland. The Golden has much going for him. He is not only good-looking and well dispositioned; he is also blessed with a jacketing that needs no professional trimming. A bath and a brush will take him anywhere. It is particularly gratifying to pet owners to observe the wonderful "self-cleaning" qualities of the Golden coat. If his owner's interest is in practical matters, the Golden can handle waterfowl superbly and upland game extremely well. He is eye-catching in the show ring, and in the Obedience ring, he has become number one, a dog apart. He outshines all in numbers of Obedience titles won, and, significantly, when in the late 1970s, the AKC introduced the title of Obedience Champion, the first three winners were Goldens.

Work qualities of the Golden are well proved. There is a fine list of Dual Champions, and there might well be more if the numerical strength of the Labradors had been less overwhelming. What is more, the working Golden and the show Golden are one in type, their activities interchangeable, venue to venue, a position as unique as it is satisfactory within the Sporting breeds classification.

The Flat-Coated Retriever (known in earlier days as the Wavy-Coated Retriever) was formed by crossings of British Setters with transatlantic imports. Virtually all Flat-Coats are in the hands of owners that use them in a practical

Labrador Retriever. *Thomas C. Pollock*

Golden Retriever. *Frederick C. Walker*

Flat-Coated Retriever.

Curly-Coated Retriever.

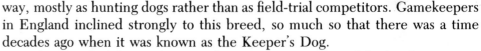

way, mostly as hunting dogs rather than as field-trial competitors. Gamekeepers in England inclined strongly to this breed, so much so that there was a time decades ago when it was known as the Keeper's Dog.

The origin of the Curly-Coated Retriever is questionable, but he is popularly believed to be descended from the sixteenth-century English Water Spaniel and from the retrieving Setter. Some maintain the Irish Water Spaniel was his ancestor, and it is more than probable that a cross was made with this Spaniel from time to time, the liver color being a recognized color for the Curly as well as black. Many assert that the Curly Retriever is temperamentally easy to train. He is affectionate, enduring, hardy, and will practically live in the water. Moreover, his thick coat enables him to face the most punishing covert. He is a charming and faithful companion and an excellent guard.

Chesapeake Bay Retriever. *Evelyn Shafer*

While some of the curly-coated Retriever breeds saw their popular support completely lost as the supply of ducks dwindled in North America, the Chesapeake Bay Retriever has continued to win approval. He is firmly in the upper half of popular breeds, and he is climbing. Several factors have contributed to this. He has dedicated breeders to produce him. He has adaptability. He is strong and sturdy, possessed of temperament qualities that discourage any who might take liberties where he guards. He is a topnotch retriever.

As his name identifies, the Chessie was born in the eastern United States. Breed formation appears to have been casual and extended over almost two centuries. How well Chesapeake Bay hunters shaped this breed to their needs is revealed in some of the wording of the current breed standard: ". . . A Chesapeake's coat should resist the water in the same way a duck's feathers do. When he leaves the water and shakes himself, the coat should not hold the water at all, being merely moist. The color must be as nearly that of his surroundings as possible and with the fact that dogs are exposed to all kinds of adverse weather conditions, often working in ice and snow, the color of coat and its texture must be given every consideration."

Exercising author's privilege, the Irish Water Spaniel is here classified with the Retrievers. Long ears he does have, but his occupational leanings are not Spaniel. Nor is his temperament, his tail, or his coat pattern, with its topknot and the all-round clothing on his forelegs. He does not cross successfully with any breed in the Sporting Group, as his original promoter in early nineteenth-century Ireland, Justin McCarthy, warned in an article in *The Field* over a century ago. McCarthy was a rare close-mouthed Irishman, not to be matched for keeping secrets to himself. So no one ever knew how he formed his breed— whether he resuscitated something ancient in Ireland, or whether he implemented some radical cross, and, if so, with what.

Irish Water Spaniel registrations in any country now are few. But over recent years, there have been some standout wins in the show ring, the most notable of which was the Best in Show at Westminster in 1979 by the delightful extrovert, Ch. Oak Tree's Irishtocrat.

The European Sporting Utility Breeds

The first thing to say of the European sporting utility breeds, which include the German Shorthaired Pointer, the German Wirehaired Pointer, the Vizsla, the Weimaraner, and the Wirehaired Pointing Griffon, is that they were originally and specifically formed, developed, and stabilized by their breeders to be able to discharge *all* aspects of hunting dog activity. In other words, they were to be completely versatile on land and in water and in tracking.

When these breeds were introduced to America, there was no slot in which to file them. There were "Bird-Dogs" here, there were Spaniels, and there were Retrievers. The European dog was none of these, and yet, paradoxically, he was *all* of them. He was a Bird-Dog, though never a horizon runner. He was a Retriever, though nonslip work was not his accustomed style. The awkward truth is that he was exactly what European breeders have made him—a dog of all skills for a hunting man to use and value.

It has been the unvarying record of the German Shorthaired Pointer that he has quickly gone ahead in public favor wherever he has been introduced. Although his American history dates only from the importations of Dr. Charles Thornton of Montana in the 1920s (first registration of the breed was in 1930), he is the most popular of the European sporting utility breeds.

German Shorthaired Pointer.
Bob Greaves

The Shorthair was fashioned in Germany in the second half of the nineteenth century. He is a dog with which an owner can expect to have sport. The ingrained versatility is remarkable; what an owner requires of his dog, it is genetically endowed to provide. Over a hundred Dual Champions have been made in the breed, reflecting the ideal of maintaining proper conformation with proper working spirit. And it should not be overlooked that the Duals attaining their show title first outnumber those that gained their field title first by nearly two to one, bringing to mind the old admonition: "A working dog you can make. A show dog you first have to breed."

The German Wirehaired Pointer was the last formed of the Germanic sporting utility breeds, and the Deutsch-Drahthaar, as the breed is known in Germany, is the most popular sporting breed in Germany today. Coat has always been emphasized in the development of the breed. He is designed to be an all-weather as well as an all-purpose dog, able to negotiate underbrush that would punish severely any dog not so characteristically armored. The coat is weather-resistant and, to a large extent, water-repellent. The undercoat is dense enough in winter to insulate against the cold but so thin in summer as to be almost invisible.

Chronologically the oldest of the European sporting utility breeds introduced to America, the Weimaraner may have had it hardest here because of the need to outlive his disastrous early promotion as a "Wonder Dog."

Known as the "Grey One," the Weimaraner was around for centuries before the rich-dog productive last quarter of the nineteenth century in Germany, and he differs radically from the dogs developed in that period in that he has no English Pointer infusion in his origins. Capable of all manner of hunting chores, including water work at which he is so good, he could and still can do modest bird work whenever such is required of him. But he has always been most used as a tracking hound.

The Weimaraner is a big dog (25–27 inches for males, 23–25 inches for bitches), different in shape and make, including underline and heavier bone, from the Shorthair or Vizsla. He was first brought to America by Harold Knight in 1929, but the initial brace proved sterile. Almost a decade later, as war clouds gathered over Europe, Mr. Knight was luckier, securing fresh, uncut dogs of which the bitch, Aura v. Gaiberg, proved to possess a prepotency that has endured down through the generations. The Weimaraner Club of America was formed in 1941, and the breed accepted for registration in 1943.

The Wirehaired Pointing Griffon was the first of the European sporting utility breeds introduced in the United States. Zolette, the first Wirehaired Pointing Griffon registered by the AKC (in 1888), was classed originally as a "Russian Setter." The standard identifies him as a dog of medium size, rather a little low on his legs, of unkempt appearance (not withstanding his short coat, harsh like the bristles of a wild boar), and with "a very intelligent air." Though few Griffons see the show ring, there is wide dispersal across the country, and those who favor them do so with enthusiasm.

The development of national dog breeds is linked with the fortunes of the nations that sponsor them. Thus, the Vizsla, the beautiful golden Pointer of Hungary, has endured periods of peace and war, surviving the sweep of invaders and the results of his people's taking the wrong side when great nations

Weimaraner. *L. M. Tomme*

quarreled. It was stabilized as a breed in the nineteenth century with the help of professional gamekeepers introduced to Hungary by aristocratic patrons who brought with them their dogs from several countries, including Pointers and Irish Setters.

America received its first specimen when Joseph Pulitzer brought his sister a gift in 1938. It would be long thereafter before numbers and interest built up sufficiently to justify official AKC recognition, which was given in 1960. Club establishment was sponsored by the late Colonel Jeno Dus, who brought two favorite dogs to the United States after World War II, having until then kept Vizsla pedigrees safely for the Hungarian club while in active service.

Described by his standard as "robust but lightly built," the Vizsla is a medium-size dog of exceptional eye appeal. His utility and versatility are best suited to trial competition outside the Pointer/Setter sphere. He wins approval for his "good field manners, enduring search, liking for waterwork and retrieving, his color attractive for field work, and with versatile skills to bring joy to the heart of the hunter." His work pattern tends to be close, about 150 feet. Climatic conditions don't bother him. He will work ducks in all but the iciest environment, and, like his far-back relative, the Pointer, he can go long periods without water. Vizsla owners have included Pope Pius XII and Zsa Zsa Gabor.

And so we have the 24 breeds of the Sporting Group, literally all of a feather in hunting usefulness but each with its individuality of type—its own special characteristics and outline, its own head properties, its own jacketing, and even its own color(s). Ours to cherish and ours to preserve.

Wirehaired Pointing Griffon.

2

The Hound Group

Damara Bolte

D' ye ken John Peel with his coat so gay?
D' ye ken John Peel at the break of day?
D' ye ken John Peel when he's far away
With his hounds and his horn in the morning?

'Twas the sound of his horn brought me from my bed,
And the cry of his hounds, has me oft times led;
For Peel's view-hollo would waken the dead,
Or the fox from his lair in the morning.

JOHN WOODCOCK GRAVES, 1795–1886

Man has hunted with dogs since prehistoric times, and if ever you've turned out early on a crisp fall morning for a hunt meet, the cheerful tune and rollicking lyrics of "John Peel" conjure up the same spirit of the chase—horses stamping and snorting, jingling bits and creaking leather, pink coats, the air filled with anticipation, and the hounds eager to be on their way. The classical sport of fox hunting, which had its inception in the mid-eighteenth century, is a little older than the American Kennel Club, but both are relative newcomers when compared to the ancient relationship of man and dog. This mutualism developed from a tentative and difficult beginning into a "togetherness" that is legendary.

36

Opposite: **Beagle.**

The breeds that comprise the Hound Group are as varied in size and shape as they are in coat texture and color, from the stalwart Irish Wolfhound to the achondroplastic Dachshunds and Basset. However dissimilar they may be in appearance, they all share the common function of hunting nonfeathered game. The hound breeds were originally classified by the American Kennel Club as "sporting dogs," but in 1928 they were reclassified as Sporting Dogs (Hounds).

In the teaching of design, the concept that "form follows function" is a basic principle. This is more than aptly demonstrated when applied to the breeds that comprise the Hound Group. Hunting mammals is the one common denominator that designates as hounds this assortment of eclectic breeds so heterogenous in appearance. These dogs hunted elk, bear, and deer and foxes, badgers, and hares. Each breed evolved and adapted itself to perform in the climate and terrain to which it was indigenous. Those that were hardy enough survived and functioned well in their given role, their lineage often perpetuated without much concern for appearance. In more recent times, perhaps as the necessity for performance became less pressing, more emphasis was given to conformation.

The Greyhound

The Greyhound is the prototype of the classic gazehound, its graceful appearance already recognizable 5,000 years ago. Appearance and great speed, together with its other attributes, gained royal favor. Commoners were not allowed to own a Greyhound, and it remained a symbol of aristocracy. Indeed, even today it adapts to the good life with alacrity. The Greyhound, brought to America by the Spanish in the sixteenth century, hunted a variety of game but excelled on hares and rabbits. With the formation of the Swaffham Coursing Society in 1776 came organized greyhound coursing in Britain. In 1885, when the first six hound breeds were admitted to the American Kennel Club registry, the Greyhound was the only sight hound among them. In North America since the 1920s, with the invention of the mechanical lure, Greyhounds have been racing on the track. As a sporting hound, as well as a companion, the future of Greyhounds looks bright. It seems almost paradoxical that the exclusive hound of the ancient kings has become almost a household word in modern times, primarily because of the buses that bear its name and logo.

The Basset Hound

Of French origin, the Basset derived its name from the French word *bas*, meaning "low-slung." Its short, well-boned legs, powerful body, and excellent scenting ability suited it well for trailing game yet made it slow enough to be followed on foot. Originally used for badger hunting in the late fifteenth century, Bassets now trail rabbits and hares instead with pleasure and skill. Can the same eyes that view the Greyhound as elegant, see elegance in the Basset? The well-proportioned, loosely skinned head, the long, soft, low-set ears, the slightly arched neck (not mentioned in the standard), and the long, strong top line finishing in a happy tail somehow achieve a harmonious, utilitarian figure with an elegance and bearing all its own. The breed first came to the United States in 1883, and the next year the first Basset was exhibited at Westminster.

Left: Greyhound. *Tauskey*

Below: **Basset Hound.**
Tauskey

TAUSKEY

When Rudolph William Tauskey died in 1979 at the age of 91, he left behind a pictorial legacy of some of the past's greatest dogs. A proud man and a unique artist, Tauskey was the only official photographer ever retained by the American Kennel Club, a post he held from 1924 to 1942.

As a photographer, Tauskey was an undisputed master who developed his own film and was an expert retoucher. Negatives of his work clearly show his efforts to portray his clients' dogs in the best possible light.

The backdrop for most of Tauskey's dog photographs was his home in Saddle River, New Jersey, where the beautiful grounds and gardens complemented the animals. Mrs. Tauskey often contributed her talents as an excellent cook to provide bountiful meals before or after a photographic session.

Born in Budapest in 1888, Tauskey emigrated to the United States at the age of 17 and was introduced to photography while serving in the U.S. Army on the Mexican border during World War I.

The American Kennel Club Library now possesses Tauskey's collection of photographs and negatives through the generosity of his son and daughter-in-law, Rudolph and Dorothy Tauskey.

Until the television public met "Cleo" in the 1950s, the Basset was relatively obscure. However, with the combination of television and Hushpuppy shoes, the Basset can boast better public relations than the Greyhound. Furthermore, hunting with Bassets either singly or in packs has a real following. The show and obedience rings are also proving grounds for the breed's versatility. But it is as a family pet that Bassets excel in America with their droll appearance, charming, easygoing manner, medium size, and easy care and keeping.

The Bloodhound

The trailing ability of the Bloodhound is legendary. Although its appearance has been developed and polished, particularly since its arrival in the United States over a century ago, that famous nose was already a recognizable type in the Middle East before the Crusades. Largest of the medium-sized packhounds, the Bloodhound is descended from the black European staghunting St. Huberts hounds of the eighth century, which were later imported to England. It is only in the last century that the Bloodhound's splendid scenting ability has been used to track down a different quarry: man. As a finder of the lost and injured, as well as of fugitives from justice, the Bloodhound has been of inestimable value. Its enthusiasm for work and its kindly disposition reveal the true sportsman to whom applies the ideal "not the laurels, but the race." It is equally gratifying to still find show champions today that can perform in the field as well as their ancestors did.

Bloodhound. *Evelyn Shafer*

The Dachshund

It is hard to believe that the little Dachshund that has wormed its way into the hearts and households of so many was developed in Germany centuries ago to hunt the tough badger. This long, strong package with punishing jaws propelled by short, sturdy legs has the spirit and determination to do the job. The breed originated before the seventeenth century and grew in popularity during the 1800s in Europe.

Dachshunds have been in America for over a hundred years and were among the first six breeds admitted by the American Kennel Club in 1885. Different sizes were developed to suit specific game. The 30–35-pound "original model" was equal to facing the badger or, in packs, to pursue even the wild boar. The 16–24-pound size, most popular in the United States, could cope with a fox. A miniature weighing 10 pounds or less had plenty of spunk to bolt rabbits or weasels.

Variety is certainly provided by the Dachshund, which not only comes in different sizes but also in three coats—smooth, long, and wirehaired—and in assorted earth colors. This delightful and adaptable little breed has continued to increase in registrations, and over the years there have been some consistently great winners in the show ring.

In order to ensure its hunting capability, so little in demand today, field trials were instituted in 1935. The Dachshund is generally an easy keeper and, because of its unique physique, easier to confine and to exercise than any of the other hound breeds. Apt to be a little stubborn, a rather prevalent characteristic in the hound breeds, the Dachshund has a companionable personality, often making it the right dog for a lot of people.

Long, Smooth, and Wirehaired Dachshunds.
Jim Callea

The Beagle

One of the best known and loved dogs in America today is the little rabbit hound called the Beagle. Popular in ancient times in Britain and Europe, the Beagle has provided excellent sport, hunting rabbits and hares for centuries. Importation of packs and individual hounds from England 120 years ago marked the turning point in the development of the Beagle, that uniformly attractive breed that closely resembles a small Foxhound.

Beagling is done either with single hounds or packs in pursuit of cottontail rabbits or hares, with the hunter following on foot. A handy little dog with a keen nose, distinctive voice, and infectious enthusiasm for the chase, the Beagle provides more sport to more people more of the time than all the other hounds put together. Their vast numbers, reflected by the number of AKC registrations, are not just the result of multitudinous packs all over the country; the Beagle has proved itself to be a delightful companion and a worthy contender in the show ring.

The two varieties under 13 inches and 15 inches allow for surprising differences in size ranging from convenient to even more convenient. The Beagle's relatively carefree coat in combinations of black, tan, white, and occasionally blue and its soft expression and easy charm contribute to its universal appeal. The Beagle's laissez-faire philosophy has been illustrated not infrequently by stories and photos of bitches suckling baby rabbits along with their puppies. Here is a neat little hound that has definitely succeeded on all fronts—in the field, in the home, and in the ring.

The Harrier

It is rather surprising that the Harrier, so obscure today, was among those six hounds initially registered in 1885. Fifty years ago over a hundred packs of Harriers hunted in Britain and were followed on foot as opposed to the faster Foxhounds that were followed on horseback. Some of these packs were made up of single hounds belonging to different individuals and were called "scratch" packs. Scratch packs and following on foot made the sport of hunting hares accessible to the common man.

The Harrier is midway in size between the Beagle and the Foxhound, which it closely resembles. No recent arrival, the Harrier already hunted here in colonial times and later was often used for drag hunts that were set by laying or dragging a scent instead of giving chase to the actual fox. Speed, therefore, was not of great importance. Although individual hounds may be kept as pets, the Harrier, like the Foxhound, is best suited to hunting in packs for which purpose it was originally bred in the thirteenth century. In the show ring as in the field, the Harrier is a handsome dog and is capable of providing top-notch competition. Unfortunately, few have achieved great distinction in bench shows recently, probably because of their relative paucity and the judges' subsequent lack of familiarity with this worthy breed.

These six breeds comprised the first Hound Group as classified by the American Kennel Club in 1885—the Greyhound, the Basset, the Bloodhound, the Dachshund, the Harrier, and the Beagle. One gazehound, four pack-hounds, and the independent but "packable" Dachshund. Each of these breeds has its own national parent club or association, which has drawn up or adopted an official standard. The purpose of the standard is to verbalize an ideal description in order to provide a blueprint with which to work. Of course, standards are subject to individual interpretation and variations developed within each breed, depending on the country and the climate in which they hunt.

The Scottish Deerhound

The red deer of Scotland often weigh as much as 250 pounds and are powerful and fleet. The origins of a big, rough-coated Greyhound strong and swift enough to chase and bring down these large stags are lost in the swirling mists of the Highlands. Bred by chieftains in Scotland for 2,000 years, the Deerhounds were identifiable as a breed as early as 1600. With the demise of the clan system, the gradual decimation of the great deer herds, and the invention of the gun, the Scottish Deerhound almost disappeared. Fortunately, through the successful efforts of Archibald and Duncan McNeill, the noble Deerhound survived. Here is a hound that lived closely with its master who cultivated its gentle and companionable nature while still nurturing its great hunting ability. The Deerhound has always been selectively owned and carefully bred to preserve its true character. Although still quite rare, it has gained recognition in the show ring, has adapted to coursing rabbits, hares, or even mechanical lures, and is generally quite affable regarding its change in circumstances.

The American Foxhound

The American Foxhound was derived originally from the English Foxhound and adapted to the American life-style. Different strains were developed and altered by later imports of French and even Irish hounds. Considerable variation evolved in these hounds as their adaptability responded to different demands. This resulted in distinct strains such as Henry-Birdsong, Trigg, and Walker, all three rather dissimilar in appearance as well as in temperament, speed, and manner of hunting. In recent years great strides have been made in establishing a uniformly representative type. Thanks to the combined efforts of the American Foxhound Club and the Hunts (which belong to the Masters of Foxhounds Association), the American Foxhound is a handsome, clean-limbed, upstanding dog and typically enjoys communal living. It is still primarily a hunter, but successful showing of individuals has brought the breed considerable acclaim.

With the admission in 1886 of the American Foxhound and the Scottish Deerhound, the American Kennel Club had in its second year a Hound Group comprising eight breeds. Over the next 98 years, 12 more breeds gained sufficient support to bring the Group to its present complement of 20 breeds.

Beagle. *Satriale*

Scottish Deerhounds. *Cecilia Arnold*

Borzoi. *Terence A. Gili*

Whippet, *c.* 1935.
Wm. Brown

Opposite:
American Foxhounds.

The Whippet

"Faster than the speed of light"—well, not quite, but faster than any other dog of equal size, the Whippet, while over 100 years old, is a relative newcomer. To its big brother the Greyhound, it doubtlessly owes its speed, grace, and above all its type; and perhaps to some contributing terriers, it owes its diminutive size and much of its keenness. The smallest of the sight hounds, the Whippet is incredible to watch on the move and delightful to observe in repose. Developed for coursing rabbits, the Whippet demonstrates versatility through its ability to be successful on all fronts simultaneously. It can course, it can show, and it can lie back in splendor on satin pillows. Three years before the English Kennel Club recognized the Whippet in 1891, the breed was registered by the American Kennel Club.

The Borzoi

Could anything personify Czarist Russia better than the regal Borzoi? Combining the type, size, and elegance of the greyhound, the Borzoi is dressed for the severe cold with a coat that would shame a sable. The time, effort, labor, facilities, and money dedicated to developing this breed over several centuries are almost beyond comprehension. Coursing became the pastime of the Russian aristocracy, and the Russian Wolfhound, as the Borzoi was called prior to 1936, was admirably suited both literally and figuratively to the sport. The Russians prized the Borzoi not only for its speed and beauty but for the intelligence and gentleness that still characterize the breed. Unlike the dog itself, Borzois got off to a slow start in this country. Recognition came only in 1891, two years after the first import, but despite the exposure provided by Wolfschmidt Vodka and by the adoption of the Borzoi as the colophon for Alfred A. Knopf books, the breed has remained somewhat exclusive.

Ownership of the great hound breeds is almost self-limiting. Although they can adapt to modest means, they were intended for a different life in a different time. The rising interest in lure coursing is bringing within reach a variation of the purpose for which hounds were conceived and adds a heretofore little explored dimension to enhance their popularity.

The Irish Wolfhound

Fortunately, the giant Irish Wolfhound has a heart commensurate with its size. It is relatively easy to identify references to this great rough-coated hound throughout its long history because it literally stood head and shoulders above the crowd. Seldom used today for its original purpose of hunting large game in northern climes, the Wolfhound is enormous, powerful, and kindly. Before the breed was resurrected in the latter part of the nineteenth century, it was bound for extinction like the Deerhound. To its detriment, it now seems headed toward the opposite extreme. At its best, this is a wonderful breed requiring lots of companionship and lots of space to develop optimally. Although the Irish Wolfhound is neither flashy nor particularly showy, excellent specimens have done well in the ring by virtue of their imposing presence and free movement. Admitted to registry in 1897, this was the last breed recognized by the AKC in the nineteenth century.

Opposite: **Irish Wolfhounds.**

The English Foxhound

The English Foxhound was brought over to this country as early as 1600, but it traces its roots back to the French Norman Talbot and St. Huberts hounds. The most salient feature of the English Foxhound is its tremendous bone structure, which provides the framework for a powerful and efficient trailer. Very few are seen in the show ring, and virtually none as household pets, for this is a pack hound born and bred to pursue game. A wonderful-looking animal with an arched neck and a strong back and the heart room and legs to run all day, this Foxhound is bigger and sturdier than its American counterpart. Probably the development and adaptation of the American versions, along with reduced interest in the English hound, accounts for the fact that the breed was not registered until 1909.

The Otterhound

Surely the rarest of the hound breeds is the shaggy Otterhound, which reached its zenith in England in the last half of the nineteenth century, came to America in 1900, and was admitted to registry in 1907. The Otterhound, designed to hunt European otters, is equipped with its own wet suit and webbed feet to cope with icy waters. Although there were a number of organized packs in England and Scotland, the Otterhound in America has been almost a collector's item. Since otters have such a fan club of their own, and now that otter hunting is banned in Britain, Otterhounds will have to make it on their own charm and whimsical good looks. Once in a great while, an Otterhound surfaces to command attention for its delightful symmetry and grace of movement.

The Norwegian Elkhound

While the Greyhounds were disporting themselves in the Mediterranean area in antiquity, the Norwegian Elkhound was a veteran at earning its keep in the frozen North. A product of its purpose and environment, the sturdy Elkhound has smoothly adapted from the role of big-game tracker to companion dog. The Elkhound was registered with the American Kennel Club in 1913, but competition in the ring was still scarce 35 years ago. Its alertness and eagerness to please, coupled with practical size and athletic good looks, have gained the Elkhound a secure position among hounds. Conscientious breeding has now produced dogs that have become highly successful in competition while still retaining that special versatile character.

The Afghan Hound

No breed has come so far so fast as the Afghan. Rooted in the mountains and plains of Afghanistan, the modern Afghan came to the United States only in 1926, almost entirely via Britain. For lack of a parent club until 1938, an interim

Opposite: English Foxhound. *David Hancock*

standard was provided by the AKC. Certainly the most glamorous of all hounds, if not all breeds, the Afghan has soared to the top as a show dog. Although it combines speed, grace, and superlative vision, its looks rather than performance have netted it fame and fortune. Independence characterizes its hunting as well as its personality, and Afghans make incredibly fascinating and decorative pets.

The Saluki

The tribes in Persia and the Near East had but one favored dog, the Saluki. Treasured for speed and adeptness in hunting the gazelle, the Saluki is probably the most ancient of all the breeds. The breed was a latecomer to the United States, and its popularity since 1927 has steadily increased, largely because of its great beauty and tractable disposition. The Saluki's smooth coat comes in a gorgeous array of colors and shadings, and its silken ear and tail feathering add an exotic look that requires little upkeep. Like its fellow sight hounds, Salukis excel at coursing, are not generally aggressive, and are delightful to look upon. Exceptional individuals imbued with showmanship have brought increasing recognition to the breed.

The Basenji

Perhaps the most intriguing and atypical of the hound breeds is the Basenji, the barkless dog of Africa. Hunting companions of the ancient Egyptians and even now of tribes in the southern Sudan, the Basenji surfaced to Western eyes as late as 1937. Independent in mind and spirit, alert and stylish in bearing, the Basenji has charmed its way into the heart of many a skeptic. The short, slick coat in red, tricolor, or black with white trim is virtually trouble and odor free. The erect ears, worry wrinkles, and doughnut tail are trademarks, and the quick graceful movement and silent reserve are almost more cat than dog. The Basenji possesses its own vocabulary but is usually quiet, and as a rule the bitches still have but one season a year. It took 15 to 20 years after it arrived in America in 1941 for the Basenji to gain real consideration in group competition. Whether in the show or obedience rings, in the home or chasing a lure, the Basenji's intelligence, humor, inventiveness, and perseverance provide a delightful challenge.

The Black and Tan Coonhound

In 1945 the selectively color-bred Black and Tan Coonhound was accepted for registry. Developed from centuries of pure hounds, the Black and Tan edition specializes in tracking raccoon and opossums. It is a fine-looking, upstanding hound whose most distinguishing features are the head with the long, low-set ears hanging in folds and the dense, short coat of the colors that impart its name. Since the Black and Tan Coonhound is primarily a dog that earns its keep, the numbers that seek distinction in the show ring are few. But there have been individuals of such obvious quality, soundness, and type as to be worthy of the tricolor rosette.

Afghan Hound. *Tauskey*

Norwegian Elkhound.

Saluki. *Carlene Kuhl*

Basenjis. *Evelyn Shafer*

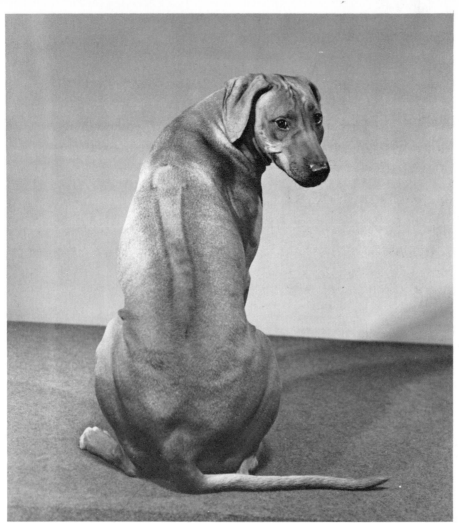

Rhodesian Ridgeback.
Alton Anderson

Ibizan Hound.

The Rhodesian Ridgeback

In 1950 the first Rhodesian Ridgebacks were imported to the United States, and registration by the AKC was granted five years later. Here is a hound that has proved itself as a companion and protector as well as a show dog. Selectively bred for the distinguishing ridge of reverse hair along its back, the Ridgeback combines the desirable qualities of several European breeds and the South African Hottentots' ridged hunting dog. The breed was brought to a defined state of the art in Rhodesia during the 1880s for hunting lion and other large game, and the standard was then drawn up in 1927. Assiduous breeding with concern for type, soundness, and temperament has made great strides in improving the quality and uniformity of this all-purpose breed since its arrival in the United States.

The Ibizan Hound

The twentieth and last breed to be added to the Hound Group is, ironically, one of the most ancient. The Pharaoh's regal hunting dog found its way to the Balearic Isles, specifically Ibiza, where the breed got its name. Brought to this country in 1956, the graceful Ibizan Hound gathered momentum until it gained acceptance in October 1979. Built on the same long, slim lines of a sight hound, the Ibizan has a charming look of astonishment owing to its large, erect ears and amber eyes. The short, sleek coat customarily comes in varying amounts of red and white. Intelligent, alert, and responsive, the Ibizan makes a delightful pet while still maintaining its ability to course and to win acclaim in the show ring.

These are the twenty breeds of hounds currently recognized by the American Kennel Club, dogs whose heritage it is to pursue game by sight or scent or both. A motley assemblage, perhaps, to some, yet each possesses a prescribed and preserved beauty that serves and is served by man.

3

The Working Group

Herman L. Fellton

The dog was the first animal to be domesticated by man, who turned to this task some 14,000 years ago, probably in the area now known as Iraq. Since that time, working dogs have served man in many capacities. They have guarded against hostile intruders, and helped us win in wartime. Working dogs have helped our police maintain law and order. They have pulled sleighs and carts, performed rescue operations, destroyed vermin, and helped to improve life for the physically and mentally handicapped. As pets and companions, they have tested our sagacity and foresight as breeders and inflated or deflated our egos as participants in the sport of pure-bred dogs.

Prior to 1983, the Working Group was the largest of the six AKC groups with thirty-two breeds. At the annual meeting of the American Kennel Club in March 1982, the Delegates voted to amend the Dog Show Rules to create a seventh Group, the Herding Group, comprised of the fourteen herding breeds. This Group is discussed in Chapter 7.

The present Working Group is composed of eighteen breeds. These diverse, even disparate breeds are to a great extent the gloried breeds. Who can forget the dogs immortalized by Jack London, or the otherwise surly Mastiff that took so readily to Little Lord Fauntleroy? Many readers will remember watching Doberman Pinschers in a variety of roles in many films. We can all picture the Saint Bernards in the mountains of Switzerland carrying small kegs of brandy, and Sir Edwin Landseer's painting of a Newfoundland, *A Distinguished Member of the Humane Society*, commemorating the many lives saved by this heroic breed.

The dogs who pulled the sleds in the early polar explorations belonged to the Working Group, as did the Siberian Huskies who made the famous 1925 "serum run" sled relay to Alaska. Doberman Pinschers were members of the Marine Corps during the second World War. Rottweilers and other breeds have splendid records as war dogs.

A team of Alaskan Malamutes. *Jim Yuskavitch*

In terms of success in the show ring, a working dog has been honored with Best in Show at the prestigious Westminster Kennel Club show only eight times since 1907. (Three other Westminster winners that were members of the Working Group when they took their trophies are now among the breeds in the Herding Group.) These eight were the Doberman Pinscher Ch. Ferry Rauhfelsen (1939), the Boxer Ch. Warlord of Mazelaine (1947), the Boxer Ch. Mazelaine Zazarac Brandy (1949), the Boxer Ch. Bang Away of Sirrah Crest (1951), the Doberman Ch. Rancho Dobe's Storm (1952 and 1953), the Boxer Ch. Arriba's Prima Donna (1970), and the Siberian Husky Ch. Innisfree's Sierra Cinnar (1980).

During the period from 1917 to 1960, Westminster also selected a Best American-Bred in Show when an imported dog won Best in Show. On only two occasions was this award won by a Working Dog—in 1926 by the St. Bernard Ch. Hercuveen Aurora Borealis, and in 1944 by the Boxer Ch. Warlord of Mazelaine. In 1960 a Pembroke Welsh Corgi—then classified as a Working Breed but now among the Herding Breeds—won the award, Ch. Cote de Neige Sundew.

Although a number of our working breeds have historically served several functions, one can, for the sake of convenience, divide them into general categories for discussion.

Police, Guard, and Protection Dogs

The Boxer

This breed is basically a descendant of the Molossus or Mastiff type, a heavy-boned dog that is the progenitor of many of the world's big, powerful breeds. The first Boxer was registered by the AKC in 1904, and the first champion, Damf v Dom, imported from Germany by Herbert H. Lehman, later governor of the State of New York, was recorded in 1915. Boxers have won more Bests in Show (four) at Westminster than any other working breed. In 1938 there was a very large entry of 103 Boxers at Westminster, and it seemed for a while that the Boxer would go the top in registrations. This did not happen, however; the breed climbed to fourth place but never rose any higher.

Boxers, originally classified as members of the Non-Sporting Group, were shifted by AKC to the Working Group in 1936. They achieved this new status because of service with the armed forces and the police of several nations. In this country Boxers have been mainly home guards and companions.

The Doberman Pinscher

Despite the popular misconception of the Doberman as a vicious dog, long fostered through the media, this is one of the most loving, intelligent, faithful, and obedient breeds of dogs. The Doberman is a "manufactured" breed, originating in Germany about 1890. It was designed to be a watch and guard dog, and the attribute of "sharpness," that is, aggressiveness, was much desired. The early Dobermans in Germany and Holland and those first imported into this country were truly "sharp." American breeders, however, have greatly modified this aspect of the breed's temperament, while retaining those

Boxer.

A Doberman Pinscher
being photographed after
winning its class.

qualities of courage, boldness, intelligence, trainability, and loyalty that enable these dogs to serve most effectively as police, military, guard, and protection animals. The Doberman is a smooth, sleek, powerful, elegant, beautiful dog. It is a working dog devoted to the service of man.

The Great Pyrenees

Shepherds of the Pyrenees once used this ancient breed to protect their flocks from the ravages of wolves and bears. For protection these dogs wore broad iron collars armed with menacing spikes. French aristocrats adopted the Great Pyrenees as the court dog in the seventeenth century and used it for guard duty as well as companionship. Specimens of this breed played a considerable role in the origin of the St. Bernard, and the Great Pyrenees was probably used as an outcross to produce the Newfoundland.

Great Pyrenees, c. 1940.

Rottweiler. *Tauskey*

The Rottweiler

A breed of great antiquity, whose name is derived from the West German town of Rottweil, these dogs were used extensively in the Middle Ages for boar hunting. They later became cattle dogs (butcher dogs) and were also used to pull small carts. In 1910 they entered the field of police work. Rottweilers are used in Germany by the police, customs, and army. In Denmark and Austria they perform mainly police work. They can also be found pulling sleighs in Finland. In this country and in England, they are valued as guard and companion dogs, and they are increasingly used for security work.

The Giant and Standard Schnauzers

The Standard, or medium-sized, Schnauzer is the prototype of the three breeds recognized in the United States—the Miniature, the Standard, and the Giant. The latter two are in the Working Group, while the Miniature is a Terrier. First exhibited in Germany in 1879, Schnauzers gained fame in this country during the First World War. The Schnauzer Club of America was formed in 1925. Since the Giant Schnauzer made his appearance here when the German Shepherd Dog's popularity was peaking, the Schnauzer had little chance to advance, especially in police work, which had become its main occupation in Germany. The Standard served mainly as a farm "yard" dog, protecting stock and eliminating vermin.

Samoyed. *Ludwig*

The Draft Dogs

Most people today don't realize the extent to which dogs were used to pull small carts in Europe. These carts were loaded with milk cans, bread, butchers' products, or vegetables. In the parks and on the country roads, the sight of a dog or a brace of dogs harnessed to children's carriages was as common as the accepted image of dogs pulling sleds over snow and ice.

The Alaskan Malamute

The most powerful of the sledge dogs, the Alaskan Malamute is used for hauling heavy loads. They are named for an Innuit tribe, the Malimiuts, in Alaska. Admiral Byrd used dogs of this breed in Antarctica.

The Bernese Mountain Dog

One of four varieties of Swiss mountain dogs, the Bernese was originally used in the Canton of Berne to pull small wagons loaded with baskets. They also worked as drovers and as watchdogs on farms.

The Samoyed

This breed of medium-sized white sledge dogs was introduced into England about a hundred years ago. Roald Amundsen used Samoyeds in his successful expedition to the South Pole in 1911, as did Shackleton and Scott.

The Siberian Husky

The Chukchi people of northeastern Asia are responsible for originating the Siberian Husky as a sled dog who could travel great distances in cold climates, with a heavy load and with a minimum use of energy, at a good speed.

Siberian Husky puppy.
Martin Miller

The Rescue Dogs

The Newfoundland

This is another large, heavily coated dog, who is as much at home in the water as on land. The breed originated in Newfoundland but attained most of its present conformation and type as a result of excellent breeding in England. Black and white specimens are called Landseers, because one was the subject of a famous painting by Sir Edwin Landseer.

The St. Bernard

This large, massive-headed breed has been the subject of some of the most romantic tales in canine history. It was used by the monks at the Hospice in the Swiss Alps to locate and help rescue imperiled travelers in the treacherous passes between Switzerland and Italy, particularly the St. Bernard Pass. Most celebrated of all Hospice dogs was Barry, who is credited with saving 40 lives during his tenure (1800–1810).

St. Bernard,
c. 1940.

Newfoundland.

Other Working Dogs

The Akita
The attractive Akita received official recognition by the government of Japan in 1931. The Akita Club of America was founded in 1956, and the breed was admitted to registration in the AKC Stud Book in 1972 and to regular show classification in the Working Group in 1973. Helen Keller is credited with bringing the first Akita to the United States.

The Bullmastiff
This breed was the product of cross-breeding between the Mastiff and the Bulldog. The idea for such a plan came from gamekeepers on large estates and game preserves who desired a dog to guard against poachers. It has been known since approximately 1860.

The Great Dane
Great Danes were first used as war dogs by Atilla the Hun and the Romans, as fighting dogs in the Roman arenas, and as hunters for wild boars. They are large, substantial dogs of considerable elegance. An early description of their characteristics called for "a combination of grace and power, and therefore the lightness of the Greyhound and the heaviness of the Mastiff must be avoided." Following the war of 1870, when national feeling ran very strong in a reunited Germany, the Germans renamed the Great Dane the "deutsche Dogge" and viewed it as their national dog.

Akita.

The Komondor
The Komondor has been native for ten centuries to the sheep and cattle areas of Hungary, having been brought there from the Russian steppes by the Huns. He is a large, white dog with a dense, weather-resistant double coat. The coarser hairs of the outer coat trap the softer undercoat, forming permanent strong cords that are like felt to the touch. Grown dogs are covered with a heavy coat of these tassel-like cords. More of a protector than a herder, the Komondor is used in the western United States to protect flocks of sheep from coyotes and other predators.

Great Dane. *Evelyn Shafer*

Komondor.

Kuvasz. *Missy Yuhl*

The Kuvasz

The ancestors of this large white dog were Tibetan, but it was in Hungary that the Kuvasz achieved its present conformation. It was used as a personal guard by the aristocracy, but many were also trained for hunting big game and sometimes hunted in packs. Later the Kuvasz was found to be suitable for work with sheep and cattle, primarily as protectors. The Kuvasz has a double coat, medium coarse in texture and cordless, that ranges from quite wavy to straight.

The Mastiff

The oldest of the British dogs, the Mastiff has been bred in England for over 2,000 years as a watchdog. A giant, short-haired dog with a heavy head and a short muzzle, it is similar in size and form to the British Mastiff and the fierce Molossian dogs of ancient Greece. Caesar encountered Mastiffs when he invaded Britain in 55 B.C., where he found them fighting beside their masters. They were later used as fighting dogs in the arenas of Rome.

The Working Group—grand breeds, one and all. No matter that many of them no longer are called upon to perform unnecessary, obsolete, or archaic duties today; our main concern is that they retain the innate ability to do so. We need to guard and sustain those attributes and characteristics that, in totality, constitute the essence of each breed and that serve to distinguish the dogs in this Group and enable them to perform their functions.

A Mastiff watches over her young charges while benched at the Westminster Kennel Club Show.

4

The
Terrier
Group

John T. Marvin

The Terrier Group arose as a generic strain of dogs bred for the purpose of going to ground. While the definitive evolution of the 23 distinct Terrier breeds consumed centuries, all share the great courage and determination that are hallmarks of the Group. The earliest mention of the Terrier as an "earthe dogge" comes from the fourteenth century, when the poet Gace de la Vigne wrote: "He goes to earth with the good Terrier dog that they put in the burrow." More than 200 years later, Dr. Johannes Caius (the latinized name of the Englishman, John Keyes) cited the "earthe dogge" in his book *De Canibus Britannicis*. His Terriers, however, were generally small hounds chosen for their aggressive characters.

The present Terrier Group includes some breeds of the Terrier stamp and blood that cannot be broadly classified as earth dogs because their size prohibits them from entering a burrow. Furthermore, several breeds once hailed as Terriers in the AKC now claim membership in other Groups through transfer; to wit, the Miniature Pinscher, the Standard Schnauzer, and the Lhasa Apso, while the once popular White English Terrier was dropped from the AKC Stud Book in the 1920s because of the absence of breed registrations. Two other Terrier breeds that are not recognized officially by the AKC but that have recognized status in other countries are the Glen of Imaal Terrier, recognized in Ireland since 1933, and the Deutsche Jagdterrier, a product of German breeding skills. Of course, the Jack Russell Terrier, an old breed resembling the Fox Terrier in some respects, is very popular in England although not recognized by the English Kennel Club.

Skye Terrier and puppies. *Evelyn Shafer*

Early-nineteenth-century
Terrier types in England,
drawn by Sydenham Edwards.

The following list of all presently recognized Terrier breeds together with the date of their official AKC recognition illustrates the diversity of the Group together with its long history. Two divisions—short-legged and long-legged Terriers—are offered for reasons that will become apparent.

Short-Legged Terriers	Long-Legged Terriers
Australian Terrier (1960)	Airedale Terrier (1888)
Cairn Terrier (1913)	American Staffordshire Terrier (1936)
Dandie Dinmont Terrier (1886)	Bedlington Terrier (1886)
Norwich Terrier (1936)	Border Terrier (1930)
Norfolk Terrier (1979)	Bull Terrier, White and Colored (1885)
Scottish Terrier (1885)	Fox Terrier, Smooth and Wire (1885)
Sealyham Terrier (1911)	Irish Terrier (1885)
Skye Terrier (1887)	Kerry Blue Terrier (1922)
West Highland White Terrier (1908)	Lakeland Terrier (1934)
	Manchester Terrier, Standard (1886)
	Miniature Schnauzer (1926)
	Soft-Coated Wheaten Terrier (1973)
	Staffordshire Bull Terrier (1974)
	Welsh Terrier (1888)

Short-Legged Terriers

The short-legged Terriers were generally bred to work in rocky dens where headroom was limited. They have broad fronts, and while digging, their slightly turned-out front feet move the debris aside to prevent digging themselves in. Most short-legged Terriers have prick or upright ears for keener hearing.

There is little question that the earliest Terrier strain (and the ancestor of all short-legged Terriers) was the Old Scotch Terrier, a stable worker that had great strength, courage, and stamina and was bred to breach rocky predator dens in the rugged Scottish Highlands. The Old Scotch Terrier has long been extinct, but its virtues are preserved in its descendants.

Skye and Dandie Dinmont Terriers are probably the oldest members of the present Group. The Skye Terrier was spawned on the Isle of Skye and gained substantial popularity as a prized companion dog in the Glasgow area during the nineteenth century. Many variants having different coat colors and textures were developed but they eventually lost favor. The modern Skye Terrier has an attractive coat devoid of silky texture and may be black, blue, gray, fawn, or cream in color.

Interest in the Dandie Dinmont Terrier was stirred by Sir Walter Scott's novel *Guy Mannering* (c. 1815). In fact, the breed gained its name from the book where "Dandie Dinmont's Terriers" were key figures. The breed has since undergone refinement, but it still closely resembles its early prototype. Three other short-legged Terrier breeds, the Scottish, the Cairn, and West Highland

Nineteenth-century painting
of Dandie Dinmont
and his Terriers.

Dandie Dinmont
Terrier.

Scottish Terrier. *John L. Ashbey*

Four West Highland
White Terrier
Champions, 1925.
Fall

White are all interrelated. In fact, before the turn of the century, all were sometimes found in the same litter. Each breed now possesses a unique temperament with the most reserved being the Scottish Terrier. All are highly affectionate and make fine house dogs.

The remaining members of the short-legged division are the Australian Terrier, produced by coupling basic, short-legged Terrier blood with local canine strains; the Norwich Terrier, a small but courageous dog whose basic blood includes English infusions; the Norfolk Terrier, which until 1979 was the drop-eared variety of the Norwich but has since then become a separate and recognized breed; and the Sealyham Terrier whose bloodlines include some local Welsh strains together with an infusion of blood from the Fox Terrier.

73

Norwich Terrier.
Copyright photo:
Constance Stuart Larrabee

Australian Terrier.
Terrence A. Gili

Long-Legged Terriers

The progenitor of all long-legged Terrier breeds known today was the now-extinct Old English Terrier. This family branch consisted basically of diggers who worked in the soil. Accordingly, they were bred with generally narrow fronts and straight legs placed relatively close together so that when digging, loose earth could be propelled between their spread rear legs. There are, however, exceptions to this general rule. The ears of most long-legged Terriers are natural and drop over to prevent loose earth from entering the ear canals.

The earliest identifiable long-legged Terriers were the Fox Terrier and the Manchester. The present Fox Terrier comes with either a smooth or a wire coat. Manchester Terriers come in two varieties, either Standard or Toy, the latter being classified in the Toy Group.

The Irish, Kerry Blue, and Soft-Coated Wheaten Terriers are all related breeds of Irish origin. All are alert, strong animals that will not back away from any adversary, and they all make excellent companions. Interestingly, the Irish Terrier varied widely in size during the period of from about 1873 to 1890. Dog shows had classes for dogs ranging from 9 pounds to 40 pounds. This wide diversity led one wit to opine:

It's wonderful dogs they're breeding now,
Small as a flea or large as a cow.

Fox Terrier (Smooth). *John L. Ashbey*

75

Irish Terriers.
Evelyn Shafer

Kerry Blue Terrier. *Ludwig*

Soft-Coated Wheaten Terriers.

Mrs. Edward P. Alker,
noted breeder of
Welsh Terriers, with one
of her Champions, 1941.
Percy T. Jones

Sometimes called the King of Terriers, the Airedale Terrier is the largest breed in the Group. An infusion of Otterhound is responsible for this dog's love of water. A popular breed, its members are fearless, affectionate dogs of stable conformation. The Welsh and Lakeland Terriers are somewhat similar. The Welsh's roots reach back to the Old English Terrier through the early rough-coated black and tan. The Lakeland is a newer breed that came originally from the Lake country, where it was first called a Fell or Patterdale Terrier. This courageous hunter is slightly smaller than the Welsh and has numerous other subtle differences from the Welsh.

The Border Terrier, originally called an Ullswater Terrier, has been known for many years but did not gain notice in America until about 1930. An excellent hunter and vermin dog, it has consanguinity with both the Dandie Dinmont and Bedlington Terriers. The Bedlington, an old breed, is distinguished by its graceful appearance and arched top line. Its background is obscure, but it surely reaches back to the Dandie Dinmont, coupled with a trace of Greyhound blood. Its colors are primarily blue, sandy, and liver. The Bedlington makes a wonderful companion and is a worthy adversary despite its mild-mannered appearance.

Bedlington Terriers, 1961. *Evelyn Shafer*

An early type of Bull Terrier, not far removed from the Bull and Terrier Dog. *H. S. Beckwith etching of a painting by Sir Edwin Landseer.*

American Staffordshire Terrier. *Ludwig*

This brings us to three related breeds, the Bull Terrier, the Staffordshire Bull Terrier, and the American Staffordshire Terrier, which, unlike the other long-legged Terrier breeds, have relatively broad fronts and well-spaced legs for balance. All of these powerful animals have infusions of Bulldog blood and were bred originally for the purpose of fighting. Despite their aggressive natures, they are highly intelligent and affectionate.

The Miniature Schnauzer, the last breed to be discussed in the Terrier Group, is of German origin. One of the most popular breeds in the Group, the Miniature Schnauzer is an affectionate and active dog. Its background includes some Old English Terrier through the Manchester, together with infusions of the German Affenpinscher and possibly a trace of wolfgrey Spitz. In their natural form, the ears are dropped, although most American dogs have had their ears cropped.

Bull Terrier (Colored Variety). *David Merriam*

Team of
Miniature Schnauzers
handled by owner,
Gene Simmonds.
Evelyn Shafer

Man bites dog. A white Bull Terrier being bitten off the badger that he is baiting, as a Blue Paul Terrier is held at right (1820).

Five Characteristics

Whether long-legged or short-legged, all Terriers possess certain characteristics that are imperative to their very existence. First among these is "Terrier fire," an elusive quality that instills the desire to work with unbounded enthusiasm, rugged determination, and great courage. Furthermore, Terriers must have keen hearing and sharp eyes, which should be dark and well protected by a strong, bony, overhanging brow. Their coats must be proper for the purpose for which they were bred. In this respect the Group runs the gamut of textures, types, and lengths, with each best serving the dog it covers and protects. All Terriers must also have good feet—tight and compact, with proper depth of pad. Splayed, open feet with thin pads are not characteristic or desirable. A full set of large teeth set in powerful jaws is another "must." Certainly, today's Terriers do not ordinarily engage in the same tasks their ancestors were so ably bred to perform. Yet these basic characteristics must be maintained in future Terrier generations, because dogs capable of doing the work for which they were originally bred exemplify proper type and temperament and uphold the reason for their existence.

In general, the Terrier breeds known today reflect these hallmarks, a heritage gained through many years of concerted effort. There is no more hardy, courageous, or interesting group of dogs than those of the Terrier tribe.

Oliver Wendell Holmes once wrote: "Heredity is an omnibus in which all of our ancestors ride, and every now and then one of them puts his head out of the window and embarrasses us."

If the early background material offered for the Terrier breeds seems vague and sometimes indefinite, it should be understood that in most instances greater direction is not available. Many early crosses that resulted in new breeds involved local dogs whose pedigrees were passed along by word of mouth. It was not until the publication of Volume 1 of *The Kennel Club Stud Book* (English) in 1874 that any formal public record became available, and even this was incomplete in many respects.

5

The Toy Group

Edd Embry Bivin

Breeds or types of dogs were developed over the years to accommodate particular needs of mankind. Dogs certainly helped man combat nature and animal foes, but man also had a more sophisticated need for companionship. Toy breeds were developed as companions, and they have always been in great demand. Like miniature paintings, they were "refined" possessions. One must remember that "toy" is synonymous with small, not with dwarf; and although toy dogs are small, they have retained certain characteristics of the larger breeds from which they are descended.

The continued appeal of toy breeds is largely attributable to their adaptability. Toy dogs are portable—whether in an ancient Chinese courtier's sleeve or in a modern sports car. Whether they served as attractors of body fleas from European noblemen or as alarm dogs for threatened nobility, toys were originally the prized possessions of a select few.

Toy breeds have been popular in America since the late nineteenth century. In the formative stages of organized dog sport, all breeds were divided into Sporting and Non-Sporting classifications. The Non-Sporting Group was limited, and little consideration was given to toy breeds. While the AKC registered Pugs and Yorkshire Terriers in 1885, classes at most dog shows did not offer opportunities for the exhibition of toy breeds. Maltese dogs first appeared at the Pet Dog Club Show held in New York City under AKC license in 1893, but national specialty shows for early toy breeds were not held until after the turn of the century.

81

A Pug's-eye view of the world. *Julie Parker*

Toy dogs received additional recognition in March 1928 when the AKC amended its rules to divide all recognized breeds into five variety Groups. In 1928 the Toy Group included the Mexican Hairless, a breed that was removed from the list of registrable breeds in May 1959, because no dogs of the breed had been registered in nearly two decades.

In the May 1924 issue of the *American Kennel Gazette*, Mr. Frank T. Eskrigge bemoaned the nonacceptance in the United States of toy dogs and compared the development of toy dogs in Europe to the furtherance of the same breeds in the United States. After they recovered from what one author described as "import fever," Americans became great breeders of toy breeds.

It was not until 1956 that a toy went Best in Show at the esteemed Westminster Kennel Club Dog Show at Madison Square Garden. The white Toy Poodle Ch. Wilbur White Swan, bred and owned by Mrs. Bertha Smith and shown by Anne Hone Rogers, was the first to break the barrier. The English-bred Pekingese Ch. Chik T'Sun of Caversham, owned by Mr. and Mrs. C. C. Venable and bred by Mrs. H. Lunham and Miss I. M. DePledge, appeared in the late 1950s and is still considered by many to be the greatest American toy dog. Under the hand of the late Mrs. Clara Alford, this toy had an outstanding career that culminated in his Best in Show at Westminster in 1960. The feats of Mrs. Alford and Chik T'Sun still stand paramount in the annals of toy dogs.

In 1961 Anne Hone Rogers guided another Toy Poodle to the top spot at Westminster. The Best in Show was Ch. Cappoquin Little Sister, owned by Mrs. Florence Michelson and bred by Barbara Heyong. It took another 18 years before another toy winner, the Yorkshire Terrier Ch. Cede Higgins, went Best in Show at Westminster. Higgins was owned by Barbara and Charles W. Switzer, bred by C. D. Lawrence, and shown by the Switzers' daughter, Marlene Lutovsky. In 1981 a Pug, Ch. Dhandy's Favorite Woodchuck, owned by Mr. Robert A. Hauslohner, bred by Mrs. W. J. Brady and Mrs. R. O. Hutchinson, and handled by Bobby Barlow, took Best in Show at Westminster. The following year—the first time in the history of the Westminster Kennel Club that a toy breed won the Best in Show title in two consecutive years—a Pekingese took the coveted award. The winning bitch, Ch. St. Aubrey Dragonora of Elsdon, was bred by R. William Taylor, owned by Mrs. Anne E. Snelling, and handled by Bill Trainor. Four of these dogs were bred in America, and each has had an impact on the direction of its own breed.

Toy dogs have come a long way through the determined breeding programs of devoted individuals. A change in attitude toward toys has been achieved by improved quality and a strong organized effort to advance the status of the Toy Group. The Progressive Toy Dog Club, which has held its annual specialty show in New York City since 1933, and the Metro Mile High Kennel Club of Denver, which devotes all of its attention to toy dogs, have been major contributors to the advancement of the toy breeds.

The Chihuahua

The only native North American toy dog is the Chihuahua, which originated in Mexico. A breed very similar to, if not the same as, the Chihuahua lived among the Aztecs and was found in southern Mexico by Cortez. For some unknown reason, the breed either was carried or migrated into northern Mexico. During Cortez's time, Chihuahuas weighed between 10 and 15 pounds. Early toy authorities speak of the breed as being larger, stockier, and lower to the ground than our present representative.

The Chihuahua has gained considerable popularity in the United States since it was first registered with the AKC in 1904. Today the breed is recognized in two coats, long and smooth. It is a clean, easy-to-care-for dog requiring little special attention, although it does have an aversion to cold weather. Chihuahuas are devoted little dogs and are best characterized by their large ears, round skull, and large, round, iridescent eyes.

Chihuahua (Long Coat Variety). *Tauskey*

Pekingese. *John Ashbey*

Chihuahua (Smooth Coat Variety) *c.* 1920. *Freudy Photos*

Toy Breeds of Oriental Origin

Historically speaking, in a general classification of toy breeds, the significance of the Chinese or Oriental group must be considered. The toys in this group are the English Toy Spaniel, the Japanese Spaniel—now known as the Japanese Chin, the Papillon, the Pekingese, the Pugs, and the late arriving Shih Tzu.

The Pekingese

The Pekingese has maintained the greatest degree of popularity over the longest period of all toy breeds in the United States. The Pekingese is known to have been bred, honored, and guarded in the Peking palaces of the emperors of China. Not only was the Pekingese guarded but it served as a guard dog. Chinese royalty modeled the breed to resemble their idea of a lion in appearance and attitude. The Peke's bowed front legs seem to have had a purpose in restricting the dog's ability to stray from the palace grounds.

It was not until the Boxer Rebellion that westerners were successful in getting the Pekingese out of China. Of the five dogs taken to England, two were presented to Queen Victoria who became a fancier of the breed. First registered in the United States in 1906, the breed quickly gained acceptance and replaced other toys as the nation's most popular little dog. Today the Pekingese still enjoys solid popularity. It is an attractive dog that is rather quiet and still protective of home and ground. Accepted in all colors, the Pekingese is noted for its characteristic head and its movements, as well as its luxuriant coat.

The Japanese Chin

Known before 1977 as the Japanese Spaniel, the Japanese Chin is really not a spaniel. Kurt Unkelback, author of *The American Dog Book*, says that the Chin came to the United States from Japan before it went to England. When Commodore Perry's expedition in 1853 opened trade relations between the United States and Japan, members of the expedition saw and liked the breed. First registered with the AKC in 1888, the breed peaked in popularity in the early 1900s. Its position was then usurped by the Peke.

A concerted effort in behalf of the breed was probably hampered by controversy over the desired size. Today the present standard provides for those under and over seven pounds. The Chin, a very unique toy dog, is almost catlike in many of its behavioral patterns. A bit wary of strangers, it even goes so far as to clean its face like a cat. When speaking of a Chin, some people say it is difficult to raise while others maintain that it is worth the effort. This very attractive black and white or red and white parti-colored dog is certainly a desirable toy companion.

The English Toy Spaniel

After its arrival from England in about 1875, the English Toy Spaniel gathered a rather popular following in the United States. Challenged shortly thereafter by the Pomeranian and then by the Pekingese, the breed slipped into

English Toy Spaniels, 1961.
Evelyn Shafer

lesser prominence and eventual obscurity. In more recent times there has been a slight revival of interest in this breed caused largely by the presence in the show ring of a few representatives of exceptional quality and high achievement.

This true Toy Spaniel had its origin in the Orient. Transported to Spain and Portugal, the breed then journeyed to France and eventually to England. It is well accepted that Mary Stuart, Queen of Scots, brought them with her when she returned from France after the death of her husband, the King of France. Her devotion to the breed and its devotion to her were acknowledged by the presence of an English Toy Spaniel hiding under her skirt when she was executed.

Today this attractive breed still traces a part of its nomenclature to Stuart and English titles. English Toy Spaniels are accepted and classified by two different varieties containing four colors. The first of the solid-color divisions is really a black-and-tan combination and is known as the King Charles, having derived its name from a major sponsor of the variety, King Charles I, a Stuart King of England. The ruby, which is a solid red dog, comprises the other half of the solid-color variety. One-half of the true broken-colored variety is labeled as the Prince Charles and has a tricolor pattern of black, tan, and white. The Blenheim derives its name from the Marlboroughs of Blenheim and is the parti-colored, chestnut-red-and-white dog.

The Pug

Considerable confusion exists concerning the origin of the Pug. Some sources say that the Pug came directly from China to Holland. Mr. James Trullinger, author of *The Complete Pug*, says that the Pug may have come to Holland from Russia and/or Portugal. It is definitely known that William and Mary brought to England a group of Pugs from Holland after ascending the English throne. Regardless of its origin the breed came to us from the English, who developed much of what we see in the breed today.

The Pug was first registered by the AKC in 1885 and has enjoyed periods of popularity in the United States. The Pug Dog Club of America states in its brochure that the Pug is appealing because of its size, attitude, intelligence, and ease of care. Pugs are certainly noticed in the conformation and obedience rings.

The Pomeranian

The Pomeranian was introduced to England and subsequently to the United States as a considerably larger dog than it is today. This arctic-type breed had its origin in Europe and received its name from the German state of Pomerania. The breed was used in its earlier form as a herd dog. Reduced in size and not truly suited in temperament for herding, the Pom became popular because it was hardier and easier to raise than either the Japanese Chin or the English Toy Spaniel. Imported to England in significant numbers around 1860 and first registered in the United States in 1888, the Pom sported a coat that was black, white, chocolate, or sable. The American Pomeranian Club, Inc., held its first specialty show in 1910. With the introduction of the orange color and the reduction in size, the breed enjoyed a surge in popularity. The Pomeranian is especially appealing as a puppy and is one of those toy breeds that many feel possesses "big dog" characteristics.

The Toy Poodle

The history of the Toy Poodle in the United States must be divided into two periods. The canine literature of the 1920s illustrates a popular type of Toy Poodle that was exemplified by the breeding of Mr. and Mrs. Thomas W. C. Hartman of Philadelphia, Pennsylvania. After Mr. Hartman died in 1929, having bred some 50 Toy Poodle champions, the breed took a rather different turn and was of no major significance until after World War II.

Having been a separate breed rather than a variety of the Poodle breed as it is today, the Toy seems to have lacked the proper impetus to achieve the same footing as the standard and miniature varieties. When the Toy Poodle Club, centered largely in southern California, began to push forward the cause of its breed, the American Kennel Club insisted upon a unification of effort under the well-established Poodle Club of America. After World War II and the resumption of dog shows, the club first offered classes for the Toy variety. In the opinion of many, this marked the beginning of the modern Toy as a descendent of small miniature poodles. Today the Toy Poodle is a diminutive of the larger standard and miniature varieties, having many of the characteristics that have made the Poodle breed so popular.

Poodle (Toy Variety), 1958. *Tauskey*

Who could be lonely with three Pomeranians? *Moments by Jane*

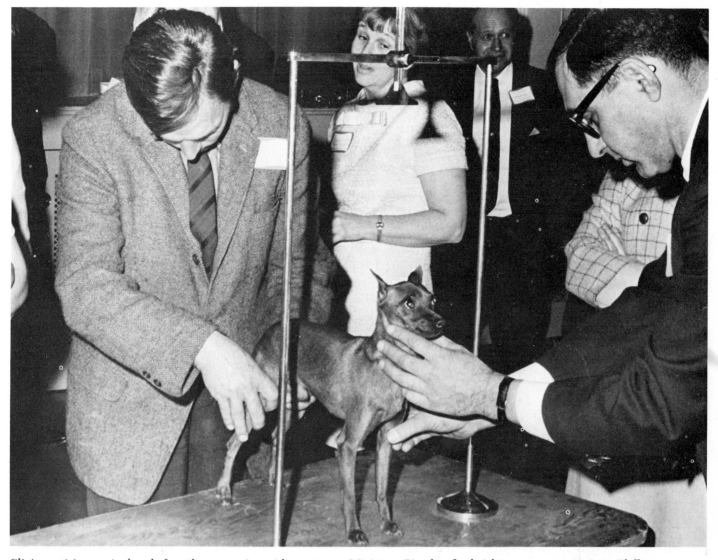

Clinic participants, in days before the measuring wicket, set up a Miniature Pinscher for height measurement using a Phillips Measuring Stand. *Hans Haehn*

Manchester Terrier (Toy Variety). *William Gilbert*

Yorkshire Terrier. *John Ashbey*

The Yorkshire Terrier

The Yorkshire Terrier came to the United States around 1880 and is certainly a major English contribution to the world of toy dogs. It is interesting to recall that as recently as the late 1970s the English and the Americans, each having a major contender in the breed, debated the qualities of breed representatives on each side of the Atlantic.

The origin of this toy breed is somewhat unclear. It is generally accepted that the mill workers of Yorkshire crossed small Terriers to produce a dog that could live in confined quarters, help rid the home of vermin, and be of general comfort to the family. Most seem to agree that the Yorkie was a combination of the Clydesdale, a Paisley Terrier, a broken-haired Scottish Terrier, and possibly a small Terrier known as the Waterside Terrier, which we no longer see today. Nevertheless, the English produced a small, long-coated Terrier of gold (tan) and dark steel-blue color that met the needs of their day.

Today the breed is noted for its luxuriant coat, sharpness of expression, and devotion to its owner. The conditioning of a Yorkshire Terrier coat for the show ring requires considerable effort and care, but many Yorkie owners don't worry about coat condition and are simply happy to have the dog around as an excellent companion.

The Manchester Terrier

Another toy Terrier developed by the English is the toy black and tan Terrier, now known as the Manchester Terrier (Toy). Its entry into the United States cannot be fixed, but a black and tan dog of this type appeared here well before the turn of the century. For many years the breed was exhibited under the general classification of "toy Terriers other than Yorkshire," and there was considerable controversy over size, amount of refinement, and bone. It seems that the coloring of a black and tan combination with pencil marking has been rather well established for a long time. In 1934 the AKC changed the name of the black and tan Terrier to the Manchester Terrier. In 1936 the organization of the American Toy Manchester Terrier Club served as a major boost to the toy variety. This clean breed is easy to live with. It has retained many of its original characteristics and still enjoys a rather small but devoted following.

The Miniature Pinscher

The Miniature Pinscher, originally known as the Rea Pinscher, is obviously of German descent. This breed predates the Doberman Pinscher by many years and is a very old toy breed. The most popular colors in this breed are solid red and a black and tan combination. The Min Pin, as this breed is often called, is noted for the neatness and cleanness of its lines. The breed came to the United States about the turn of the century; it is believed that these dogs were brought over by German immigrants.

In 1929 the Miniature Pinscher Club of America was formed and became a major contributor to the public acceptance of this breed. The Miniature Pinscher was briefly shown in the Terrier Group, but it was then moved to the Toy Group where it has remained a major contender for many years. The

Shih Tzu. *Tauskey*

Silky Terrier. *Hal Boucher*

American-bred Miniature Pinscher has made tremendous progress in quality in recent years and is generally accepted as the world's best. As a clean companion and an alert alarm dog, the Miniature Pinscher has a growing following in the United States.

The Shih Tzu

The most recent addition to the Toy Group is the Shih Tzu. Originating in China, the breed made its way into England and Scandinavia in the early 1930s. Recognized by the English Kennel Club in 1934, the breed became more popular in England after World War II. Returning U.S. military personnel are credited with bringing the breed into the United States. The AKC recognized the Shih Tzu in 1955, but it was not until 1969 that the breed first competed for championship points. On its first day of regular competition, Chumalari Ying Ying, a dog owned by Rev. and Mrs. D. Allan Easton, was awarded Best in Show at the New Brunswick Kennel Club event. The Shih Tzu has since become very popular as a show dog and as a pet. It is an attractive breed in appearance and in temperament and is very adaptable to different living conditions.

The Silky Terrier

The Silky Terrier is a combination of the Yorkshire Terrier and the Australian Terrier. A picture of the first pair brought to the United States appeared in the February 1936 issue of the *National Geographic*. The breed again received national publicity when a puppy bred by Mrs. Merle C. Smith appeared on the cover of *This Week*. The Silky Terrier Club of America was officially organized in California in 1955, and the AKC recognized the breed in 1959. The first national specialty show was held in California in 1961. The Silky Terrier is one of the toy breeds in which the emphasis has been less toy and more Terrier. The Silky is a moderate and natural breed with a blue and tan coat.

The Italian Greyhound

One of the older toy breeds, the Italian Greyhound is the smallest of the gaze hounds and is believed to be as old as 2,000 years. Of Greek and Turkish origin, the breed spread through Europe from Italy and became a favorite of the aristocracy. Although small, the breed has retained many of the characteristics of a hound. The combination of its size and its ability to live with people has made this toy breed much revered in objects of art.

The Italian Greyhound has enjoyed a select and rather small following. The first dog was registered by the AKC in 1886, but a strongly organized effort for the breed did not come until 1954 with the organization of the Italian Greyhound Club of America. Since that time, several individual dogs have enjoyed rewarding show careers and have helped to draw attention to the breed. Accepted in all colors except black and tan and brindle, the Italian Greyhound is an elegant toy hound whose quiet manner makes it a welcome addition to many homes.

The Papillon

Another toy breed whose origin is interesting, if a bit confusing, is the Papillon. It is believed by some that the Spaniards mixed a small Chinese dog with a Chihuahua type from Mexico. This cross would explain the large ears that, when erect, give the breed its butterfly appearance and its French name. Although the Papillon bears a French name, the English have contributed heavily to the development of the breed. The AKC first registered the breed in 1912 and in 1915 awarded a championship to a dog from the first Papillon litter bred in the United States.

The Papillon has a rather small but devoted following. The breed is characterized by its large ears, which may be either erect or drop (Phalene). The erect ear has always had more appeal to the American fancy. The Papillon is not a complicated breed to care for. The flat silky coat is easily brushed, and its bright, alert expression makes the breed very attractive.

The Brussels Griffon

Another toy breed that comes in two coats is the Brussels Griffon. The breed was introduced to the United States from Belgium largely through the efforts of Mrs. Olivia Cedar of New York. The Griffon was first registered with the AKC in 1910, and the first specialty show of the Brussels Griffon Club of America was held in 1918.

The rough-coated Griffon, which must be cared for properly, requires more in time and effort than does the smooth-coated dog. The Brussels Griffon, probably developed as a small ratter and companion dog, usually weighs between 8 and 10 pounds and should not exceed 12 pounds. It is sometimes confused with the Affenpinscher from which it is descended, but the Griffon is different in several ways. The Griffon's rather large head, large black eyes, and upturned lower jaw are distinct characteristics of this toy breed.

A basketful of Papillons, 1956. *Clint Grant*

The Affenpinscher

The Affenpinscher was first registered by the AKC in 1936. It is reasonable to assume that the breed's German origin and the timing of its AKC registration in relationship to World War II did not particularly help its "popularity campaign." While still not overwhelmingly popular today, the Affenpinscher has made recent gains. Receiving the title of "Monkey Dog" from the rough translation of its Teutonic name, the breed, in the opinion of some, bears resemblance in expression to a monkey. Black is the predominate color in the breed, but black and tan, red, gray, and other combinations are acceptable. The breed's head, its coat, and its natural, almost unkempt appearance account in part for the breed's attraction.

Maltese.
Boice Studio

The Maltese

The Maltese is among the more glamorous of the toy breeds. Its coat is described in the official breed standard as covering the body "from head to foot with a mantle of long, silky, white hair." While the modern techniques of caring for and preparing the coat for the show ring have added to its glamorous appearance, this ancient breed has long possessed many of the characteristics found today. The Maltese dog was depicted on ancient Greek and Roman works of art dating back to approximately 500 B.C. The breed obviously derived its name from the island of Malta, but beyond that fact, confusion exists about the origin of the breed.

The Maltese arrived in England about 1840 and came to the United States around 1875. It was first registered with the AKC in 1888 as a Maltese Terrier, but the terrier portion of the name was dropped prior to 1928. This four-to-six-pound toy enjoys worldwide popularity today, and Americans are credited with having developed the breed to what many consider its highest degree of quality. The Maltese's white coat is considered difficult to keep by some, but the reward is obvious for those who make the effort. The contrast between the white coat and the coal-black eyes and nose makes the breed especially attractive and much in demand.

Portable and adaptable, spirited and protective, the toy breeds are an important part of the pure-bred dog scene in the United States.

6

The Non-Sporting Group

James E. Clark and Anne Rogers Clark

There is nothing quite as negative as a "non." That "non" simply precludes the existence of whatever condition is tacked on to it. Non-slip. Non-fattening. Non-alcoholic. Not even a little bit can be a part!

And so it was in the eyes of the men who were to direct the AKC and the affairs of dogs. In their eyes a breed was either of a "Sporting nature" or else it was relegated to being a "Non-Sporting" dog. That was that. There was no gray area.

The Sporting Division could and, in fact, did include hounds and terriers, and shortly after the turn of the century, the constitution and by-laws of the AKC provided for the classification of breeds listed below.

As time passed, the AKC classified further. The then-existing Sporting Division got shaken down to the Sporting Group, the Hound Group, and the Terrier Group. The Toy Group received their own special recognition, diminishing the Non-Sporting ranks considerably. The breeds whose primary purpose was (and is) to guard, or herd, or pull a sled were designated as working dogs and became the Working Group. (Note: Many of these breeds remain a part of the Non-Sporting Group in several registry bodies around the world today.) The Skye Terrier was elevated to the Terrier rank. "Foreign" dogs either vanished or took their places in one of the five Groups. Toy Terriers did not answer the call.

Boston Terrier. *Ludwig.*

Poodle (Standard Variety) relaxes before judging.

RULE XXVII

Special prizes can be classified and judged under the following division of breeds:

SPORTING DIVISION
Airedale Terriers
Basset Hounds
Beagles
Bedlington Terriers
Black and Tan (Manchester) Terriers
Bloodhounds
Bullterriers
Chesapeake Bays
Dachshunde
Dandie Dinmont Terriers
Foxhounds
Foxterriers (Smooth)
Foxterriers (Wire)
Sealyham Terriers
Greyhounds
Harriers
Irish Terriers
Otter Hounds
Pointers
Retrievers
Scottish Deerhounds
Scottish Terriers
Setters
Spaniels (Clumber)
Spaniels (Cocker)
Spaniels (Field)
Spaniels (Irish Water)
Spaniels (Sussex)
Spaniels (Water, other than Irish)
Springers (Welsh)
Whippets
Welsh Terriers
West Highland White Terriers
White English Terriers
Wolfhounds (Irish)
Wolfhounds (Russian)

NON-SPORTING
Boston Terriers
Bulldogs
Chow Chows
Collies
Dalmatians
English Toy Spaniels
Foreign Dogs
French Bulldogs
Great Danes
Griffons (Bruxellois)
Italian Greyhounds
Japanese Spaniels
Maltese Terriers
Mastiffs
Newfoundlands
Old English Sheepdogs
Pekingese Spaniels
Pomeranians
Poodles
Pugs
Schipperkes
Skye Terriers
St. Bernards
Toy Terriers
Yorkshire Terriers

The seven remaining breeds comprised the Non-Sporting Group. They were joined much later by four more breeds to swell the ranks to 12, including the two varieties of poodles—a distinction made quite recently. And so the Non-Sporting Group—by far the smallest—must distinguish itself by being so versatile and of such superior quality that it can hold its own to all comers.

The Bulldog

In the mid-1800s the Bulldog faced extinction. Bullbaiting had lost favor in England and, without reason, the dogs that had been bred for that special job were being allowed to slip away. The breeding that went into the development of the Bulldog was extraordinary in that it produced an animal with a head structure enabling it to hang on to a bull's nose while still being able to breathe; a body conformation providing the massive forequarters necessary to house the heart and lung; and, most important, a temperament providing the courage and tenacity so much admired in this dog. A group of British fanciers joined together to save the breed, forming the Bulldog Club of England in 1875. Several dogs were exported to the United States and the first Bulldog was registered here in 1886. Then the Bulldog Club of America came into being in 1890. These were dedicated people on both sides of the Atlantic, and this dedication continues today, ensuring a strength of quality that guarantees a high spot for the breed in competition.

The Boston Terrier

The Boston Terrier has its roots in a Bulldog-Terrier cross that can be traced back to post–Civil War days. Several of these dogs—they were, in fact, mongrels—made their way to the United States from England on trading vessels. A Mr. Hooper from Boston bought one from a sailor and bred her. The refinement of the resulting offspring established a breed called Roundheads—a name later changed to Boston Terrier. The first dog was registered in 1893 and was to herald one of the very few breeds of any Group to be developed in this country. The distinctive look of "The Boston Gentleman" caught on quickly, and the breed continues its popularity today.

The French Bulldog

The other short-faced breed in the Non-Sporting Group, the French Bulldog, was also the result of a Bulldog cross; this time, however, the cross was made on the Continent. Bulldogs of small stature were exported from England to France where fanciers crossed them with any of several short-faced Mediterranean breeds, working until they produced a small bat-eared dog resembling the Bulldog but having a size and temperament that made it an ideal pet for small quarters. First registered in this country in 1898, the "Frenchie" rose to immediate popularity. A staunch group of supporters protect the future of this little dog.

The Chow Chow

At the turn of the century, the Chow Chow found welcome in the AKC Stud Book. A dog named Yen How was registered in 1903. Before the birth of Christ, the breed had been a guard and hunting dog in China. The Chow is a dog of many distinctive traits, and its black tongue is its trademark. By the 1920s the Chow Chow was a status symbol, and while aloof with strangers, it was a faithful family guardian. Superior examples of the breed continue to win strongly at shows throughout this country.

Bulldog. *Ludwig*

Chow Chow, c. 1938. *Tauskey*

Keeshond. *Ludwig*

The Keeshond

The Keeshond, like the Bulldog, faced extinction as recently as 1917. The only existing examples of the breed then were to be found on the barges in Holland where their Dutch masters depended on these hardy, trustworthy dogs to protect their working craft. The Baroness Van Hardencroek was able to select enough "typey" animals from these working dogs to reestablish the breed. In 1930 the first Keeshond was registered in this country, and the breed was immediately taken up by astute fanciers who have jealously guarded the superb temperament and impish smile—those appealing traits of the correct Keeshond.

The Schipperke

The other breed to make its mark as a barge dog—the Schipperke—did not come into its own in this country until about 1930, although the first dog, named "Snowball," was registered in 1904. The word *Schipperke* means "Little Captain," and its trim, black uniform, complete with *jabot* and *culottes* and its military bearing, show this dog to be well named. The fanciers of the breed are legion and devoted.

The Dalmatian

So many dog people want to take credit for the Dalmatian that it's difficult to pinpoint the dog's origin. Is its ancestor the spotted dog of India, or one or more of the native dogs of Italy, Egypt, or Yugoslavia? Or perhaps dogs owned by gypsies who roamed the Balkans? Wherever this breed came from, its "way with horses" is justifiably famous. The Dalmatian will steady the skittish filly, guard the coach, and add a touch of class to the immaculately turned-out tandem. What self-respecting fire company would answer the alarm without their coach dog as a part of the team? The breed was first registered in this country in 1888, and the clean lines and distinctive markings of the Dalmatian make this breed welcome in the city as well as in the stable.

The Lhasa Apso and the Tibetan Terrier

The two Tibetan breeds, the Lhasa Apso and the Tibetan Terrier had similar beginnings with Llamas in their native land, and both were thought to bring good luck. The Lhasa was known as the Talisman Dog or Lhasa Terrier until 1935, when the first Lhasa Apso was admitted to the AKC Stud Book and its name officially changed. The Lhasa made its show debut in the Terrier Group and was shown in that Group until 1955, when it became a part of the Non-Sporting Group. The Tibetan Terrier, a taller dog than the Lhasa, did not make its appearance in this country until 1956. It is one of the most recent breeds to be admitted to the AKC Stud Book—the first Tibetan having been registered in 1973.

The Bichon Frise

Among the many breeds to emerge from the Mediterranean area is the Bichon Frise. The Bichon Frise and the Teneriffe were interchangeable names given to a low-on-leg, long-coated white dog tracing back to 250 B.C. Brought to this country in the late 1930s, the breed was not a serious part of the dog scene until a parent club was formed in 1964. The first member of the breed was registered in 1972. A dog of great appeal, the Bichon is sought after as a rewarding pet, and its successes in the show ring document the dedication of the fancy.

The Poodle

Of super intelligence and amazing versatility, the Poodle was busy retrieving in Germany, dancing in the circuses of France, and being carried by stylish ladies all over the Continent as long ago as the seventeenth century. Like the Dalmatian, everyone wants to lay claim to its beginnings—and just maybe they can. What has emerged is a breed that comes in three sizes (the smallest of which appears in the Toy Group), all colors, and a classic clip sculpted from a profuse coat. First registered in this country in 1887, the Poodle has had a slow, steady rise in popularity until 1960 when the breed took over first place in registration figures—a position it continues to hold—showing that the Poodle's intelligence and versatility appeal to all people.

And so, without design, an elite group has come together to make up the Non-Sporting Group. No other Group can boast participants with a more interesting heritage. Where else can we find guards, and hunters, and barge dogs, and ratters, and dancers—from China, and France, and Tibet, and maybe Egypt? If these are *Non*-Sports, maybe it is not so bad to be Non-Sporting after all!

Dalmatians await their turn in the show ring.

Schipperke, *c.* 1946.

Bichon Frise with protective wrappings gets final grooming touches.

Lhasa Apso gets a lift from the grooming area to the show ring.

The frontispiece from Louisa M. Alcott's *Under the Lilacs* shows a turn-of-the-century curly-coated Poodle clipped in Continental trim—then, as now, one of the four acceptable clips for the show ring.

Poodles must be groomed to the show clip.

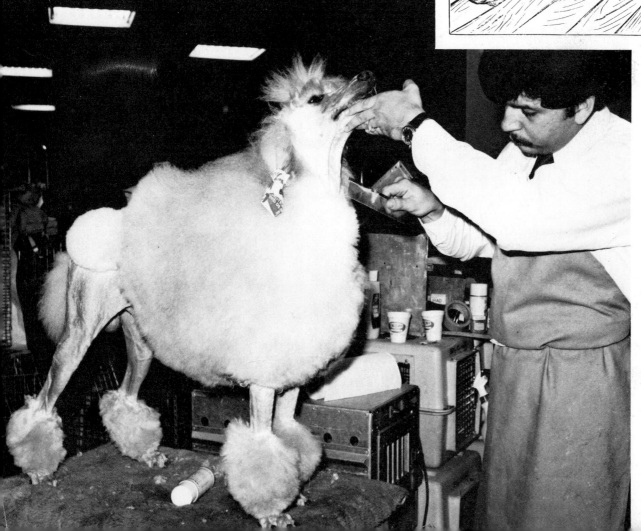

Old English Sheepdog. *Terence A. Gili*

7

The Herding Group

Herman L. Fellton

"But should you, while wandering in the wild sheepland, happen on moor or in the market upon a very perfect gentle knight clothed in dark grey habit, splashed here and there with rays of moon; free by right divine of the guild of gentlemen, strenuous as a prince, lithe as a rowan, graceful as a girl, with high king carriage, motions and manners of a fairy queen; should he have a noble breadth of brow, an air of still strength born of right confidence, all unassuming; last and most unfailing test of all, should you look into two snowcloud eyes, calm, wistful, inscrutable, their soft depths clothed on with eternal sadness—yearning, as is said, for the soul that is not theirs—know then that you look upon one of the line of the most illustrious sheepdogs of the North."
—"Owd Bob"

Alfred Olliphant's romantic description of a nineteenth-century British sheepdog in his fictional biography of Bob, Son of Battle, could be applied in general to the "Colley" dogs of the British Islands which, with their interrelated family trees, could include today's Collie, Rough and Smooth, Shetland Sheepdog, Bearded Collie, Border Collie, and, by way of the Bearded Collie, the Old English Sheepdog or Bobtail, all of which were used to herd sheep.

The present Herding Group consists of fourteen breeds that differ greatly in appearance, size, and conformation. These are the storied breeds—Albert Payson Terhune's Lad, and the other Collies from his many books; Bob, Son of Battle mentioned above, the Collie, Lassie, from literature and television and, for older readers, the German Shepherd, Rin Tin Tin from the silent movies and early talkies.

Herding dogs are movers and shakers for the farmer and shepherd. As their generic name implies, their main duty has been to drive live-stock from one place to another—from the range into the pen, or from the pasture into the

105

milking shed. Their instinct to herd, which must always be done under the direction of a herder, makes them unsuitable for full-time flock guarding as practiced by breeds such as the Great Pyrenees, Kuvaszok and Komondorok. Classified by AKC within the Working Group, these three breeds have been referred to as "the lions who lie down with lambs."

The Herding breeds are easily trained because of their natural responsiveness to man. They make excellent farm watchdogs and devoted companions in the home.

British Sheep and Cattle Dogs

The Bearded Collie

An old breed that has recently regained prominence and popularity, Beardies were and are used as sheepdogs and as drovers' dogs to move cattle. They gained AKC approval to compete for championship points in 1977.

The Collie

The Collie was one of the first pure-bred dogs imported into the United States when an organized interest in the sport of exhibiting grew among dog lovers here. The first breed registrations appear in Volume 2 of the AKC Stud Book in 1885. The Collie Club of America was organized in 1886 and was the second parent club to join the AKC. The dogs were exhibited at the second Westminster Kennel Club Show in classes for "Shepherd Dogs or Collie Dogs."

In 1899 Collies and Old English Sheepdogs were included in the same breed classification. At the Collie Club of America Specialty Show that year, the first three places in Open Dogs went to Old English Sheepdogs, much to the annoyance of Collie owners! (The judge was Henry Jarret, an early Old English Sheepdog fancier.)

The Old English Sheepdog

Its closest relation being the Bearded Collie, this breed, also known as the Bobtail, was originally registered in this country as "Sheepdog, English Old-Fashioned Bobtailed." The first separate class for Old English Sheepdogs was at the Westminster Kennel Club Show in 1890. Early Bobtail owners and exhibitors were among the wealthiest individuals in America, people like J. Pierpont Morgan, the Goulds, Harrimans, Guggenheims, and Vanderbilts. The Old English Sheepdog Club of America was organized in 1904 by, among others, Henry Tilley of the famous and influential Shepton Kennels in England. The parent club was recognized by the AKC in 1905.

The Shetland Sheepdog

This is a working Collie in miniature, not a miniaturized Collie. It was developed from the small working Collie, which was also the progenitor of the modern show Collie. A substantial, balanced little dog is desirable, with a weather-resistant Collie coat, Collie type and expression, and Sheltie size, charm, and character.

The Welsh Corgi

There are actually two Welsh Corgis, the Pembroke and the Cardigan. They are two distinct breeds, although considerable intermating once existed in Wales in their respective shires. The Cardigan has a tail and carries a little more size and substance. Corgis have existed on farms in southwest Wales for hundreds of years, primarily as herders. They drive cattle to and from the pastures or to market, guarding against intruders, checking the leaders, and persuading the sluggards by biting at their heels and avoiding the kick that followed by ducking quickly out of the way—a stratagem that earned the dog the description of "heeler."

The Three Belgians

In Belgium sheepdogs developed into four breeds or varieties—the Groenendael, Lackenois, Malinois, and Tervuren. They vary from each other in coloration and nature of coat. Here in the United States the AKC has recognized three of these breeds—the Belgian Sheepdog (Groenendael), the Belgian Malinois, and the Belgian Tervuren.

Other Sheep and Cattle Dogs

The Australian Cattle Dog
Recently recognized by the AKC, this breed of small, tough heelers was developed in Australia to control unfenced herds of cattle. Australian Cattle Dogs are the result of the cross-breeding that took place during the period from 1830 to 1840. The Smithfield dog was crossed with the Dingo (the so-called wild dog of Australia), then with the smooth blue merle Collie, and then with some Dalmatian and black and tan Kelpie blood. They were known as Queensland Heelers and Australian Heelers before Australian Cattle Dogs became their breed name.

The Bouvier des Flandres
The Bouvier served primarily as a cattle driver in southwest Flanders and on the French northern hills. Almost destroyed in Europe during the First World War, a survivor named Ch. Nic do Sottegem, who possessed excellent type, left many descendents. The breed is now mainly a police, defense, and army dog in Belgium. In the early 1970s, when I judged a Bouvier Specialty Show in Johannesburg, South Africa, I was surprised and delighted at the large number of high-quality dogs exhibited. After some reflection, however, I realized that the Boers, who were the early settlers there, came from that part of Europe where the Bouvier was most numerous and popular, and must have brought with them from Europe the ancestors of the very dogs I was judging.

The Briard
This preeminent sheepdog of France is probably the most ancient of the sheepdogs, although the name Briard was first used in 1809. The breed was accurately described in the fourteenth century and was mentioned in records as far back as the twelfth century in France. They have been used primarily to herd and guard sheep, but they also have excellent reputations as police dogs and as war dogs who accompany patrols and carry food, supplies, and even munitions to the front line. Double dewclaws on their hind legs are a unique breed characteristic shared only with the Great Pyrenees.

Collie (Rough Variety),
c. 1946.

Collie (Smooth Variety).

A Shetland Sheepdog eagerly heads off a sheep. *Carol Bradley*

Australian Cattle Dog. *Jim Callea*

Belgian Tervuren. *Evelyn Shafer*

Pembroke Welsh Corgi.

German Shepherd Dog
in a painting
by Ward Binks.
Gouache on paper,
1934.
AKC Collection

The German Shepherd Dog

The German Shepherd Dog is a natural beauty that has a close association with man. Originally a herding and farm dog, this breed has become a police dog par excellence. Its control, application, and courage are second to none, and it is outstanding for crowd control. The German Shepherd Dog has performed wartime duties with great distinction in this country and abroad, and it is now widely used to detect contraband drugs and explosives. Its work as a guide dog for blind people has been well publicized. The Shepherd is a dog of great versatility, as well as a family and companion dog. Unfortunately its great popularity has caused injudicious overbreeding, resulting in some temperament and other problems that first appeared in the 1930s. I vividly remember, though, the imported Ch. Dewet v d Starrenburg lying majestically on his bench and trotting faultlessly across the show ring in the mid–1930s. A dog of excellent substance, balance, and temperament, he was very much what was needed for the restoration of the German Shepherd Dog in this country.

The Puli

A medium-sized dog probably descended from the Tibetan Terrier, the Puli is solid in color (black, rusty-black, shades of gray and white) and has a weather-resistant double coat that tends to cord. It was originally used to herd and drive sheep. The Puli gait is springy and efficient, and it is delightful to see a properly balanced dog, with topline level and coat touching or almost touching the floor, moving along at a fast trot with ease.

Puli. *Diane Pearce*

PART TWO
The Sport Of Pure-Bred Dogs

Previous page: **Bloodhound performs in a tracking test.**

Westminster 1982: Breed judging in progress at Madison Square Garden.

8

Show Dogs and Great Shows

Steve Cady

At the edge of the crowd, a matronly woman lowers her voice to what seems like gleeful confidentiality. ¶ "My sources tell me an Afghan's going to win," she whispers. "The big handlers already are starting to sweep a lot of the local people out." ¶ "Listen," her male companion says, nodding in agreement, "most of the experts can tell you in October who's going to win at Westminster the following February. No problem."

It is barely 10:00 A.M. in West Springfield, Massachusetts, but rumors of so-called "political" judging have been circulating amiably for two hours around the three acres of floor space where 2,176 contestants are trying to look their best. To hear some of the gossipers talk, an uninitiated visitor might think the day-long competition is being conducted by Ali Baba and the Forty Thieves.

But these are not suspicious horseplayers discussing the latest race-fixing scandal. Not at all. The gossipers are simply indulging in a favorite sidelight of their favorite sport, a sport where winning or losing has always depended on personal judgments so subjective that almost any major decision can invite controversy. Such is the nature of dog shows.

The three-show "cluster" arrangement, reflecting a growing trend to fight inflation by sharing a common site, qualifies as major league with 1,868 dogs for the South Windsor Kennel Club on Friday, 2,176 on Saturday for Windham County, and 2,669 for the Springfield Kennel Club on Sunday. Many of the contestants are well-publicized dogs that "do a lot of winning," as the fanciers say. They are being shown by big-name handlers whose annual incomes sometimes approach the six-figure bracket. And they are being evaluated by noted judges from as far away as Texas.

By AKC standards, the contests are similar to a dozen or more additional all-breed events taking place this same weekend at sites around the United States. The Massachusetts action, naturally, can't compare in prestige with glittering showcase presentations such as Westminster or Santa Barbara. And it bears little resemblance, on the surface anyway, to the outdoor splendor of Morris and Essex when that most elegant of dog shows was drawing crowds of up to 50,000 during a golden 30-year era that lasted through 1957. Beneath the surface, though, the essence of the competition in the drab, hangarlike Better Living Center is basically the same as Westminster or any other all-breed show: a glorification of the pure-bred dog. In a sense, South Windham is every dog show—past, present, and future.

For the patronizing cynics who regard dog shows as little more than a frivolous exercise in vanity, the weekend activity will offer nothing new. There will be no long touchdown passes, bases-loaded home runs, or slam-dunk baskets to excite the crowd and no bone-jarring violence to serve vicarious needs. But that's not what the dog fanciers have come to see. They have been drawn by the same magnet that draws them to any dog show: their love of dogs, spiced by the added flavor of competition. Eleanor Robson Belmont, whose husband was President of the AKC from 1888 to 1916, described the feeling memorably in 1957 when she wrote: "If you own animals of any kind, aside from the pleasure they give you personally, it becomes agonizingly important, once entered, how they fare in a contest."

Make no mistake about it. Show dogs may be the snobs among America's 14 million registered pure-breds, but they are athletes competing in athletic contests. In addition to being outstanding specimens of their breeds, top dogs must have the temperament to handle the stress of crowds, the stamina to survive constant travel by land and air, and the showmanship to exude happiness in the ring day after day. They must look like a winner and act like a winner. As dog judges have put it, "Show dogs are like show girls. They've not only gotta have it, they've gotta *show* it."

For pure snobbery in the world of pure-bred dogs, there's no business like show business. Earn 15 points, and you can have a "Ch." (designating "Champion") placed in front of your aristocratic name. Go Best in Show or even Best of Breed at a prestigious event like Westminster, and you can become a snob for life. The dogs, of course, won't ever go around bragging about it. Dogs are innocents, after all, and that's part of the appeal of dog shows. At West Springfield, in the foothills of the Berkshires, the message comes through clearly on the bumper stickers of cars, vans, and motor homes in the parking lots outside the low-slung building.

"*Support Your Local Bloodhound, Get Lost!*" one of the stickers reads.

"*Chesapeakes Are More Fun,*" argues another, competing for attention with a pair of decals—"*Hug a Husky*" and "*Goldens Got It All.*"

Two arrivals from Rhode Island, a van and a station wagon, carry the parochialism all the way to their license plates. One plate says *CHOWS*, the other *CHOWZ*. On rear windows there are heart-shaped "*I Love*" tributes to English Springer Spaniels and half a dozen other breeds among the more than 125 recognized by the AKC.

But a bumper sticker on a car from Vermont ignores special-interest propaganda and brings the whole occasion into impartial focus with the exuberant declaration: *"This Vehicle Stops at All Dog Shows."* It has stopped on this particular Saturday in late November at the annual Windham County Kennel Club Show, the second of three all-breed events being held on consecutive days at the Better Living Center of the Eastern States Exposition Grounds.

That's what they are doing now inside the Better Living Center, where the search for Best in Show proceeds on schedule. While troops of dogs parade for breed judges in 20 rings, spectators check the identifying numbers worn by the handlers against the entries listed in the catalog. The scene suggests a wall-to-wall kaleidoscope: a blend of circus, fashion show, barbershop, beauty pageant, gambling casino, class reunion, political caucus, picnic, even a children's music recital, with the proud parents beaming their approval and encouragement.

Despite the commotion, the dogs display a remarkable friendliness and tolerance toward one another and toward the humans. Outside the judging areas, hundreds of dogs either snooze or rest in their carrying cases or makeshift pens. Others are patiently standing, sitting, or even lying on their sides on grooming tables, as their beauticians prepare them for the ring with brushing, clipping, trimming, fluffing, spraying, and combing. There are oils and lotions to be applied, drops to clear the eyes, plastic curlers for the ears, elastic bands for unruly hair. The dogs gaze shamelessly at passersby, whose smiles or greetings are enough to set a tail wagging. There are exceptions, to be sure. Not all dogs, even if they're physically qualified, can adjust to pressures of the show ring.

"This has got her bonkers," one woman exhibitor says, leading an early loser toward an exit. "All this stress. You're not seeing the real dog."

Yet most of the dogs seem to relish the attention they are getting. At a dog-portrait concession booth, the artist greets a friend who is holding a Welsh Corgi.

"He says he came from England when he was sixteen months old," the owner informs her.

"Ask him if he's got his naturalization papers yet," the artist replies, patting the dog on the head and cooing. "Hi, sweetheart, how are ya?" The Corgi looks pleased.

As the nineteenth-century British novelist Samuel Butler noted, "The great pleasure of a dog is that you make a fool of yourself with him and not only will he not scold you, but he will make a fool of himself, too." Dogs have not changed in this respect, even the dignified ones that compete in the serious business of dog shows.

The visit to West Springfield has been made as part of a search for the answers to questions such as the following: Who are the greatest show dogs in the history of the sport? Which shows are the greatest? Is it really possible for Group and Best in Show judges to measure closeness to one breed standard against closeness to another breed standard? Can a breed become too popular for its own good? In particular, does Best in Show at Westminster lead to ultimate ruin, as critics have sometimes charged, for the breed whose representative wins it? Is political judging—in which a judge pays more attention to a dog's owner, breeder, or handler than to the dog itself—a serious problem? Would it be fairer to have Best in Show selected by a panel of judges instead of by just one person?

Those same subjects would be pursued by further research at AKC head-

Handler Bill Trainor gaits a Pekingese, one of the six Group Winners at the 1982 Westminster Show. *Callea Photo*

Best in Show Judge Nancy Lindsay looks over the finalists. *Callea Photo*

The Peke wins it! *Callea Photo*

Ch. St. Aubrey Dragonora of Elsdon
nestles in her trophy. *Callea Photo*

quarters in New York City and during interviews with prominent dog people such as Haworth F. Hoch, Leonard Brumby, and Howard Tyler.

At West Springfield, as in almost every all-breed dog show, the big field will be narrowed to six Group winners and then to one Best in Show. For a Best in Show judge, the responsibility is enormous. No other sporting event puts so much authority in the hands of a single official. There is no jury—and no appeal. Spectators can cheer for their favorites, but that doesn't count. Somebody has to make the decision. And that's what stirs the debate. If Albert Payson Terhune himself were judging Best in Show, there probably would be howls of anguish from some of the dissenters. Yet the ritual happens every weekend at the 900 all-breed shows held annually under AKC Rules, a schedule that has tripled since the mid-1960s. Best in Show, criticized in the distant past by the purists as an absurdity, has become as important to all-breed dog shows as peaks are to mountain climbers.

"It's part of the mystique," says Anne Rogers Clark, one of the country's foremost professional handlers before she turned to judging. "People want a Best in Show, and your top judges know how to find it for them."

Yet by nightfall on Sunday, the weekend results at West Springfield will have provided a classic example of the uncertainty inherent in dog shows. Three different dogs, each of them entered on all three days, would account for a Best in Show. That's what can happen when different judges look at the same dogs.

"They could see the same dog in a different light at the same time," says William F. Stifel, President of the AKC, "but that's the game. You put the whole question of relative merit up to one person at one particular time."

The one person on this particular Saturday will be Mrs. Dona Ehrich Hausman of Stamford, Connecticut. But she will not be making her decision until about 6:00 P.M. And that is still eight hours away.

America's response to "dog show" in a word-association test would undoubtedly be "Westminster." If there is one event in the dog world that catches the general public's attention, it is the Westminster Kennel Club's two-day competition every February at Madison Square Garden in New York City.

It's not that dog shows aren't popular in other areas. They are. They can be found from Cape Cod to San Jose, from Tallahassee to Honolulu. Places like Topeka, Dubuque, and Las Vegas have shows. So do Shreveport, Myrtle Beach, and Texarkana. Dog shows are staged in coliseums, field houses, arenas, armories, and auditoriums, at racetracks, hotels, and shopping malls, and on college campuses and private estates. But the ultimate showcase is Westminster, whose inception in 1877 makes it the second oldest continuously held sporting event in the United States. Only horse racing's Kentucky Derby, first run in 1875, is older. Like the Derby, Westminster is the event that owners, breeders, and handlers want to win more than any other.

After Westminster, which one would they like most to win? Here the answers tend to diverge. Most dog people, of course, speak reverently about the past glory of Morris and Essex. Many of them rate Santa Barbara, an outdoor show in California, as second now in prestige to Westminster. Beyond that there is disagreement over which shows have prestige and which just have "numbers," the word used by dog people to denote the size but not necessarily the quality of the entry list.

A poll by the *American Kennel Gazette* indicated that a large percentage of fanciers consider the year's second most prestigious dog show to be the national specialty show of the particular breed with which they are associated. Hardly anybody, though, disputes the preeminence of Westminster, named for the old hotel at Irving Place and Sixteenth Street in Manhattan. It was there that a group of men who enjoyed sporting dogs, especially Setters and Pointers, used to meet regularly. In 1876 the group decided to hold a dog show under the banner of what they called the Westminster Kennel Club.

Westminster, it seems, was a hit right from the start. The first show, in May of 1877, was so popular with exhibitors and the public that it was extended from three to four days. It took place in Gilmore's Garden, sometimes called the Hippodrome, a former railroad depot at Madison Avenue and Twenty-sixth Street that became the original Madison Square Garden in 1879. Occupying the site today is the 40-story New York Life Building, which houses the present headquarters of the American Kennel Club. The first show drew 1,201 dogs, and a report in *Forest and Stream* noted: "We question if on any other occasion has there ever assembled in this city such a number of people at one time, and representing as much of the culture, wealth and fashion of the town."

In those days, the dogs had fancy price tags but much plainer names than they have today. Before the 1883 Westminster, for example, the cover of *Harper's Weekly* carried photographs of 11 dogs that included an Irish Water Spaniel named Mike, an English Mastiff named Turk, and a Pug named Ch. George. AKC regulations nowadays permit as many as 25 letters in a name, and the results can run to the likes of Ch. Show Biz Missy No Home, Hearthside I'm a Regal Beagle, and Hell's a Blazen Be Kinda Kool. All three of those dogs were competing at West Springfield.

Because of its far-reaching prestige, Westminster has the capability of making a breed too popular for its own good. Repeated success there by the same breed can cause at least temporary problems. Trends and popularity always have had an effect, for better or worse, on various breeds. Unusual popularity has sometimes led to a short-term decline of a breed's quality as a result of indiscriminate "backyard" breeding. When the demand slackens, the breed usually improves. Cocker Spaniels, Poodles, Doberman Pinschers, and Boxers are among the breeds that have gone through this cycle one or more times. So have German Shepherd Dogs, a breed that has never been Best in Show at Westminster.

Concern about the problem goes back as far as the turn of the century, when the artist Homer Davenport criticized what dog-show fads were doing to Collies, among other breeds. Speaking of some prize-winning Collies, he warned: "Their heads are long, narrow and flat, with no room for the brains the breed once had. Instead of being able to drive sheep or cattle, they now cannot follow their owner through a small country town without being lost."

Serious dog people have nothing but contempt for opportunistic backyard breeding in general. What they say in particular about the so-called puppy mills, the assembly-line factories that breed dogs for pet shops, is largely unprintable. It was puppy-mill greed that helped send Cocker Spaniels down-hill after the Best in Show Westminster victories by Ch. My Own Brucie in 1940 and 1941.

"They're happy, marvelous little dogs now," said Ted Young, a leading

For sheer elegance, nothing
has ever equaled
Morris and Essex.
Evelyn Shafer

With its flower
arrangements, new-mown grass,
ocean breezes,
and colorful tenting,
Santa Barbara has
a reputation for
beauty and quality.

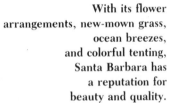

Del Monte Kennel Club Show
at Pebble Beach, California.
Julian P. Graham Studio

Cocker Spaniel handler, "but that's because the backyard breeders eventually got out of it and only the real breeders were left. The whole country sees a dog win at Westminster, and a lot of people say, 'I want one of those.' When every Tom, Dick, and Harry can make money on this, the breed can be harmed. Pet shops were breeding Cockers any which way so they'd have a lot of them."

That opinion is shared by Leonard Brumby, Jr., retired senior vice president of the AKC and a past president of the Professional Handlers' Association. During an interview at AKC headquarters, Brumby recalled a profit-minded female client who had brought two Cocker Spaniels to his kennel on Long Island in the 1950s to have them bred.

"They were nervous, ill-tempered wrecks," Brumby said. "If you went near them, they started screaming. When I told her I wouldn't touch them, she was indignant. She said, 'They should be perfect. They're brother and sister.' "

Most researchers agree that the first dog show for conformation purposes took place in the Town Hall at Newcastle-on-Tyne, England, in June of 1859. It presumably was more democratic than the exhibition of Pugs nine years earlier at which exhibitors were listed in order of their social standing and the dogs were fed cake at tea tables by liveried footmen. There is somewhat less of a consensus on when and where the first dog show in America was held. At one time it was thought that a bench show in Chicago on January 26, 1876, was the first. More recently, evidence has turned up for three shows staged in 1874 in Chicago; Mineola, New York; and Memphis, Tennessee.

Through the decades, the Show of the Eastern Dog Club shown here at the old Mechanics Hall in Boston has been one of the nation's foremost shows. *Evelyn Shafer*

124

GENERAL VIEW OF THE BENCH SHOW IN THE HIPPODROME, ON THURSDAY, MAY 10TH.

"DAGMAR." "OSCAR"
QUEEN VICTORIA'S DEER-HOUNDS, VALUED AT $100,000.

D. P. FOSTER'S "LION"

JONES'S SIB. BLOODHOUND "BRUNO" 1° PRIZE

MR. JONES'S SIBERIAN BLOODHOUND "BRUNO."

McDONNA'S "ROVER" $50,000.00

"MUNGO"
THE REV. MR. MACDONNA, WITH HIS DOG "MUNGO."

WAGNER'S "NELLIE"

MISS B. WEBB'S "REX" $1000.00

JNO. MATHEWS'S "DUKE" $1000.00

JOHN MATTHEWS'S "DUKE," VALUED AT $1,000.

MR. JOHN E. T. GRAINGER'S SETTER "NELLY" AND HER PUPS, VALUED AT $5,000.

ESQUIMAUX DOG

TWO-LEGGED DOG.—PUG "REX."—THE ONLY ESQUIMAUX IN THE SHOW

The above sketch of the first Westminster Kennel Club Show appeared in Leslie's Weekly, in the year 1877

THE FIRST AMERICAN KENNEL DOG SHOW HELD IN THE UNITED STATES.

The first Westminster Kennel Club Show, 1877, at the Hippodrome, New York City. *Courtesy of Herm David*

The 1874 Chicago show, staged by the Illinois State Sportsmen's Association on June 4, involved 21 Pointers and Setters with names like Nelly, Dolly, Bridget, Frank, and Joe. Almost all of them were exhibited as pairs, and the reports of the judges did not note any individual award for Best of Breed.

There is support for the Mineola show, on October 7 of that year, as the first "successful" bench show for dogs in the United States. That show, organized by Dr. Nicholas Rowe and restricted to Pointers and Setters, is thought to be the first at which the dogs were judged and placed.

The excitement generated by good show dogs has not faded over the years. Nowhere was it more evident than at the Morris and Essex Kennel Club's annual show, held from 1927 to 1957 at the Giralda Farms estate of Mrs. Geraldine Rockefeller Dodge in Madison, New Jersey. For sheer elegance, nothing before or after has equalled Morris and Essex.

Outdoor shows tend to be more pleasing to the senses than indoor events, and Morris and Essex was the epitome of bucolic pleasure. The 1939 edition, whose 4,456-dog entry still stands as the largest in the history of American dog shows, was typical. Picture the wide green expanse of a polo field. Now hoist 160,000 square feet of canvas for the tenting, more than double the footage required by the Barnum and Bailey, Ringling Brothers Circus at that time. Put up six enormous tents for the six Groups, with orange and blue pennants or American flags snapping from the pole tops in a summer breeze. Set up more big tents for a public cafeteria and a special area where 4,600 exhibitors, judges, and other officials can be served lunch by a famous caterer. Now stake out 57 judging rings, with a colorful beach umbrella over each judge's table. Hire 70 special policemen to handle traffic control for a crowd of 50,000. Then stack 383 pieces of sterling silver on the trophy table—and bring on the dogs.

At Morris and Essex, the event itself always stood out above any particular individuals or breeds. The winners invariably were good dogs, and that was enough. As one impressed journalist observed more than 40 years ago: "Their names are etched largely, for a moment, against an azure backdrop, and then they drift skyward into the sunset that always smiles on Morris and Essex."

Sketches from *Harper's Weekly*, 1879, of the Westminster Kennel Club Dog Show at Gilmore's Garden (also known as Madison Square Garden). *Courtesy of Herm David*

"CHARLIE"—NEWFOUNDLAND.

"FLO"—JAPANESE SPANIEL.

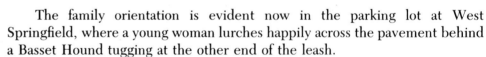

"PRINCE"—GREYHOUND.

The closest thing today to Morris and Essex's sun-kissed splendor is probably the Santa Barbara Kennel Club's annual outdoor show in July. Dog people regard Santa Barbara with the same kind of nostalgic affection horse people have for tracks like Hialeah, Keeneland, or Saratoga. From its inception in 1919, the California show has benefited from community support and scenic sites that include Hope Ranch Park, the Santa Barbara Polo Club, and Robertson Field at the University of California at Santa Barbara.

Over the years, with its flower arrangements, new-mown grass, ocean breezes, superior judging slate, and colorful tenting, Santa Barbara built a reputation for beauty, elegance, and quality that justified its billing as the Morris and Essex of the West. Now it's fighting to preserve that beauty and quality in the face of soaring expenses, and the nation's largest outdoor show (4,442 dogs as far back as 1975) has had to trim its entry list and streamline its operation. But it's still Santa Barbara. "If you're in dogs," one regular exhibitor put it, "it's part of your life and that's where you should be on that particular weekend."

Other outdoor shows of more than average prestige include Westchester County and Westbury in New York, Trenton in New Jersey, Old Dominion in Virginia, and Montgomery County, an all-Terrier event since its 1929 start, in Pennsylvania. On the indoor circuit, there would be votes for Chicago International and Detroit in the Midwest, Golden Gate and Beverly Hills in California, Eastern (of Boston) in New England, and Philadelphia. A number of shows, among them Dallas–Fort Worth in Texas and Tampa in Florida, have big numbers and are improving steadily in quality.

Two-day shows are becoming a rarity, and so are benched shows, at which the dogs must remain on public view in partitioned stalls for all or part of the day. Economics have helped change the fancy, as some prefer to call their clan, from a club for millionaire bluebloods with 150-dog kennels and full-time kennelmen to a more down-to-earth pastime geared to family participation. A lot of the "kennels" in today's show world consist of only one or two dogs, and about 60 percent of all show dogs are handled in the ring by their owners.

The family orientation is evident now in the parking lot at West Springfield, where a young woman lurches happily across the pavement behind a Basset Hound tugging at the other end of the leash.

"Is he in Obedience?" a bystander asks.

"Obedience?" she says, laughing. "For heaven's sake, he can't take two steps. No, he's a breed dog."

She speaks with affection, and the same good-natured tone prevails inside the Better Living Center as the breed judging continues into early afternoon. In a modest mezzanine-level cafeteria, judges and other officials dine with plastic forks and knives on a late lunch of cold cuts, macaroni salad, rolls, and cheese. Only about 10 percent of the dogs in the Windham County show will do any meaningful winning, with breed or Group ribbons or points toward a championship. And there will be only one big winner, a single number 1. But that doesn't discourage anybody, most of all the gossipers. They are still at it, concentrating now on the rumor that a top Miniature Schnauzer has been dismissed because he "measured out" (was too high at the withers) and the speculation that several Airedales have had their coats illegally dyed darker. J. Monroe Stebbins, the AKC field representative at the show, reportedly is checking.

"A person who shows one dog can run around all day gossiping," says Bill Trainor, a professional handler who went 28 years before his first Westminster Best in Show winner in 1979, and then won it again in 1982.

Asked if he has heard the rumor about an Afghan going Best in Show, Trainor laughs.

"HARROLD"—SMOOTH ST. BERNARD.

"I've been too busy," he says. "Look, there's favoritism from time to time at dog shows. Alva Rosenberg, the famous judge, said once if he had two dogs of equal quality and one of them was being shown by a friend, he'd put up his friend's dog. It happens. But I don't think there's ever been more than two or three cases of actual attempted bribery."

Dorothy Poole, a longtime Dachshund breeder from Carlisle, Massachusetts, is asked if dog people could agree on the top 10 or 20 champions in dog-show history. She says they couldn't, but she likens all top show dogs to performing artists who know how to project an image of vitality.

"The great dogs," she says, "what I would call the ultimate dogs, all have charisma. They seem to have a little more oomph than the others. And they are able to relax and behave at a show. Some people love to perform, but others just die on stage. It's the same with dogs."

Mrs. Poole illustrates her point with a story about a friend's Great Dane. The dog was extremely regal-looking at home, standing at attention to peer out windows or doorways if a car noise startled him. But whenever the woman went to pose him, as though at a dog show, he fell apart.

"TINY"—PUG.

"He simply didn't respond," Mrs. Poole explains. "He knew what she was doing."

Lining the walls on three sides of the Better Living Center, rows of concession stands offer a cornucopia of dog merchandise that includes powders, shampoos, skin lubricants, dog food, leashes, stickpins, porcelain statues, and books. The books range from classics like *Bob, Son of Battle* to specialized offerings such as *The Complete Collie* or *The New Doberman Pinscher* and a few irreverently titled volumes like *From Riches to Bitches, and a Cadillac for Your Vet.*

Near the book racks, a salesman in a yellow corduroy jacket stands behind a line of free-sample bins from which spectators are filling paper bags with scoopfuls of dry Gravy Train chunks.

"If you've got five dogs or more and want to save some serious money," the salesman brays, "ask the man with the Action Plan, the man from General Foods."

It's just another normal day at a typical dog show, and the best is yet to come. In another hour or two, when all the breed winners have been determined, it will be time to start judging the six Groups: Sporting, Non-Sporting, Working, Hound, Terrier, and Toy. From those contests will come the six finalists who will battle for Best in Show.

When the Westminster Kennel Club calls its only triple winner a "he" instead of a "she," a researcher can appreciate the hazards of trying to draw up a definitive list of great show dogs.

Westminster's 100th anniversary book, published in 1976, noted dutifully that the club's first Best in Show award was made in 1907 to a Smooth Fox Terrier named Ch. Warren Remedy. It added that the same contestant also won in 1908 and 1909, "making him the only dog to have won three Best in Shows at

"PATCH" AND "TATTERS"—SKYE TERRIERS.

Westminster." Considering the fact that Warren is a boy's name, the description seemed logical. But a nine-column report on the show in *The American Field* of February 23, 1907, contained the following disclosure: "Open bitches brought out the wonderful champion, Warren Remedy, which later on won the championship for the best dog of all breeds in the show. We may look for a long time for one to beat her."

Mix-ups such as that only underscore the fleeting nature of show-dog fame. Edd Embry Bivin, who had flown from Texas to judge the Terrier and Toy Groups and eight breeds in the Windham County show, pointed out that it was harder for a show dog to be remembered the way great racehorses are.

"The dog game is more fleeting," he said. "They come and go, and they get shuffled out. You don't have the same absolute gauge of success that you do with racehorses."

What, then, is the gauge of greatness for a show dog? One method might be simply to list the dogs that have been number 1 at Westminster, and let the search end there. Or the list could be limited to dogs that had topped Westminster more than once. That group would include, from 1931 or earlier, in addition to Ch. Warren Remedy, the Wire Fox Terriers Ch. Matford Vic, Ch. Conejo Wycollar Boy, and Ch. Pendley Calling of Blarney. Since 1940, the double-winners would be Ch. My Own Brucie, the Cocker Spaniel; Ch. Rancho Dobe's Storm, a Doberman Pinscher; and Ch. Chinoe's Adamant James, an English Springer Spaniel. But most dog experts don't accept the notion that a Westminster champion should automatically be considered greater than a top dog that failed at Westminster. Howard Tyler, one of only several dozen "all-rounders" qualified to judge every breed, expressed the consensus view during an interview at his home on Cape Cod.

"You can't use Westminster or any other single major show as a barometer for evaluating the greatness of a dog," Tyler said. "Top dogs often get beaten in the breed at Westminster."

One such dog was Ch. Nornay Saddler, a Smooth Fox Terrier imported from England in the late 1930s and defeated for Best of Breed by Ch. Flornell Spicy Piece of Halleston, a Wire Fox Terrier bitch, in a classic 1938 confrontation at Westminster. Leonard Brumby, the retired AKC executive, remembers it well. His father was Saddler's handler.

The younger Brumby calls it "the most dramatic decision I ever saw," because the general feeling was that whichever dog won the breed would go on to take the Terrier Group and Best in Show. George Hartman, the judge, finally lined them up together, Brumby recalled. "Then he said, 'All right, gentlemen, drop those leashes.' He wanted the dogs to stand by themselves. Well, Saddler happened to lean a little backwards, upright, and the bitch leaned forward, which was the right kind of assertiveness for a terrier. The judge picked the bitch." Brumby remembers Hartman saying later that Saddler was the best dog he had ever seen, "but at that particular moment, Spicy was better." She did go Best in Show.

Nornay Saddler, in a painting by Edwin Megargee.

Another yardstick for measuring a dog's greatness might logically seem to be its record: how many breed, Group, or Best in Show victories. Such a list would have to include the only four dogs to have won more than 100 all-breed bests. They were the Boxer from California Ch. Bang Away of Sirrah Crest, whose 1951 Westminster victory made him the first dog from west of the Mississippi to win the Silver Bowl; the Pekingese Ch. Chik T'Sun of Caversham, also number one at Westminster; and two that never managed to top Westminster—the Standard Poodle Ch. Lou-Gin's Kiss Me Kate and the English Setter Ch. Rock Falls Colonel.

But that system, too, has weaknesses. With so many more all-breed shows than there used to be, the opportunities for fattening a dog's record are much greater. Furthermore, many top dogs never gain national recognition because their owners don't have the money (as much as $30,000 or more) to campaign them coast to coast at up to 75 or 100 shows annually. Several top performers have been flown around the country in their owners' private jets.

Still another measure of greatness might seem to be celebrity status. At least three show dogs have had their pictures on the covers of national magazines: Brucie, Bang Away, and Chik T'Sun. But popularity might be the wrong criterion. As Brumby remembers Bang Away: "The first time I saw him, when he was only eleven months old, I said to myself, 'He's not a Boxer, but he's going to do a heck of a lot of winning. He's a showin' fool.' "

Haworth F. Hoch, former chairman of the AKC and one of the country's busiest Best in Show judges, doubts the wisdom of trying to compare dogs from different eras. He noted that styles change, sometimes so drastically that the parent clubs of the various breeds are urged by breeders and exhibitors to change the written standards. For example, Boxers today are slimmer and more streamlined than they were 40 years ago.

"A show-dog Hall of Fame would be quite unfair," Hoch said in a telephone interview from his home in St. Louis. "You wouldn't have floor space enough for all the names. Bang Away was a great Boxer, but there have been other great Boxers. Storm was a tremendous Dobe, but there were other tremendous Dobermans, even in the same era. And who's to say My Own Brucie was a better Cocker than some of the Cockers who are winning today?"

Hoch will always remember Ch. Dersade Bobby's Girl, the Sealyham Terrier he named Best in Show at Westminster in 1977. Yet his respect for her is no greater than for less-celebrated dogs such as Ch. Sam of Blaircourt, a black Labrador Retriever who competed in the 1960s. A week after arriving from England, Sam won five Groups and four Best in Shows during a five-day span at Woodstock, Vermont, and at other sites on the scenic New England summer circuit.

"He was the greatest Lab I've ever seen in my life," Haworth Hoch said. "He made such an impression on me that I'm still looking for another Lab as good as Sam."

Nevertheless, Hoch insists it would be foolish to call Bobby's Girl or Sam of Blaircourt or any other dog the greatest of its breed.

"There are some great dogs none of us alive today have ever seen," he said. "And there is always somebody who will tell you, 'No, that one isn't the standout. This one is.' "

In the gathering darkness at West Springfield, the time has come for the Group judges to decide which dogs are the standouts and which are not. Nobody else's opinion will matter. At least not today.

Inside the Better Living Center, the Best of Breed winners in the Windham County show are waiting: 125 of them, each a proud representative of its breed. The earlier judging has weeded out the dogs with the most obvious major faults. Did the contestant have cow hocks, flying ears, a goose rump, or a gay tail? Was he or she too "leggy," too "shelly," too "lippy," too "weedy"? If they were, they probably would not have received report cards good enough to have gotten this far.

Now the Group judges will be looking for lesser flaws and keeping an eye out for any "flat-catchers"—show-offs whose great style and flashiness can sometimes camouflage structural deficiencies from an unpracticed eye. It won't be easy. Measuring look-alike dogs against the Standard of Perfection for their particular breed is one thing. But what happens when 20 or 30 breed winners, all of them presumably close to their own tribe's standard of excellence, compete against one another in a Group showdown? And what happens when the six Group winners go into the ring for Best in Show?

How, for example, do you judge one sunset against another sunset? Is Beethoven's *Fifth Symphony* greater than the Brahms *Fourth*? Is Michelangelo's massive St. Peter's Basilica in Rome a greater work of art than Giotto's much smaller Campanile in Florence? When you get to a point of ultimate beauty, style, and composition, is it fair to judge one masterpiece against another? Is a near-perfect St. Bernard of 200 pounds or a near-perfect Irish Wolfhound that stands three feet high at the shoulders any more or less deserving than a near-perfect Chihuahua or Yorkshire Terrier weighing only a few pounds?

Those are the kinds of questions dog-show judges must answer every weekend, and that's what makes the process so subjective. Would it be fairer to have Group awards and Best in Show determined by a panel of judges instead of by just one person? Most dog people say it wouldn't, and history appears to support that conclusion. Multiple judging was tried at Westminster during a five-year experiment that began in 1924. Two judges selected Best in Show that year, and the panel grew to four in 1925 and to five in 1926, 1927, and 1928. In 1928 it took the five judges an hour and twenty minutes to reach a compromise and select Ch. Talavera Margaret, Reggie Lewis's Wire Fox Terrier. That was enough for the AKC, which went back to the one-vote system the following year.

They are calling for the Terrier Group now at the Windham County show, and Edd Embry Bivin, whose judging reputation has brought him from Texas, is calmly awaiting the assignment. With so many different breeds to consider, he is asked: Are oranges being compared with apples?

"Not really," Bivin says. "When some judges get into a Group, it becomes more difficult to evaluate different dogs against different breed standards. Is this Peke closer to his standard than that Pomeranian is to his? But there are judges who can make the transition from breed to Group and Best in Show. It can be done."

Dog-show judges usually emerge from the ranks of exhibitors, breeders, or professional handlers. And they carry their personal preferences to the show ring. They always have. Consider the following excerpts from an editorial complaining about what it called the "injudicious selection" of judges.

"Many cases are on record," the editorial said, "where dogs which have won under one judge have lost under another judge, with the same competition. This is all wrong. Breeders and fanciers are entitled to something more than individual opinion. . . . As judging is conducted at present, personal preferences weigh in the balance more than standards."

The complaint could have appeared last month. Actually, it appeared more than three-quarters of a century ago, in a 1907 issue of *The American Field*. The AKC's current President, William F. Stifel, concedes that the grumbling has not subsided.

"There's still a Sore Loser Syndrome that leads a lot of people to write a lot of letters," he said at his New York headquarters. "They're generally very sincere letters. The typical one starts, 'When is the American Kennel Club going to step in and do something about judges who don't know one breed from another?' We try to explain to them what a dog show is all about."

Stifel acknowledged that the AKC occasionally had problems with judges who don't know when it's time to retire. One elderly multibreed judge, he recalled, caused a stir once at a major show by asking: "Do you want to bring those Irish Wolfhounds in?" They were Scottish Deerhounds. The judge's license was lifted temporarily. Another judge confided to the AKC that she was "frankly scared" of German Shepherds. She was assigned to toy breeds.

"Sometimes they'll say, 'When I get like that judge over there, remind me to quit,' " Stifel said. "But when they get to that point themselves, they have usually forgotten."

But there are checks and balances, and the best judges get the most assignments. At least 80 percent of the judging in any given year is done by about 15 percent (approximately 400) of the 2,600 judges approved by the AKC.

Like any nomadic subculture with a routine of frequent traveling, parties, and overnight stays, the dog-show fraternity generates its share of gossip about who is running around with whom. More often, though, the gossip involves those rumors of suspected collusion on the part of "political" judges who supposedly either favor their friends or accept favors from certain owners, breeders, or handlers.

"Most of what you hear is just talk," said Howard Tyler, the "all-rounder" and former professional handler. "I think you get more honest opinions from judges today than in the past. There's less collusion. They're making progress at the AKC."

Tyler sees nothing wrong with "good" politics in the dog world, as opposed to "dirty" politics. He defined the two varieties as follows:

Good Politics: Start with a very good dog; put the dog with a good professional handler; go to all the big shows; advertise the dog and publicize its good victories; be affable and pleasant, a regular guy, at shows and social functions, but don't fawn over judges or send them presents, because that "kind of repulses" most of them.

Dirty Politics: Start with a very good dog; ingratiate yourself with judges by handing out cases of liquor, Virginia hams, and other lavish gifts; buttonhole judges at cocktail parties and swing the conversation around to promoting your own dogs; offer to help the judges get good assignments if they treat you right.

Both Tyler and Haworth F. Hoch agree that some judges pay too much attention to the advertisements they see in dog magazines. The result, they said, is that those judges start looking for dogs whose pictures they saw in the magazine ads and not for what's good and bad.

"Those full-page color ads are ridiculous," said Hoch. "I don't look at all those breed magazines they send to judges. I give 'em away. I get three different Afghan Hound magazines every month. *Three* of them. If you want to know who's making money in dogs, it's not the judges. It's the magazine publishers."

PASS THE DRAMAMINE

The *American Kennel Gazette* of October 1909 reported on what was claimed to be the first (and probably the last) international dog show ever held on the high seas.

When the White Star liner *ADRIATIC* was some 800 miles from Sandy Hook en route to Europe, Dr. C. Y. Ford of Canada interested the owners of the several canine artistocrats that chanced to be aboard in holding a dog show. The Adriatic Kennel Club was organized, and the exhibitors pledged to make the show an annual fixture.

Under the patronage of the ship's captain, and with Dr. Ford as judge, the 16 entries were gaited on the forward deck, which had been decorated for the occasion. Souvenir silver cups, engraved "Adriatic," that had been purchased from the ship's barber were awarded to the winning dogs described as follows:

"Lilly"—
Griffon Soyeau—
First Prize
Dalmatian
Golden Fox Dog
Blenheim Spaniel
Austrian Pomeranian
Miniature Pomeranian
Aberdeen Terrier
Scottish Terrier

It was reported that much amusement was occasioned by an attempt to enter the ship's two cats as "nice hounds."

Dog Show Scenes

Dogs in their crates arrive at a show.

While the handler adjusts front leg, judge examines the hound's hindquarters.
John L. Ashbey

Some dogs arrive in style in their owners' RV's.

Handler baits Boxer in show ring
to keep up his interest.

Judge records his choices in his book.
John L. Ashbey

Giant Schnauzer gets
a sponge bath.

Tibetan Terrier gets a final look
before heading for the ring.

All spruced up
and ready to go.

A well-deserved snooze.

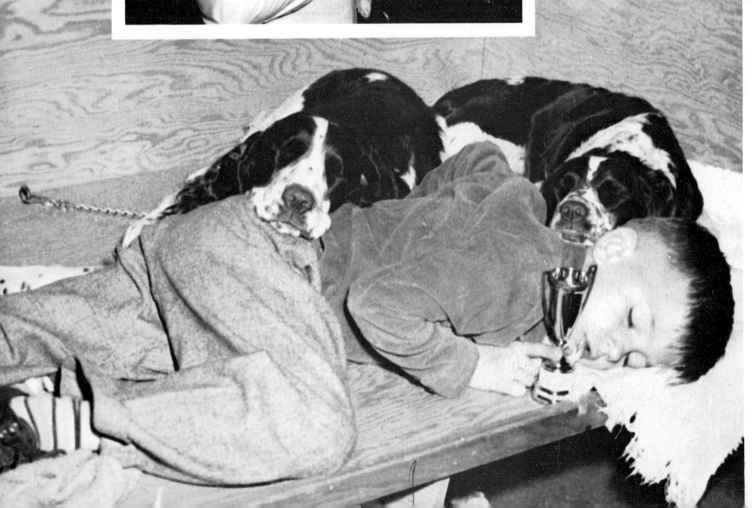

"It's OK—we'll win tomorrow."
(Soft-Coated Wheaten Terrier puppy.)

By 6:00 P.M., the 2,176-dog field that began the Windham County contest ten hours earlier has been cut to six finalists. Instead of 20 rings, now there is only a single large one. In it stand the Group winners who will be competing for Best in Show.

The finalists do not include an Afghan, a development that has quieted the gossipers. Also missing is the Lhasa Apso who went Best in Show the day before. Typically, the crowd has thinned out. At all but the biggest dog shows, spectators don't always feel compelled to stay to the end. Taking part in the fun is what counts, and they know that whoever wins will be a worthy representative of its breed.

Mrs. Hausman, the Best in Show judge, takes note of what she has been given: an English Springer Spaniel, a Pekingese, a Scottish Deerhound, a Bichon Frise, a Newfoundland, and a Lakeland Terrier who will eventually be chosen Best in Show on Sunday. First together in a line and then one by one, the dogs are paraded around the ring and back and forth on black rubber matting. The judge evaluates them and studies the rapport between handler and dog.

By sight and by touch, she checks for style, balance, conformation, condition, soundness. She is doing what AKC-approved show judges have been doing for a hundred years—trying to find the dog that comes closest to perfection, a dog you could write a breed standard about and say, "This is the ideal."

There is more gaiting, more posing, with the handlers keeping their athletes alert by flashing bits of oven-dried liver in their free hands as bait. The deliberations take no more than about 15 minutes. Suddenly the judge steps forward and points to the brown-and-white English Springer Spaniel. The others are hustled offstage by their handlers, leaving Ch. Salilyn's Private Stock, tail wagging joyously, prancing by himself in the center of the ring to the cheers of the crowd.

"He knows he won it," a woman says. "Look how he's so happy."

Photographers move in for the presentation of the top award, a silver-plate punch-bowl set. They remain in the ring to snap promotional shots of the winner and his handler. In a moment or two, all of them are gone. The ring is empty, waiting for another day, another field of finalists, another Best in Show.

9
Obedience and Tracking

James C. Falkner

The story of Obedience began in America at Mt. Kisco, New York, in October 1933, when eight dogs were entered in a "test" on the estate of Henry J. Whitehouse. The organizer and promoter of this test was Mrs. Helene Whitehouse Walker whose Poodles did well in the show ring but were disparaged by her friends as "sissies." Mrs. Walker believed that her beloved Poodles were as smart and competent as any sporting or working dog and set out to prove it. Since there was no such thing as an obedience test open to Poodles in 1933, she organized her own—and a new sport began.

Perhaps the interest in Obedience had been sparked at the close of World War I when Lt. Lee Duncan returned to the United States with a young German Shepherd puppy that had been abandoned by the retreating German army. Duncan was an experienced dog trainer, and this waif became Rin Tin Tin, the first of a long line of canine movie stars. He was followed by Strongheart, Yukon King, Lassie, Boomer, "Broadway Sandy," and many others up to our present-day Benji. These stars, loved by movie goers across the country, helped greatly to create an interest in the trained dog.

Like all good ideas, the sport of Obedience needed someone with desire, time, and the means to make it happen. A "good press" was as important in the 1930s as it is today, and so Mrs. Walker wrote articles for a number of key publications to stimulate interest in Obedience and received in return enthusiastic coverage of the early events by prominent dog writers. Through Mrs. Walker's efforts, the North Westchester (N.Y.) Kennel Club, on June 9, 1934, became the first all-breed club ever to offer obedience tests at a show. The publicity before and after the fact dramatically increased the impact of the event.

Henry J. Whitehouse with an early
"Carillon" Poodle.
Howell Book House

Helene Whitehouse Walker puts two Poodles
through their paces. *Edwin Levick*

The historic Walker trailer and Buick. *Howell Book House*

First all-breed Obedience Trial, Westchester County, New York, 1934. *Morgan*

Leaving no boulders unturned, Mrs. Walker wrote to the AKC *Gazette*: "This is a great step forward, and I understand some of the prominent fall shows are planning to follow suit . . . Anything you can do . . . to bring these tests before the public will be of great assistance. . . ."

In fact, only the Somerset Hills (N.J.) Kennel Club, in September 1934, did follow suit, and obedience tests were not offered again until the North Westchester Kennel Club staged tests in 1935.

Training was a problem. There were a number of American trainers who specialized in dogs of the larger working breeds for guard and protection work. Field trials for the sporting breeds were well established, and many fine trainers worked as professionals. The contributions of these trainers to Obedience can never be underestimated, and the Field Trial connection can be seen in many of our present exercises.

But it wasn't enough. A month following the historic all-breed test at North Westchester's show, Mrs. Walker left for England to study under the best trainers there. When she returned to America, Mrs. Walker pulled Blanche Saunders off a tractor on the family farm and named her kennel manager. This young lady became one of the outstanding obedience trainers in America, as well as a great teacher and author. In her Bedford Hills Training Class, Mrs. Walker taught Blanche and a few others what she had learned in England. Within a few months, Blanche was doing the teaching. When World War II began, Mrs. Walker shut down her kennel, and Blanche went to help the great trainer Josef Weber in his war-dog training program. Her methods are still in use today by most trainers.

In an effort to persuade the AKC to place obedience tests under its authority, Mrs. Walker compiled a file of clippings and correspondence that revealed nationwide interest in obedience training. She also wrote a small pamphlet that outlined the "Procedures for Obedience Tests," including the stipulation that all dogs entered in Obedience must also be entered in at least one breed class. She gave the pamphlet to the AKC, and it became the basis for the first "Regulations and Standard for Obedience Test Field Trials." These regulations were approved by the Board in March 1936, but they contained no such stipulation. The first licensed test held in accordance with the original regulations took place at North Westchester Kennel Club's show on June 13, 1936. It is truly amazing how closely the original regulations have been followed through the years.

In March 1936, Mrs. Walker and others in her Bedford Hills Training Class formed the Obedience Test Club of New York, the first obedience club in the country, and held its first all-breed test in 1937. In spite of its name, the Obedience Test Club of New York had members in 13 states from Maine to Hawaii. Failing in its bid to be a "parent" club for Obedience in the United States, the O.T.C. did not apply for membership in the AKC but instead served as a buffer between the AKC and the obedience community. At that time Obedience was popularly thought of as a "specialty," and in 1940, with 500 members, the O.T.C. was considered the "largest specialty club in the U.S."

Recognizing the need for instruction and demonstration of training techniques around the country, Mrs. Walker and Blanche Saunders set off in 1937 with three Standard Poodles, a Buick sedan, and a 21-foot trailer. They traveled 10,000 miles over a period of ten weeks—to Cincinnati, Wichita Falls, Dallas, Ft. Worth, San Antonio, Galveston, Houston, El Paso, Hollywood—and the gospel was spread. They scheduled obedience exhibitions in connection with shows and made it possible for others interested in the sport to see trained dogs and established standards. The Obedience Test Club of New York, with 15 affiliates, disbanded in the early years of World War II. In June 1941 the New England Dog Training Club became the first obedience club approved as a member of the AKC.

In all of her writings on the concept of obedience competition, Mrs. Walker stressed two related points that, like the earliest rules, have survived through the years: Obedience should be accessible to the amateur owner of a single dog, and the tests should be designed and executed with the next generation of exhibitors—the spectators—in mind. For example, a virtue of the Group exercises, in Mrs. Walker's view, was "saving time and not boring the spectators."

Obedience became a factor in the defense of the country during World War II. The influence of those prominent in the sport helped to establish the K–9 Corps. This tragic event in the life of the nation eventually gave Obedience the great boost it needed. As is so often the case, from the ashes of war great movements arise.

The United States had never before used dogs in war. There were plenty of suitable dogs, but they were in private hands and untrained. Only a handful of Obedience and Field Trial trainers were available. But what happened next was another example of American ingenuity.

With the whole-hearted approval of the AKC, a volunteer organization known as Dogs for Defense was formed. The Fancy rallied behind this organization, which eventually supplied some 17,000 dogs to the armed services. These were family dogs, donated by the American people.

The greatest school for young soldier trainers that ever existed was the K–9 Corps, where they absorbed the knowledge of America's great trainers, most of whom were over age for service but were employed by the armed services as civilians. The K–9 Corps made people aware of the potential of trained dogs as never before. Exhibitions were staged all over the country by select groups of servicemen. The papers were filled with stories of the heroism and courage of our canine soldiers, and the people loved it.

The dogs of the K–9 Corps epitomized the meaning of Obedience. Dogs of many breeds were trained to guard American forces and to attack the enemy on command. They were used to patrol the front lines and headquarters units. Messenger dogs carried vital information from the front lines back to headquarters by backtracking on the scent of their handlers.

Many of the dogs in the K–9 Corps were true war heroes. A good example was Chips, the son of a Husky and a Collie-German Shepherd cross, who was loaned to Dogs for Defense by his owners, the Edward J. Wren family of Pleasantville, New York. Chips was the leader of the first K–9 detachment to cross the Atlantic Ocean. Landing at Fedallah, French Morocco, Chips quickly learned from his handler how to dig his own trench in the sand while under enemy fire.

Later in his career, Chips landed on a beach in Sicily under artillery fire, charged an enemy pillbox, and singlehandedly captured a four-man machine gun crew.

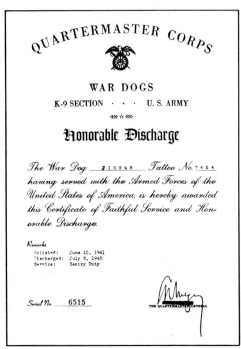

War Dog's certificate of Honorable Discharge from the U.S. Army.

In every situation in which dog serves man, some sort of basic Obedience is the foundation necessary for whatever task the dog is selected to perform, be it in the show ring, bomb and drug detection, the K–9 Corps, guiding for the blind and the hard of hearing, and in tracking and field trialing. In each of these endeavors the responsible breeder and the amateur Obedience enthusiast has contributed immeasurably.

Training for Obedience demonstrates the purpose for which the dog was bred. Obedience training is one of the most powerful means of producing responsibility, both for the dog and the owner, thereby fulfilling their responsibilities to society.

The AKC's Obedience Regulations state that

The purpose of Obedience Trials is to demonstrate the usefulness of the pure-bred dog as a companion of man, not merely the dog's ability to follow specified routines in the obedience ring . . . The basic objective of Obedience Trials is to produce dogs that have been trained and conditioned always to behave in the home, in public places, and in the presence of other dogs, in a manner that will reflect credit on the sport of Obedience.

It is also essential that the dog demonstrate willingness and enjoyment of its work, and that smoothness and naturalness on the part of the handler be given precedence over a performance based on military precision and peremptory commands.

Put another way, Obedience really comes down to owners making good citizens of their dogs.

Obedience Trials are broken down into Novice A and B Classes, Open A and B Classes, Utility Class, and Obedience Trial Championship. Most dog owners interested in making good citizens of their dogs set as their goal a C.D. Title (for Companion Dog), which is issued by the AKC to dogs that have been certified by three different judges to have received qualifying scores in Novice Classes at three Licensed or Member Obedience Trials.

The Novice exercises include: (1) Heel on Leash and Figure Eight; (2) Stand for Examination; (3) Heel Free; (4) Recall; (5) Long Sit; and (6) Long Down.

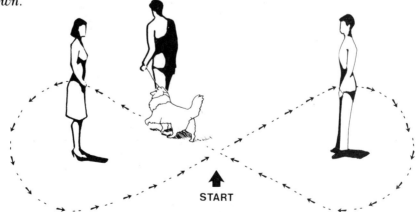

START

Principal feature of the Heel on Leash and Figure Eight Novice Class exercise is to demonstrate the ability of dog and handler to work as a team.

The coveted C.D.X. (Companion Dog Excellent) and U.D. (Utility Dog) certificates are sought by the most serious Obedience trialers.

Word of his exploits spread, and Chips's company commander recommended the dog for the Distinguished Service Cross. Chips was awarded the Silver Star for gallantry in action and the Purple Heart for a wound he sustained. General Eisenhower later congratulated him in person; when the General tried to pat the dog, Chips nipped his hand.

Chips's story was widely reported in American newspapers, and Dogs for Defense made much of his record as representative of the K–9 Corps. But a storm of protest arose over conferring decorations on an animal. Chips was the subject of two speeches in Congress and the eventual cause of a War Department order prohibiting the awarding of decorations to animals. Nevertheless, Chips and many other brave K–9 dogs played a major role in World War II.

In a nostalgic article called "Jigger," which appeared in the January 1977 issue of the AKC *Gazette*, I talked about the K–9 dogs who were *not* publicly acclaimed:

> . . . The book is written on the "dogs of war." The heroes are immortalized on the printed page and their story still told but I cannot help but think of all those great ones who live only in the memories of their human buddies who served with them. The ones who walked the beaches night after night all alone with their handlers. The ones who manned the lonely outposts all over the world where nothing ever happened. Maybe, just maybe, that's why nothing ever happened—they were there. Their human counterparts were the ones we call "good ol' guys" nowadays. They were the "good ol' dogs."

When the war ended, young trainers spread out over the land. Many found a profession in dog training, while others pursued the sport as competitors and judges. They organized clubs and they taught. Obedience after the war took on a new aspect—training the family pet to be a good citizen.

Much refinement and clarification have taken place in Obedience over the years, and much of the credit for the evolution of the sport goes to a series of Obedience Advisory Committees, composed of knowledgeable people from around the country, who have met as needed to review all aspects of the sport and make recommendations to the AKC's Board of Directors. Although strictly an advisory body, the Committees' influence has been profound.

Among the most important contributions of these Committees is the standardization of judging procedures. By 1947 "Suggestions" had become "Standards" for judging, and in 1972 "Regulations" consisted of some ten pages. Quite apart from language added to the official regulations book, a separate pamphlet—"Guidelines for Obedience Judges"—was first published in 1973 and a program of regional seminars was set up to discuss the regulations, and guidelines with judges, prospective judges, and exhibitors. Dozens of these seminars have now been held around the country.

The revised regulations in 1947 also stated that dogs entered in obedience tests had to be of pure breeding and that castrated males and spayed bitches could compete.

Another revision in 1947 moved Tracking as an exercise in the Utility Class to a separate event with its own title and certificate. Some 30 years later, the Tracking Dog Excellent test and title were initiated. The special requirements of Tracking, both in terms of training and testing, had become a problem as more and more urban and metropolitan dwellers embraced Obedience. Track-

Official AKC publications
on Obedience Trials.

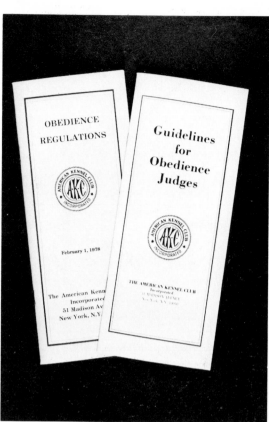

Blanche Saunders in role of Obedience Judge. *Basil A. Hernandez, Jr.*

FIRST AKC
TRIPLE CHAMPION

Cariad's Kutya Kai Costa, a Vizsla was the first dog to become a Triple Champion— a title the AKC first authorized in 1981—by winning his championship in all three sports; show, obedience, and field.

ing tests were few and far between, and few judges had real knowledge of Tracking. Dogs were entered with little or no preparation. A judge once was asked by an exhibitor at the starting flag where the scent was to be found. Told that it was on the ground, the exhibitor got down on hands and knees and sniffed the ground loudly to show her dog how it was done.

Despite the separation of Tracking from mainline Obedience, the vast majority of tracking enthusiasts are also Obedience devotees, and many trainers consider a dog's career unfinished until he has earned his "T." Outside the world of obedience competition, however, tracking has gained wide acceptance, especially within law-enforcement agencies. More than once the AKC has been approached to certify the registration, pedigree, and tracking proficiency of individual police department tracking dogs so that their actions might be submitted as testimony in courts of law.

More than 700 U.S. police departments use some 4,000 dogs in K–9 units for tracking, trailing, and other scent work to find suspects, missing persons, bombs, or narcotics.

Milo Pearsall,
noted tracking authority,
critiques a
performance.

The AKC Regulations state that:

The purpose of a tracking test is to demonstrate the dog's ability to recognize and follow human scent and to use this skill in the service of mankind.

Tracking, by its nature, is a vigorous noncompetitive outdoor sport. Tracking Tests should demonstrate willingness and enjoyment by the dog in his work, and should always represent the best in sportsmanship and camaraderie by the people involved.

The regulations require that each track be designed to test dog and handler with a variety of terrain and scenting conditions. The dog is not asked to find the tracklayer, but he must overcome a series of typical scenting problems and locate objects dropped by the person whose track is being followed.

The AKC issues two Tracking certificates, the T.D. Title (Tracking Dog) and the T.D.X. (Tracking Dog Excellent), which received AKC Board approval in 1980. The accompanying charts diagram the exercises that must be mastered for dogs to earn Tracking certificates.

Exercises have been changed to create more uniform and meaningful tests of a pure-bred dog's usefulness to man, as well as his willingness to perform as required. The advisory committees have guarded the early premise that exercises should represent everyday routines that might confront dog and master. In the advanced classes, exercises are representative of a dog performing field, police, sentry, or other work.

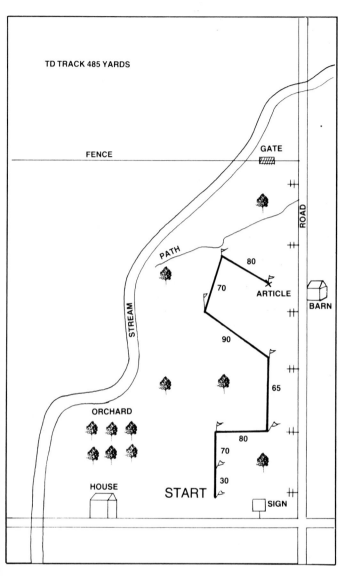

Example of a T.D. track.

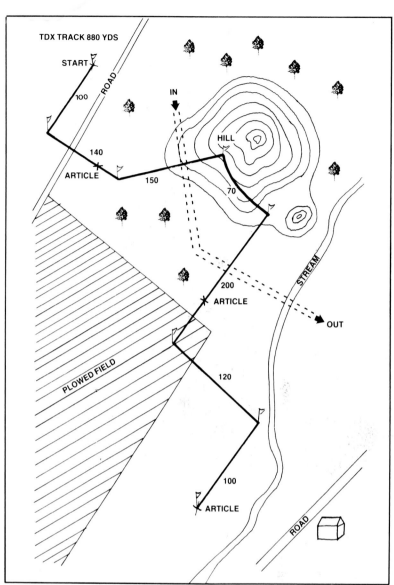

Example of a T.D.X. track.

In 1972 the AKC set up an Obedience Department with well-known judge Richard D'Ambrisi as first director. Following his untimely death a short time later, the Dick D'Ambrisi Award was established by the Association of Obedience Clubs and Judges to honor persons for significant and truly outstanding contributions to the sport. In 1974 the first three D'Ambrisi Awards were given: One recipient was Helene Whitehouse Walker.

In 1974 an official award for the Highest Scoring Dog in the Regular Classes was instituted and is known as HIT for "High in Trial." The names of the winners of these awards—the "Best in Show" of Obedience—are published in the Show Awards section of the *Gazette*.

In 1977 the AKC created the title of Obedience Trial Champion and specified that its abbreviation, O. T. Ch.—unlike all other Obedience titles—could be used preceding the name of the dog rather than in the suffix position. It immediately became a hit with the exhibitors and caused a spurt of interest in the Open B and Utility Classes because it brought back into competition many dogs that were facing retirement or who had already been retired.

Dogs competing in the Utility Class for a U.D. Title must qualify in Scent Discrimination. In this exercise the dog must select from among identical articles the one carrying the handler's scent.

Bulldog.

Komondor. *Ludwig*

Scottish Deerhound. *Percy T. Jones*

Dogs competing in the Open A Class for a C.D.X. Title must qualify in the Retrieve over High Jump and Broad Jump exercises.

The future looks bright for Obedience, both inside and outside the competition ring. The AKC has some 200 member and licensed clubs in 45 states and Puerto Rico, with many more working toward accreditation. More than 90,000 dogs compete annually in some 1,300 trials, and more than 1,000 take part in tracking tests. The AKC each year grants more than 10,500 obedience titles to dogs in almost every registrable breed and more than 450 tracking titles to nearly half of the registrable breeds. Some 50 dogs annually achieve the Obedience Trial Championship, with over 35 breeds now represented.

At the same time, the practical application of Obedience continues to expand in such areas as guiding the blind and aiding the hearing-impaired and in promising new medical-research programs where scent discrimination is employed. From the rim of Mt. St. Helens to the subway platforms of New York City, dogs are being put to work for man in new settings. With "no pet" clauses being enforced in more and more cities, concerned dog owners look to obedience training for all dogs as one way to fight back.

New projects await only the ingenuity of man's mind. Meanwhile, ever-increasing numbers of dog owners faithfully attend weekly training classes and then go on to compete in matches and trials. They are discovering the special joys of training one's own dog to be a good canine citizen.

The challenge of Obedience training . . .

© 1982 United Feature Syndicate, Inc.

10
Field Trials

A. Hamilton Rowan, Jr.

Golf is a delightful accomplishment, but the love of hunting is almost a physiological characteristic. A man may not care for golf and still be human, but the man who does not like to see, hunt, photograph, or otherwise outwit birds or animals is hardly normal. He is supercivilized, and I for one do not know how to deal with him. Babes do not tremble when they are shown a golf ball, but I should not like to own the boy whose hair does not lift his hat when he sees his first deer.

ALDO LEOPOLD, 1887–1948

Field Trial fashion.
Club pins adorn a trialer's hat.

AKC Field Trial Rules.
The twenty-two eligible breeds
require three books
of running Rules.

Tests for dogs in the field were developed to allow hunting dogs to compete with each other with the object of improving their performances in the field. It is generally agreed that these tests originated in England.

151

Veteran campaigners watch a field trial.

In order to pick up the thread in this country, we turn to a wounded Civil War soldier named P. H. Bryson from Memphis, Tennessee. He was released after the war ended and permitted to go home to die so that he might have a decent burial. When he reached home, his family physician advised him to buy a shotgun and a bird dog and get as much exercise as possible. In time he recovered, became a dedicated sportsman, and, through the sporting journals of the time, began to advocate the holding of dog shows in the United States.

Bryson formed the Tennessee Sportsmen's Association and organized a combined Dog Show and Field Trial held on October 7 and 8, 1874. The only breeds represented at the show on the first day were Pointers and Setters, and the entries totalled 95. The old soldier's Setter, "Maud," was awarded Best in Show.

Fourteen Pointers and Setters competed in the field trial on the second day. The winner was an all-black Setter, and the results are recorded in Volume I of the National American Kennel Club's Stud Book.

Today the American Kennel Club licenses some 2,000 Dog Shows and over 1,100 Field Trials. But while the AKC acts as the licensing body for field trials in exactly the same manner as it does for dog shows and obedience trials, the Rules under which field trials are run present a complicated problem.

The Dog Show Rules, for instance, apply equally to every dog in the show ring—all 125 breeds eligible for AKC registration. In field trials, while 22 different breeds are eligible to compete, the problem is that these 22 breeds cannot compete at trials under one set of AKC Rules.

Why is this so?

Field trials are divided into four basic categories based on the hunting characteristics of the breeds involved.

The pointing dogs are made up of ten different breeds. They assist the hunter in the field by stopping or pointing the very moment they scent the presence of a game bird, permitting the hunters to walk past their dogs on point and flush the birds into the air.

The scenting or trailing hounds pursue the cottontail rabbit or hare at trials either in packs or in pairs or braces.

Retrievers do just what their name implies—fetch or retrieve from both water and land all game shot by the hunter.

Flushing dogs are expected to search for feathered game within gunshot range of the hunter. When game is located, they must flush the bird into the air and retrieve it on command if it is shot.

Several other national dog organizations in this country also license formal field trials and award their own championships. However, only in AKC-licensed competitions can a dog be awarded the title of Dual Champion. In order to achieve this AKC title, a dog must complete the requirements for both a Field and a Show Championship. The existence of this coveted title will always set AKC events apart from those of other dog organizations. The Dual Championship title also serves an an incentive for sportsmen to breed dogs capable of doing equally well on the bench and in the field.

A Brittany striving for Dual Championship honors. At 3:00 P.M. *(left),* **he competes in a field trial; less than five hours later** *(right),* **he appears in the show ring.**

Beagle Field Trials

Robert F. Slike and Robert A. Bartel

It was a century ago when one hunter said to another, "My hound is better than your hound." The gauntlet was down. The weapons chosen were two small, eager Beagle hounds. The referee was a third experienced hunter. The contest began with the three men following a pair of Beagles trailing scent left by a cottontail rabbit.

One handler exerted himself to be in a position directly behind his hound. He would never admit that, on occasion, his favorite would backtrack—pursue the trail in the opposite direction of the quarry—but he placed himself strategically to prevent this from happening.

His opponent, noticing the behavior, remarked, "Hey, you can't do that!" The reply was, "There is no rule against it and, anyway, you have the advantage since that guy judging is a friend of yours." At that moment the Beagle field trial was conceived, leaving only rules, regulations, and qualified judges to follow.

The Beagle is the smallest of the dogs of the chase that go under the general denomination of hound. It is, in fact, a miniature Foxhound. Although the Beagle is slower than the Harrier, or Foxhound, its scenting ability is equally acute, and it pursues its game with boundless energy and perseverance. The Beagle traces every winding and twisting of the scent line with a degree of accuracy that must be seen to be understood properly. While on an enticing scent line, it would be intolerable for the Beagle to run mute—its soft and dulcet tones must proclaim the chase for all to hear.

The Beagle that came to America was an animal that hunted in a pack. Selective breeding in England had produced small hounds with a variety of skills that allowed them to be hunted together in a pack as a team. Some could pursue the quarry with speed and drive, while others were adept at unraveling the puzzling maze left by a tired but clever rabbit. Some American breeders have maintained this pack tradition.

154

Beagle field trials, a sport found only in the United States and Canada, started with this announcement in the *Sunday Boston Herald* on October 26, 1890: "A group of Beagle owners would hold a Beagle field trial in Hyannis, Massachusetts, in a fortnight." This group called themselves the National Beagle Club of America, and the advertised trial was held on November 4, 1890, with 18 entries—15 dogs and 3 bitches.

Shortly thereafter this group applied for membership in the American Kennel Club, which was then just six years old. They were denied because a group of show enthusiasts known initially as the American English Beagle Club already held membership.

The men in the National Beagle Club refused to give up. Finally, in May 1891, the American Beagle Club (formerly the American English Beagle Club) merged with the National Beagle Club. The new group called itself the National Beagle Club, and it became the Parent Club for the breed. At that time, the AKC was completely show oriented, and an interesting sidelight on the club's admission to AKC membership was the AKC's strong objections to the Parent Club's involvement in both field trials and shows. H. F. Schellhass, then president and AKC delegate of the National, told the AKC: "This club was formed for improvement in the field and on the bench of the Beagle hound in America, and will enter the AKC with its constitution unchanged, if it enters at all." The AKC dutifully backed off.

Participants in the first Beagle Field Trial, 1890. *Courtesy National Beagle Club*

Today the sport of field trials for Beagles has something to offer any Beagle owner who can compete with his hound in any one of five different kinds of trials. The most popular trials are those in which the hounds compete by sex in pairs, or *Braces*, in pursuit of the ubiquitous cottontail rabbit. They can also compete in *Small Packs* of up to seven hounds, either with or without being tested for gun-shyness. In the northern tier of states, where the varying, or "snowshoe," hare is found, Beagles may be trialed in *Large Packs*, where a pack of 30 to 60 hounds or more in a single class is not uncommon. Lastly, there are the traditional *Formal Packs*, which are either privately owned or supported by subscription from local Beagle devotees.

Three Formal Packs were entered at the National Beagle Club's meet in 1896. Today, 24 such packs are registered with that club. They are hunted as three-couple (6), four-couple (8), and eight-couple (16) packs. At a Formal Pack field trial, each pack is judged as a unit or team, and its performance is measured against that of other packs entered in the trial. The packs are foot handled, with the Huntsman and his (or her) assistants, called Whippers-in, all resplendent in green jackets, white pants, knickerbockers or skirts, and black-velvet caps. Packs are identified by the uniquely colored piping on the Huntsman's jacket.

The ultimate competition for the Formal Packs is held annually at the Mecca for all Beaglers—the National Beagle Club's Institute Farm in Aldie, Virginia. It's here that pack Beaglers practice the most ancient of all Beagle competitions by chasing on foot after the dogs who, in turn, are chasing a rabbit or hare. As in all Beagle trials, the hounds rarely catch up with the quarry. But catching the rabbit really isn't the point of any Beagle trial. As the AKC Standard for judging says: "The Beagle is a trailing hound whose purpose is to find game, to pursue it in an energetic and decisive manner, and to show a determination to account for it."

Usually, after a rabbit has given the Beagles a merry chase, it goes to ground, safely, in its hole.

Participation in the sport of Formal Pack Beagling has always been limited to relatively few people. The interest and contribution of our two hunters of a hundred years ago was in the development of an individual hound that could trail the hare or rabbit effectively and efficiently without the assistance of variously endowed pack mates. Beagles, selectively bred with this concept in mind, were referred to by the pack men as "singles." To this day, it is not unusual to hear this term on the running grounds of the National Beagle Club when reference is made to Beagles run in braces.

In a sense the merits of a Formal Pack were to be discovered by testing, the traditional method of evaluating the abilities of working dogs, sporting dogs, and hounds. But rather than putting them to tests, most Americans always prefered to put dogs in competition on a head-to-head basis. In fact, the AKC *Beagle Field Trial Rules and Standard Procedures* states it this way in the foreword: ". . . the holding of field trials at which pure-bred dogs may be run in competition . . . has been found to be the best method by which the progress which has been made in breeding can be shown."

A strange thing, however, happened on the way to the twenty-first century. Early on, Beaglers became aware that industrialization and development for business and housing were reducing the availability of hunting and training

A Formal Pack of Beagles with Huntsman and Whippers-in heads out from the National Beagle Club's Institute Farm in Aldie, Virginia, to meet the judges.

Master of Beagle Hounds.

grounds. The purchase of land by the now-burgeoning Beagle clubs was encouraged and even mandated by the AKC. In contrast to field trials for breeds in which domestically raised game can be released for the trial, the Beagle field trial is limited to the pursuit of a quarry that must be acclimated to the terrain. Beaglers became ardent conservationists. Natural food and cover programs on the Beagle club grounds became necessary to maintain a natural supply of rabbits for training and trialing. In many instances, clubs reclaimed marginal land; soil fertility was measured and improved; and the term "rabbit farming" became the by-word at any progressive Beagle club. Today more than 550 Beagle clubs either own or lease land in excess of 150 acres each.

This commendable achievement, however, had its Trojan horse. The building boom that followed World War II introduced new hazards to Beagles intent on the chase. Too often the rabbit could take them across a new road or superhighway. Most clubs were forced to fence their land for the safety of the hounds. This, of course, also enclosed the rabbits, who developed running traits quite unlike their "wild" cousins outside the enclosures.

In order to get hounds that could effectively trail the "enclosure" rabbit, houndmen bred for a slower, more precise working dog. Gradually, the old, one-on-one competition to see who could get there "fustest with the mostest" was replaced by an appreciation of the "style" in which the field-trial Beagle tracked a rabbit. This was significant in light of the fact that nearly 90 percent of the 400 clubs holding AKC licensed trials were running Brace events. At these trials the hounds whose "style" most impressed the judges were given the ribbons. Through selective breeding, the Beagles used at field trials run in Braces became slow and meticulous tracking specialists.

However, what was not anticipated was that the rabbit hunter, still the most numerous of all who take wild game in the United States, found that the slow "stylish" field-trial Beagle was totally undesirable as a hunting dog. By the early 1970s, the need developed for a real gundog, or hunting Beagle. This movement gathered momentum, and its breeding programs reflected the trend to hark back to the early days.

At all Beagle Trials, height determines whether the hound will compete in the 13- or 15-inch class.

The gallery at a Sanctioned Beagle trial concentrates on a brace of tracking specialists. *Art Slike— Hounds and Hunting*

Meanwhile, the situation was somewhat different for those northern clubs that ran their hounds in Large Packs on hares. They continued to pride themselves justifiably on producing hunting Beagles and believed that their trials showed the Beagle to such an advantage.

The promoters of the "gundog" or "hunting Beagle," however, did not believe that the Large Pack was the most acceptable method to pursue the cottontail rabbit. Instead, they chose to use a running standard that was already in the AKC Rules. This was the Small Pack in which hounds are run on rabbits in packs of from four to seven hounds, with the judges selecting the outstanding performers to be run in a second series and then finally in a Winners Pack. To prove beyond a doubt that they were competing with "hunting Beagles," the AKC in the late 1970s permitted the additional testing of their hounds for gun-shyness and searching ability in what became known as the Small Pack Option, the fifth and newest type of competition for Beagles. By the end of 1981, 5 percent of all Beagle clubs were conducting licensed and sanctioned trials in this manner.

With the sport of Beagle field trials so diversified, and with traditions dating back almost one hundred years, how has the AKC coped with its administration of the five distinctive competitive standards for Beagle trials, recognizing that pure-bred Beagles are the objects of competition in all five standards? It took a unique mechanism.

In order to understand this administrative evolution, the reader must know that an AKC Member Parent Club for any breed, such as the venerable National Beagle Club of America, has not only the responsibility to approve the dates of events held by local clubs for its breed but also to propose the standards by which its breed is judged in conformation and performance.

In 1936 the National Beagle Club voted to abrogate part of its responsibilities as a Parent Club and ceased granting consent for field-trial dates. Instead they recommended that the AKC appoint a ten-member Advisory Committee from among the delegates of the Beagle AKC Member Clubs whose purpose would be to advise the AKC's Board of Directors on the matter of granting licenses for Beagle field trials. A member of the AKC's Executive Staff was to chair this Advisory Committee.

Hounds and handlers head
for start of Large Pack
Beagle trial where the quarry
is always the Varying
or "Snowshoe" hare.

And so for almost 50 years a Beagle Advisory Committee (BAC) has been responsible for advising the AKC's Board of Directors on meeting the challenge of the administration of the dynamic and evergrowing sport of Beagle field trials. Evolution has played its part, and there have been some significant changes in the BAC's structure. For instance, it's now a committee of 12 members, 11 of whom each represent some 40 Beagle clubs from across the nation. The twelfth committee member belongs to the National Beagle Club of America. An AKC Executive still chairs the meeting. The system has worked well.

Thus in their wildest dreams, our two hunters of a century ago could not have foreseen where their challenge to compete would lead. When speculating about the next hundred years, the only possible advice is: "Wait and see."

Basset Hound Field Trials

Marjorie Skolnick

My hounds are bred out of the Spartan kind,
So flew'd, so sanded; and their heads are hung
With ears that sweep away the morning dew;
Crook-knee'd, and dew-lapp'd like Thessalian bulls;
Slow in pursuit, but match'd in mouth like bells.

WILLIAM SHAKESPEARE
A Midsummer Night's Dream

It may come as a surprise to many people to discover that the heavy-bodied, low-slung, long-eared, easygoing hound with the comically sad expression can be a determined hunter exhibiting endurance and devotion to the business of trailing rabbits. The Basset is the Dr. Jekyll and Mr. Hyde of the hound world. He lies like a blob of jelly on the rug, and he can look *barely* able to lumber ten feet to his sunning board in the kennel. He is capable of considerable devilment, yet he looks *so* innocent or *so* proud that his misdemeanors will be forgiven. This is the Basset's "at home" personality. He may at first be difficult to train or "break" to the hunt, but once he gets going, a magical transformation takes place and a serious, hard-working Basset hound emerges, revealing his heritage as a venerable hunting dog.

The Basset has inherited an acutely distinctive nose for picking up scent. This short-legged fellow, with his resilient skin, can wriggle into tall grass and brush that man can't cut through. The field-trial Basset weighs from 30 to 70 pounds with the average being 45 pounds. Once he has found the line, he works very fast for such a short-legged dog. His stamina coupled with a stubborn resolve are important features of his performance.

The Basset's bell-toned voice as he trails game (called "giving tongue") is music to the ears of the hunter. Years ago, Buck La Follette, a Basset trialer, followed his favorite hound, Tulpehocken Tip Toe, with a tape recorder, so that when his Pennsylvania farm was deep under winter's snow, Buck could sit by the fire and listen to the sound of old Tip Toe's melodious voice.

The Basset look. *Ludwig*

A brace of Bassets
on the trail.
Sally Foster

Is the Basset an intelligent hunter? Consider the story of one field trialer who had a Field Champion Basset that hunted both rabbits and game birds. When the trialer decided to keep rabbits on his land for field-trial training, the Basset quickly caught on and only trailed pheasants and quail when her master brought a gun on their hunts! Whoever takes a Basset out for a hunt, that person will win the hound's special devotion, because once he's started, a Basset loves the hunt above all things.

Basset Hounds as hunting dogs have a long history. There is some evidence that low and heavy hounds with great scenting abilities were bred in ancient Egypt and Greece. The origin of the Basset has been traced to the hounds bred by St. Hubert, a French monk of the seventh century. These were hounds with heavy bodies and short legs, not swift, but good at scenting. They were described as having "bagging lips" and "hanging ears reaching down both sides of their chappes." These hounds hunted all small game including badger, and by some accounts they also chased wild boar and wolf. Bassets today will usually track deer, but most owners prefer that they do not!

By the sixteenth century the breed had acquired the name Basset, a French word meaning "low-set." Many varieties were bred in France, including long-haired and wire-haired dogs. Low, heavy, hunting hounds were known in Britain as early as the eleventh century. Sir Everett Millais was one of the best known breeders of the nineteenth century. Though his hounds were bred mainly for showing, numerous British packs were developed from these hounds.

It was from the French hunting strains that the first American imports were acquired. George Washington's friend Lafayette sent him hounds for pack hunting in America, and these hounds were probably the so-called Old Virginia Bench-Legged Beagles. Other imports in the early nineteenth century were obtained from France, but some also came from British packs, especially the Walhampton Pack. Gerald Livingston imported from the Walhampton Pack in the 1920s forming his well-known Kilsyth Pack. Another early importer was Carl Smith of Ohio. During the Great Depression, Smith acquired the Starridge Pack, and when economic conditions improved, he was able to supply a new demand for hunting Bassets. Loren Free of Ohio, one of the earliest field trialers, imported Walhampton Lively in the 1920s, and his Shellbark Bassets competed in the early field trials.

Hunting in pack has remained an interest in the United States, and from 10 to 15 packs have been maintained during the past several years. In the early days of the Basset Hound Club of America, Mrs. Consuelo Ford maintained the Bijou Pack. Other well-known packs include the Brandywine, Stockford, Timber Ridge, Coldstream, Tewksbury Foot, and Skycastle among many others over the decades. Occasionally, individual hounds were run in Brace trials and some achieved Field Championships. Daisy's Dopey, a hound from the Tantivy Pack, achieved its Dual Championship in 1971.

The American Kennel Club registered Bassets in 1885 and recognized them as a breed in the United States in 1916. After AKC recognition of the Basset Hound Club of America in 1937, show and field-trial activities grew and spread rapidly. The first Basset field trial was an AKC sanctioned trial held at Hastings, Michigan, on October 24, 1937, by the then newly formed Basset Hound Club of America. It attracted seven Bassets. The hounds were run in Braces (pairs) under the AKC Rules and Procedures already in use for Beagle trials.

Young handler cools off his charge after a run.

Soon thereafter, two AKC-licensed Basset field trials a year were held in either Michigan, Ohio, or Pennsylvania, with a growth to about 30 to 40 entries per trial. By 1964, 97 Bassets had fulfilled the requirements for the Field Championship title. The sport spread rapidly to New York State, Massachusetts, New Jersey, Maryland, Kentucky, Illinois, California, and Texas, with many trials attracting over 100 entries. Today some 20 Basset Hound Clubs hold 30 trials each year, and the Basset Hound Club of America gets the best of the Bassets together each spring and fall for a national event.

There have been only nine Dual Champion Bassets over the years. The first, Dual Ch. Kazoo's Moses the Great, won his second of the Champion titles in 1964. Although they are but a small number of the Basset fancy as a whole, those working their hound toward a Dual title make it up in dedication.

A hound must behave quite differently for each type of competition. There is an old story, still circulated, about a Show Champion hound named Belbay Extra Handsome competing in a field trial. As he ran past the large gallery of observers, Handsome assumed they were there to admire him, and he slowed down, raised his head, and strutted on by, resuming the chase only after he had passed the gallery.

It is nearly 50 years since the birth of Basset field trials. Today, as then, the thrill of competition, of testing your special hound at a trial, is as attractive as ever to both man and Basset. Win or lose, chances are that each season they'll come back to the friendly group of Basset trialers to swap training hints, pups to start, breeding plans, patches for the jacket, decals for the car—and tall stories about short hounds.

Pointing Dog Field Trials

Robert H. McKowen

When the last hot days of summer give way to the first hints of autumn, pointing dogs and their masters start getting restless for one of the most exciting activities in the sporting dog world—the field trial.

The pointing dog field trial is a combination sporting event and social gathering. It also is one of the most important functions of the American Kennel Club. In this activity the AKC performs both as a registration body and as a regulatory authority. This authority has helped to establish and maintain stability in a sport that could easily have gone off in many directions.

While shows are concerned with conformation, the field trial is the proving ground for the function of the dog. It must not only live up to an established criteria for performance but must also compete against other dogs.

Although the principal reason given for field trials is the development and continuance of the class bird dog, trials probably came into being as the result of bragging. The by-product of this competition is a better hunting dog for the average hunter.

We don't know where pointing breeds really originated. They all trace back to wild animals. But the English made an art of developing bird dogs, and Americans later turned trials into a way of life.

There have been pheasants in England since the year 1000, and it follows that where there are game birds, there must be dogs to hunt them. And where there are dogs, there are men who think they have better dogs than other men.

The English are not an impulsive people. So, not surprisingly, it took them until 1876 to stage their first-recorded bird dog trial.

Even though bird dogs have been in the United States since revolutionary times, Americans were too busy fighting Indians, the British, and each other to get down to the serious business of formalizing field trials. So it was not until 1884, eight years after the British started field trials, that the first-recorded trial was held in the United States: near Memphis, Tennessee, when H. C. Pritchett's Setter, Knight, was immortalized as the first winner.

Weimaraner points its game.

At the zenith of the sport in the 1920s, one of the real hotbeds of field trials was northeastern Pennsylvania, where it was not uncommon to see grudge matches for $500 purses. Bird dog men sat around in taverns in Wilkes Barre and Scranton boasting about their dogs. Inevitably there would be a match staged to settle a bet. The contestants, surrounded by the usual onlookers, would cast off their dogs in the Pennsylvania woods in search of native grouse. Sometimes they would go for days until one dog gave up.

Those early Setter and Pointer trial dogs also were shown on the bench for conformation, and it was not until the 1920s that the split began between field and show in those breeds.

The AKC, which began registering bird dogs in 1884, held its first licensed trial in 1924. It was conducted by the English Setter Club of America in Medford, New Jersey. Trials are still held there today, although farm fields are slowly shrinking the running area.

The continental breeds—Shorthairs, Wirehairs, Brittanys, Vizslas, Weimaraners, and Griffons—really caught hold shortly after World War II, although Dr. Charles Thornton of Montana began importing Shorthairs as far back as 1928. Much of the Shorthair's impact on field trials is due to the work of such veteran trialers as Dick Johns of Benton, Pennsylvania, who brought in some of the top winners from Germany after serving there in World War II. The first AKC Shorthair trial was held in 1944, and other continental breed trials soon followed.

The major controversies in trials today—too much emphasis on run versus bird work, for example—existed almost from the beginning. In most trials today much emphasis is put on horseback handling, but it was not until 1961 at the old Empire State Shorthair Club near Pawling, New York, that the AKC first permitted horseback handling.

The real joy of field trials is watching spirited dogs perform and learning some of the tricks used by crafty old campaigners. Some examples:

• It's a trial near Akron, Ohio, on a cool October day. The handlers were whooping and whistling over the last few hills before entering the bird field. Suddenly a Shorthair came over the hill and into the bird field and locked upon a solid point. The second dog appeared and seeing his bracemate on point in the distance, immediately slammed into a back. After several minutes, the backing dog sneaked a look over his shoulder and, seeing no one, took off in a sprint past the first dog and stole his point. He knew when his handler hove into sight that he would see good old "Doc" standing on point and credit him with the find.

A professional handler checks his large string of dogs. Staking dogs out in this manner is routine at trials for Pointing Breeds except in inclement weather. *Below:* The gallery aboard the dog wagon follows the action.

Handlers and dogs on the breakaway.

• Somewhere in New Jersey, a great old Shorthair was way out in front of the handlers and gallery. He came over a low rise into the edge of the bird field where he slammed onto point on a planted pheasant. He stood there for four or five minutes and still there was no handler in sight. Finally he could take it no longer. He broke, scooped up the pheasant, and carried it around the bird field with great joy. Then he heard the whistles of the group drawing close. He ran to the edge of the bird field where he originally pointed, dropped the bird, backed off, and pointed it again.

• At the age of 12, Jack was still running big and winning all-age stakes in Shorthair trials. How did he do it? The old campaigner would leave the breakaway on the dead run and head out to the nearest objective, a hedgerow or tree line. Once out of sight, he would drop on his stomach and take a couple minutes of rest. Then, as the group on horseback approached, he would go flying out the other side of the cover. The judges would only see a dog going hell for leather toward the next objective, a running fool. Once at the next spot of cover, Jack again took a rest until the gang approached. Jack had been hanging around humans too long.

Today thousands of dogs compete in AKC trials every year, and most of them are continental breeds. The Pointers and Setters, which were the backbone of the sport in the early years, now mostly compete in trials sponsored by the American Field because of the definite split of field types versus show types. Fortunately, the continentals still produce many Dual Champions. But there have been shortcuts taken by some field trialers seeking an edge in run who have developed cross-breeds that barely resemble the standards.

A Vizsla covers the ground. *Jayne Langdon*

Mounted gallery follows the action at a Brittany National Championship. *Dan Buster*

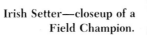
Irish Setter—closeup of a
Field Champion.

The classic pointing
stance shown by a Pointer.
Evelyn Shafer

While field trials are essentially the same all over the country, great rivalries exist between different sections. But all clubs everywhere are facing the same problems: The dogs are running bigger because handlers are riding faster, and there is less ground and fewer birds.

The tall tales are legion and the great performances are few, but what else is there to sustain the true bird dog man on the long winter nights, with his faithful dog lying at his feet as he sits in front of the fire?

He dreams of that great old Pointer who ran big and always stayed on point until released by his handler. He finally disappeared in the late fall and was not found again until the snow had melted in the spring, his skeleton still locked on point.

High heads, cracking tails, rigid points, cackling pheasants, and soft-whirring quail, all in the great outdoors in sunshine and rain—these are the things pointing dog field trials are all about.

A Day At a Field Trial

AKC Field Representative reviews the Rules with the judges.

Below right: A handler releases her dog with a shout of "Hie-on!"

Below: The dogs are ready as the sun comes up.

The Game Steward hides
a hen pheasant
in the tall grass.

A little encouragement
never hurts.

Judges and gallery follow the dogs.

The essence of a pointing breed trial: the point and the back.

Judge marks his book with the names of the placed dogs.

The Winners.

Spaniel Field Trials

Evelyn Monte Van Horn

Field trials are one of the most absorbing, exciting, stimulating, and highly competitive of all dog sports. Because they simulate hunting, they are held outdoors under natural conditions of varying terrain, cover, wind, and weather. It's usually very invigorating weather, too, since for most of the country, fall and early and late winter are the times of the year for trials.

Springer Spaniel trials are particularly thrilling for there is complete action—the bold seeking, finding, and producing of game, the control in being steady after the flush, and the retrieve to hand with a tender carry, for a Spaniel is also a retriever. His first job is to seek, find, and flush game. His second is to bring the game to bag. Therefore, he must be able to mark well the fall and to persevere in trailing wounded or crippled game and bring it promptly to hand. Natural ability is the most important quality. Then there are those other qualities—responsiveness and control, which are instilled by training.

Horses are not used in Spaniel field trials. A Spaniel must hunt to the gun, that is, cover his ground within gun range. Therefore, handlers, the "guns," judges, stewards, and gallery are on foot and the going may be rough, for a Spaniel must attack punishing cover with boldness.

Since medieval times meeting new forms of the chase, or hunting, brought changes in our sporting dogs. In early days the name Spaniel covered several types of dogs used in hunting. A print from the 1300s shows Spaniels springing into the air, scaring birds into flight for the talons of a hawk. With the development of wing shooting, the Spaniel served the same purpose, flushing game for the arrow and, later, the gun. Today the Springer (and that is why he is so named, of course) still springs game into flight for the gunner. The Cocker Spaniel, whose looks beguile and whose name derives from its wide use in hunting woodcock, does the same.

An English Springer Spaniel flushes a pheasant at a National Championship in California. *Callea Photo*

American sportsmen used Spaniels for hunting game birds and waterfowl long before there were Spaniel field trials. The Cocker Spaniel, recognized by the Kennel Club of England in 1892, had no trouble gaining stature in the United States.

The breed even had a sponsoring club early in the game—the American Spaniel Club, a strong organization founded in 1881, which eventually took all the sporting Spaniels—the Clumber, the Sussex, the Irish Water Spaniel, the Field and the Springer Spaniel—under its wing.

The Cocker was always designated as a hunting dog. There were other small Spaniels, the pets of ladies, but they were not the ones "which, if taught to keep within gun range make the best dog among hassocks and briars."*

The first stakes for Cocker Spaniels were held by the Hunting Cocker Spaniel Field Trial Club of America, a club that was largely the creation of Mrs. Ella B. Moffit, a well-known sportswoman from Poughkeepsie, New York. In her book† on the breed she described the club's first trial, held at Verbank, New York, in 1924:

> The stakes were puppy, novice and all age. We had so few dogs that each stake was practically a repeat. The puppy stake was won by Rowcliffe Diana. Only seven months old, she was so small she provoked merriment from the gallery . . . but the way she retrieved a grown cock pheasant bigger than herself turned the ridicule to respect and thus began a new era for the cocker spaniel in America.

That new era endured for a long time. Meanwhile, English Springer Spaniels were catching on at a great rate. Freeman Lloyd, a respected journalist and gundog authority who wrote for sportsmen's magazines and the AKC *Gazette*, had seen Springers at a field trial in Canada and wrote glowingly of this "rare" new breed's ability as a hunter and retriever. It wasn't long before nearly every ship from England and trains from Canada carried Springers to their new American owners.

In a few years the name Hunting Cocker Club was changed to Cocker Spaniel Field Trial Club of America. The catalog of its trial on October 28–29, 1931 shows that the judges were David Wagstaff and Capt. Paul A. Curtis. Other luminaries of the Spaniel world who officiated as guns or stewards included Ralph C. Craig, Henry Ferguson, Elias Vail, Dr. Samuel Milbank, and H. E. Mellenthin, breeder of My Own High Time, which became a Dual Champion, and of the famous My Own Brucie.

There was never any conflict between the Cocker people and the Springer people. From the beginning, trials held by the Cocker clubs included stakes for Springers. Likewise, Springer clubs throughout the country held Cocker stakes, and American and English Cockers competed in the same stakes without breed distinction.

Field trials were the perfect showcase for the Springer. The first field trial for Spaniels in the United States took place late in 1924 at Fishers Island, New York. The setting, a narrow island off the coast of Connecticut, was ideal for game and a natural sanctuary for pheasants. Moreover, the land was almost all privately owned, and its owners delighted in playing host not only to the trial but to the renowned British authorities brought from England to judge and advise.

*From *Recreations in Shooting*, a book published in England in 1800 "designed to aid the young sportsman."
†*The Cocker Spaniel*, 1st ed., Orange Judd Publishing Co., 1935.

A Cocker Spaniel
retrieving a pheasant.

An English Springer Spaniel eagerly enters the water for a retrieve under the watchful eye
of the legendary trainer, Larry McQueen.

There was always a "bench show," or conformation judging, held in conjunction with the early trials at Fishers and judged by a show judge. This was dropped in later years, but there still exists the Horsford Dual Challenge Cup, presented in 1926 by William Humphrey of Shrewsbury, England, for the "Best Looking, Best Working Dog" in the trial. The trial judges now select the winner. Other impressive trophies of long standing are the British Challenge Cup and the International Gun Dog League of England Challenge Cup.

With this auspicious beginning it seemed only natural that the English Springer Spaniel Field Trial Association, founded in 1926, should become acceptable to the American Kennel Club. No other national breed club in the United States has the field-trial connotation in its name.

Field trials went into a decline from 1934 to 1945, but then came a strong rebirth of interest and the Cocker Spaniel scored high. During the 1950s and early 1960s, entries in the Cocker stakes sometimes outnumbered those in the Springer stakes. For nine years there was a National Cocker Championship, the last one held in 1963 at Amwell, New Jersey. Then came a drop in interest and this time a deep one. For one thing, breeders of field Cockers were limited and they had no place to go for outcrosses. Some turned to Springers and Springer trials. Besides, the American Cocker had become too satisfactory and successful as a show dog.

At one of the field trials in the late 1950s, a breeder of both top-show Cockers and field Cockers brought one of his show champions to a trial. He put the dog on the ground to exercise. A few minutes later he called to people nearby. "Look! That poor dog hasn't been able to move two feet. He's all tangled up in the brush." Long coats and short faces do not work in "hassocks and briars" or in retrieving big cock pheasants.

The Cocker Spaniel Field Trial Club of America is a flourishing, active club today, and its 57th annual licensed trial was held in October 1981. But there were no stakes for Cocker Spaniels—only for Springers. Although many sportsmen still use Cockers as gundogs, there hasn't been a field-trial stake for Cockers since 1965, which was the last year in which there were enough dogs to fill a stake. The Springers, however, were forging ahead strongly in the Midwest, in the East, and on the West Coast.

All this interest in Springers naturally led to a National Championship stake, the first of which took place at Marion, Illinois, in 1947. Forty-one dogs qualified by getting a placement in a licensed all-age stake during the calendar year, and 34 were entered. In 1980, 95 dogs qualified and 63 were entered.

During the 1950s the amateurs were being heard from, and in 1960 the American Kennel Club adopted changes in its Rules to provide for amateur all-age stakes to carry points toward the title Amateur Field Championship. Three years later the first National Amateur Championship was celebrated. The event carries the same qualifying requirements and all the luster of the Open National. In 1981 there were 61 starters in the National Amateur.

What of the other sporting Spaniels? A good many are taking advantage of the Working Certificate Tests inaugurated by the Springer Parent Club in 1960 in response to requests from show Springer owners and breeders who desired to keep the hunting instincts of the Springer alive and well—not with the inspired genius of a topflight field-trial dog but acceptable as a worker in the field. It is

Henry P. Davis *(left)*, noted sporting writer and field trial judge, at an early Spaniel trial with Dr. Samuel Milbank, a President of the Westminster Kennel Club and an avid trialer, 1956.

not competitive, but dogs are scored on the way they find a bird, respond to their handler, and retrieve from land and water.

In 1964 the title Working Certificate Excellent was added for those dogs that showed more advanced ability.

Pigeons are the usual source of game, but clubs or groups may also use chukars or pheasants. Entries of all flushing Spaniels are accepted, and many have taken part—Welsh Springers, Cockers, English Cockers, American Water and field Spaniels, as well as Springers. In essence, passing a Test means that the dog is not gun-shy, can hunt well enough to find a bird, and retrieve on land and from water.

It was a Springer stake in a Spaniel field trial. A swiftly flowing stream bordered one side of the course where the whirling flash of a tail could be seen as a hard-driving Springer bore through the high, heavy cover.

Suddenly he caught the scent and swiftly and unerringly thrust a pheasant to squawking flight. He promptly sat and with eager intensity marked the bird's flight and, with the shot, the fall of the bird into the fast-moving river. On his handler's command to fetch, the dog took off speedily and saw the bird being carried very fast downstream. He ran along the bank, checking on the moving bird as he ran. The bird was carried along, faster and faster.

The dog increased his speed and dived into the water just ahead of his quarry, swept it up, swam back to land, and brought the bird to his handler. This kind of performance—a dog showing not only ability but initiative, intelligence, and reasoning on his own—is what makes the work of a Springer Spaniel so thrilling.

Retriever
Field Trials

Richard A. Wolters

In 1931, when the American Kennel Club was approaching its fiftieth year, Retriever field trials in this country had just begun. They grew directly out of the elegant sport of English and Scottish pass shooting, which was and still is the shooting sport in Great Britain for the aristocracy. The dress was the Norfolk jacket and tweed knickers, and it was an honor to receive an invitation.

In America hunting was a democratic endeavor, and its origins had more to do with survival than sport. A dog that only retrieved upland game seemed a waste. In the early twentieth century you couldn't tell the banker from the farmer by his field dress except that one carried a fine handmade gun and the other a seven-dollar mail-order gun. It wasn't until the 1920s in the Jazz Era, the flapper society, the time of the Charleston and great financial fortunes, that the wealthy sportsman became smitten with the British aristocracy. Americans were introduced to British pass shooting with all its glamor and tradition. Somehow these men did not "fit" in our rough-and-ready upland shooting sport. With their wealth they could do anything, and they literally imported the British sport lock, stock, and barrel.

They imported fine English guns, fine English clothes, and even the gamekeepers and their dogs. They turned their estates into shooting preserves, and weekends on these estates became fashionable affairs with lunch on the lawn and fine dinner parties. In that era the shoots were more like Hollywood productions and, to simulate the pass shooting in Scottish style, bird boys were stationed in gullies in the field and threw pen-raised birds as fast as they could toward the advancing line of guns. Labradors were used to retrieve and were handled by the Scottish gamekeepers. It was all done in the style of an F. Scott Fitzgerald story. But this came to an end with the Great Depression. It was only natural that Retriever field trials would become a by-product of the imported shooting because it was a sport the gamekeepers knew from home.

Field trialing in America started as a closely held sport by a few dozen wealthy families. The first trial was deliberately held on a Monday, December 21, 1931, so it would not attract a gallery. The trial was held by the newly formed Labrador Club under the management of the George Foley Organization of Philadelphia and run on Robert Goelet's Glenmore Court Estate in Chester, New York.

Although the first program stated that it was held under AKC and Labrador Club Rules, eyewitness accounts relate that the trial was run under British rules. There was a line of guns, judges, and beaters, and handlers. Each judge tested two dogs at a time. As in a typical British walk-up hunting situation, when a bird was flushed and shot, the line stopped and the judge picked a dog to run. The object was to retrieve the bird. If the dog failed, a second dog was sent. If the second dog came up with the bird, the first dog was eliminated.

To simulate the pass shooting in British trials, two boys in a gully threw two birds toward the advancing line. When the two birds were down, the line stopped and the retrieving was started. Dogs were on their own to work out the problems of the wind, terrain, and the ways of a running bird. Tests were simple single retrieves, and the dog lucky enough to receive a running cripple and then work out the tracking problem would invariably be the winner.

Neither the general dog public nor the hunter took much interest in the new game. There were very few dogs available; it was a "closed" game, and the use of the dog as an upland Retriever was foreign to American needs. Had things continued this way, it is more than possible that retrieving dogs would have become extinct. But the Retrievers were saved and the game of field trialing flourished because of a fluke in the early trials.

In 1932, the second year of Retriever trials, the Chesapeake Bay Retriever entered the scene. Their club trials placed heavy emphasis on water work, and the Chessies skunked the Labradors badly. This shook the gamekeepers into action, and they took their Labs home and retrained them for water retrieving. By the next year they were back and beat the Chessie at his own game. It was this chance beating that made Retrievers popular. The Lab, already a fine land worker, became spectacular in the water. Now hunters took note and saw a dog that had real potential. The Lab's popularity and future was assured.

In 1937 the Golden Retriever Club held its first trial. Dog people and hunters alike were greatly impressed by the hunting ability and the temperament of the Labrador and the Golden. They were not only fine workers but excellent house pets as well. Now Retrieving dogs would achieve a broad base in this country, and field trials would have to change.

Judges evaluate possible test site near Silver Creek, Idaho.

The popularity of the three retrieving breeds increased so fast that the British rules could no longer accommodate the number of dogs entered in U.S. trials. In America the AKC stipulated that trials were open to all comers. In England, even today, the names of the dogs to be tested are drawn from a hat, and the field is limited to 24 for a two-day trial. Because entries in America might go over 100, tests became more difficult and of a different nature in order for the judges to find the winner. Gradually we got away from using upland hunting and pass shooting as the basis for our tests.

To accommodate the large entries, we eliminated the tracking of wounded game, which could take up to an hour for one retrieve. We took all the luck out of the sport and gave each dog the exact same test. Instead of the participants moving over many hundreds of acres to find the game, as the British still do, we run each dog from a line and bring the game to the area. It is all done in a democratic way. All "falls" are exactly the same, and if a bird does fly out of an area or is only crippled, the dog is given another chance.

Year by year the tests have become harder as the dogs become better and better. What winning dogs did during the fifties became child's play for the dogs of the sixties. Today the dogs are almost like machines. They will remember

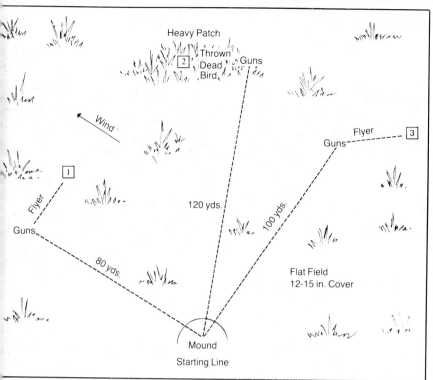

Heavy Patch

Thrown
Dead
Bird

2

Guns

Wind

Flyer

3

Guns

1

120 yds.

100 yds.

Flyer

Guns

80 yds.

Flat Field
12-15 in. Cover

Mound
Starting Line

Typical land triple mark retrieving test.

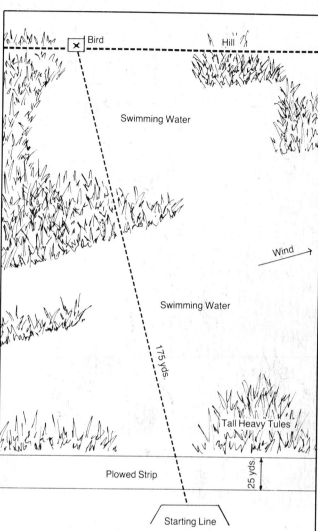

X Bird

Hill

Swimming Water

Wind

Swimming Water

175 yds.

Tall Heavy Tules

Plowed Strip

25 yds.

Starting Line

Typical water blind retrieving test.

three falls without trouble. Even now judges are using four or five falls on occasion. The dogs learn to mark and remember the spot with uncanny success. All sorts of diversionary tactics are incorporated in the series, testing not only the dogs but the imagination of the judges. The sky is the limit, just as long as it simulates a real hunting situation.

A blind retrieve on land or water, when the dog does not know where the bird is down, is an example of precision obedience. The dog is given a line (a direction) and sent off. He's expected to run or swim in a direct line until he reaches "Philadelphia." He only stops when the handler blows his whistle if the dog has deviated from the "line" by 15 or 20 degrees. The dog is put back on course with hand signals until he scents the game. Blind retrieves over all kinds of terrain and through all sorts of water situations can be up to 200 to 300 yards. A good field-trial dog has to be seen to be believed.

In the half century since its inception, the sport of field trialing has grown more than a hundredfold. Today there are 133 clubs from coast to coast running trials under the Rules of the AKC. Countless people who had no interest in hunting became field-trial buffs. Today it is a sport unto itself.

Lab enters the water
with courage and style.

Judges score a retrieve on a snow-covered hillside. *Percy T. Jones*

Gallery of spectators
at a Retriever National
Championship in Delaware.
Evelyn Shafer

A Dual Champion Chesapeake Bay Retriever.

Golden Retriever being sent on a retrieve.

Dachshund Field Trials

George C. Wanner

Few people have observed a field trial for Dachshunds for there are only ten such trials held each year involving some 200 entries. But these trials do provide a select group of trialers with the opportunity to see their Dachshunds do what they were bred to do—hunt game.

In the early 1930s, the short-lived U.S. Dachshund Field Trial Club held the first organized field trial for Dachshunds. The hounds were put to ground in artificial rabbit burrows and were judged by Rules brought over from Germany.

In 1935, under the leadership of the renowned and respected Dachshund fancier Lawrence A. Horswell, the Dachshund Club of America, the Parent Club for the breed, held its first trial at Lamington, New Jersey, under revised Rules tailored for American competition. It remained the only club holding field trials for Dachshunds until the Dachshund Club of New Jersey held its first trial in 1966. Today eight Dachshund clubs hold some ten trials each year in Connecticut, New York, Ohio, and California.

In the early days, with only one trial a year to go to, by far the greatest challenge for any Dachshund owner was to keep his beloved field-trial prospect alive long enough to earn the 25 points for its Field Trial Championship.

The AKC Rules for Dachshunds specify that the judging be based on the following standard of performance:

In all Stakes the principal qualifications to be considered by the Judges are good noses, courage in facing punishing coverts, keenness, perseverance, obedience and willingness to go to earth. Should a rabbit lodge in any earth, or run through any drain large enough for the Dachshunds to enter, the dogs should, of course, be expected to enter without hesitation; and failure to do so should automatically render them ineligible for first award, even though their performance was in all other respects outstanding.

186

It takes a game little dog to meet this standard of excellence in the field, and once a dog has been exposed to the sport, his enthusiasm for it will be ample reward for most owners.

Since Dachshund trials must be held on live rabbits or hare, they are always held on the grounds of an existing Beagle club where game is usually plentiful. Like Beagles, the Dachshunds compete in pairs, or Braces, and the dogs both seek and pursue their game with obvious delight. However, unless the scent is particularly "hot" or the quarry is in sight, most Dachshunds run mute—a trait that would not have excited John Peel.

All varieties and sizes of Dachshunds—Longhair, Wirehair, and Smooth— and both Standard or Miniature compete in the field on an equal eligibility basis. At a trial a Dachshund is a Dachshund regardless of coat or size, and all varieties have done their share of winning over the years. The AKC record books also show that seven Dachshunds have achieved the ennobled designation of Dual Champion, thereby proving to all breeders that function can follow form, or vice-versa.

Dachshunds and their handlers await their turn to compete.

Although in America Dachshunds no longer pursue the badger as they once did in the fifteenth century in their native Germany, they have retained an accurate nose for trailing and tireless courage in punishing cover. Field-trialing experts in this breed claim with considerable pride that no special training is required by either the field-trial handler or the hound. All that a Dachshund needs to bring out the best in his inherited hunting instinct is some rabbit country and a fresh "Tally-ho."

Opposite: A brace of Wirehaired Dachshunds being released on the line.

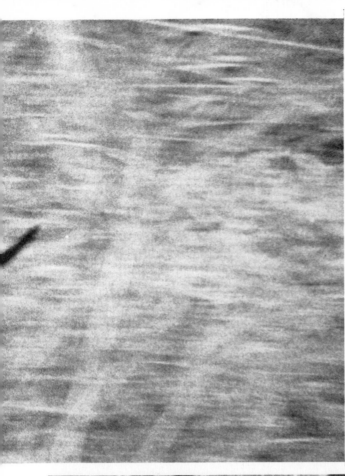

A Dachshund in full cry.

PART THREE

The Dog In Life And Art

Previous page: "Highland Tod (Fox) Hunter," 1859, by Richard Ansdell, R.A. *AKC Collection*

A St. Bernard on avalanche rescue duty. *Photos by Hal*

11
Dogs Serving Man

Roger Caras

Since, in all likelihood, man has been maintaining dogs for somewhere between 150 and 200 centuries, there must be some very good reason for so lengthy a commitment. It must be remembered that pure-bred dogs have been kept, refined, and deeply cared for during famine and times of drought and through wars, plagues, and migrations. Throughout the world, under every imaginable social order and disorder and in the face of restrictive laws, we have had dogs. Despite threats and derision, people have kept their canine companions. There must be a reason.

There are, in fact, many reasons. If one were to search for a special single reason why dogs have meant so much to so many hundreds of millions of people in so many extraordinarily diverse cultural settings, one would almost certainly fail. There are so many reasons that they blend together and form a fabric of man-dog relationships that approach the mystical.

Clearly, there have always been economic reasons. The stockman's dog in Scotland, in Australia, and in many other parts of the world are not niceties. Working dogs of the stock-guarding, stock-herding, and droving types have made it possible for man to keep livestock safe in many parts of the world. Bandits, wolves, and bears have all been held at bay by working dogs, making animal husbandry practical.

We know that Pulik and Komondorok played significant roles in stock-keeping in Hungary a thousand years ago. It probably is not overstating the case to say that it would have been impossible without dogs. The Kuvasz, the Great

193

Australian Cattle Dog herding sheep. *Callea Photo*

GREYFRIAR'S BOBBY

This statue stands in Edinburgh, Scotland, in commemoration of a dog's devotion to a man. Every day for fourteen years (1858–1872) Bobby stood vigil over his master's grave in Greyfriar's Churchyard.

Pyrenees, the Rottweiler, and the German Shepherd Dog served and still do. The Australian Cattle Dog, newly recognized by the American Kennel Club, is far more than a companion today in the Australian outback.

There have been the sled dogs, too. It is true that many of today's Arctic peoples use snowmobiles and even aircraft, but that is only in the last five minutes of their history. Before now, movement by clans and families where goods and food had to be transported would simply not have been possible without sled dogs. In Siberia, the Samoyed served the Samoyed peoples. The Husky is descended from dogs whose being meant life itself to their owners in the same region. The Alaskan Malamute was essential to cultures in the Alaskan Arctic. The Norwegian Elkhound served so long and in so many ways that we can only speculate now on the degree to which Viking explorers depended on them. Life in the Arctic for Arctic peoples would have been far, far different, perhaps even impossible, were it not for the strength and the intelligence of dogs and their ability to survive where machinery (once it became available) and other animals would fail.

Once man from temperate regions decided to explore the high latitudes north and south, he turned to dogs. Explorers who did not use dogs often did not return. His refusal to use dogs killed Robert Falcon Scott and gave the prize of the South Pole to Amundsen, who had warned Scott that it was madness to even attempt 90° South without dogs in harness.

Not very long ago, as we recognize history and the development of man, survival hunting accounted for 99 percent of man's economic activity. Today it accounts for less than one percent and it is easy for us to forget the origins of the sight and scent hounds and how vital their roles were. Long before rifles and telescopic sights, there were men, primitively armed, seeking food to keep their families alive. By their side were dogs. Pure-bred dogs go back further than agriculture, or at least came into being at about the same time, with dogs almost certainly having the edge.

The use of dogs in recreational hunting today is economically significant in many areas, and the use of trained retrievers is a humane and an ecological factor. Crippled ducks help no one, serve no purpose. Retrievers like the Labrador, the Golden, the Chesapeake Bay, the Flat-Coated, and the Curly-Coated still serve now as they were designed to serve rather long ago.

Today's dogs serve as the eyes of visually deprived men and women throughout the more advanced regions of the world. It is impossible to project and really understand what it would be like to be blind and not have a dog, but blind friends with whom I have talked and who have been guests in my home, their dogs by their side, say they would perish inside without their guiding companion dogs. And now work is progressing rapidly in developing a program for dogs for the deaf. No deaf person need fear an approaching car, a fire alarm, or an intruder at the door or window with a dog to warn and alert them to things their own ears would miss. It would seem that being the eyes and ears of man would be enough of an excuse for everything man has put into his canine companions through all of history.

Pope John Paul II greets Joseph Stancampiano, who is accompanied by his guide dog, "Olive."
Pontificia Fotografia Felici

NEW YORK'S FINEST

On March 7, 1972, Brandy, a German Shepherd Dog trained to sniff out explosives for the New York City Police Department's Bomb Section, responded to a call at Kennedy International Airport. An airborne 707 jetliner had been called back after a bomb threat. After one minute of searching, Brandy alerted her handlers to a briefcase in the cockpit of the plane, smuggled in as crew baggage, which was found to contain a time bomb and four and a half pounds of plastic explosive.

Within twelve hours an identical bomb hidden in a first-aid kit in the cockpit of another plane exploded in Las Vegas, causing $1.5 million in damage. This plane had not been searched by dogs. Several days later the circumstances of this incident were simulated to test whether an explosives detection dog could have found the bomb. Two pounds of plastic explosive were hidden in the first-aid kit of a jetliner, and with an FAA official looking on, Brandy and her partner, Sally, a Labrador Retriever, were tested separately. Brandy found the bomb in seven seconds; Sally found it in five seconds.

During her career Brandy responded to over 1,000 calls and discovered over 50 explosive devices, never missing one.

The hearing dog serves as its owner's ears, letting her know when the range timer goes off.

I have watched luggage come along the conveyor belts at the airport in Singapore while dogs dash along those belts checking every bag and parcel for drugs. I have watched dogs climbing mountains of baggage at John F. Kennedy International Airport in New York City and seen them set up a terrible uproar when they detect what to them is the unmistakable smell of narcotics.

Dogs are trained to locate explosive materials and to announce their presence. Drug smuggling on an internationally destructive scale and terrorists using explosive devices against innocent people may be relatively new episodes in mankind's struggle toward humanity, but dogs have been able to respond when called upon. Drug dogs and bomb dogs are noteworthy standards with police departments around the world.

In at least two terrifying world wars when the world itself appeared to go mad, dogs were again called upon, and uncounted thousands of them gave their lives as sentries, as messengers, and as draft animals carrying medical supplies and even ammunition. German Shepherd sentry dogs and Airedale and Irish Terrier messenger dogs have served, have died, and have been honored. War is not honorable, but many of the men, women, and dogs who serve are.

"Rico," a German Shepherd Dog, sniffs out marijuana and hashish at a Customs mail facility in California.

Dogs, of course, have gone into space. Some of the earliest travelers in the Russian space program were dogs, and they have become legendary figures. It is true that space-traveling dogs were not volunteers, but serve they did in ways unique and, in the eyes of Russian scientists at least, essential.

Dogs have been a part of our world for so long that they have become symbols and play an important role in commerce as advertising devices and trademarks. They have served the artist since the days of the cavemen and have appeared in more paintings, etchings, prints, and sculpture than can be cataloged. They have even had religious significance at different stages of human development, including, of course, the god Anubis in Egypt. All of this, including adoration in Madison Avenue commercialism, reflects the importance we have attached to dogs.

U.S. Marine Corps "Devil Dog"
in training during World War II
to accompany Marines in amphibious
landing operations. *U.S. Marine Corps*

World War II recruiting poster for
"Dogs for Defense."

Siberian Husky in service with
U.S. Army carrying light machine gun
and tripod in 1942.

Jack Russell Terrier closes in on a barn rat. *Copyright, David Hancock, Little Aston, England*

There have been special uses for dogs, generally limited to one place and often a relatively short period of time. Although we can no longer determine how much was fact and how much fiction, St. Bernards are said to have trailed lost alpinists and located travelers buried in avalanches. Although now properly despised, gaming with dogs goes far back, and the very word *fancy* as used in *dog fancy* means to "wager." And dogs did not just kill rats in gaming pits. The small terriers did double duty. They were often used to bolt the fox from underground in fox hunting, and they kept their masters' turf relatively free of rats and other vermin. Few cats outdo terriers when it comes to ratting.

As burglar alarms there can be no estimation of the number of human lives saved or the amount of property preserved by dogs, which are naturally territorial and will announce the presence of unwanted strangers bent on mischief or worse. In the hands of trained personnel, properly trained guard dogs have protected commercial as well as military property for a long time. It is only when amateur handlers put ill-chosen dogs in the hands of amateur owners that problems occur with the attack dog.

Bloodhounds have been rescuing lost children, campers, mentally ill patients, and confused elderly people at a ratio of four to one over the criminals they have tracked down and helped bring into custody.

But, strangely, the most important value that dogs have ever had for people is just now being recognized for the first time. Without realizing why they were doing it, people have been keeping dogs because they probably lengthen our life span!

Medical science did not really begin to understand the role of stress in human disease until quite recently. Ulcers, diverticulitis, and even strokes and heart disease were sometimes attributed to stress, but stress was little understood and often ignored. Now we know far more about stress. Many forms of heart disease, many cardiovascular accidents and medical complications are stress related. Stroke is probably brought on by stress in a high percentage of cases, and stress may indeed predispose some people to some forms of cancer. The more we learn about the human body and its potential failings, the more we come to appreciate the role of the mind. And the mind is where stress is likely to register earliest and stay longest.

Pictured above is Owney, the peripatetic mascot of postal clerks around the world.

It was the spring of 1888 that Owney first appeared at the door of the post office in Albany, New York. This Terrier-type dog soon became the friend of local postal clerks, who shared him with their colleagues by attaching labels to his collar and forwarding him to other post offices around the country. From Chicago to St. Louis to Denver, then on to San Francisco, El Paso, Atlanta, and elsewhere. In 1895 Owney set off by steamer from Tacoma around the world, arriving in New York on Christmas Eve. Just five days later, back in Tacoma, he was given a hero's welcome after arriving by train from a 132-day circuit around the globe.

An old dog, Owney met his end in Toledo, Ohio, having been "mailed" there to make a celebrity appearance. Owney bit the clerk who met him at the station, and the police, deciding he must be dangerous, ordered Owney destroyed.

Thus was Owney unceremoniously "returned to sender." Owney, now stuffed, remains on view at the Smithsonian Institution in Washington.

From Henry N. Ferguson's article in the *Basset Babbler*, April 1982.

Perhaps by coincidence, our understanding of what stress does to us has grown just as we have begun to examine the role of companion animals in alleviating stress. It has been known for some time that people who live apart and do not bond to other people get sick more often, contract more severe forms of diseases, and generally die younger than people who are able to bond to others in some meaningful way. It is now becoming apparent that bonding to a companion animal may work as well, or nearly as well, for a great many people. A group of 53 people, all of whom had had one heart attack, were kept under observation in a University of Pennsylvania study. All 53 people in the group owned companion animals or were given them. Of those 53 people, three died within the first year of a second heart attack. A control group was then established of 39 non-pet-owning people who had had one heart attack, and they were also watched. In that group 11 people died of a second heart attack during the first year. The mortality ratios of 3 to 53 (pet-owning) and 11 to 39 (non-pet-owning) were far too dramatic to ignore. The study, in fact, correlates with other evidence that suggests pets—especially dogs—play a role in human longevity.

In Maryland patients with severe hypertension were watched through one-way windows while they wore remote-reading blood-pressure cuffs on their legs. On signal, technicians entered their rooms and put puppies or kittens in their laps or grown dogs by their sides. Reflexively the subjects of the study began petting the animals, and doctors watched in amazement as the remote readout tubes showed their blood pressure dropping steadily toward near-normal levels.

A Handi-Dog helps its owner with such tasks as retrieving a dropped spoon. *Barbara Tellman*

Nothing's better for relieving stress than a visit from a friendly dog. *PPP/WSU Photo: Ken Porter*

The Bulldog serves many masters as the symbol of toughness, tenacity, and dependability.

Corporate symbol of Mack Trucks, Inc.

Lance Corporal Chesty, Mascot of the U.S. Marine Corps.

Handsome Dan, Yale University Mascot.

A home for severely alienated alcoholics in Connecticut assigns incoming residents Labrador Retrievers to care for and finds that the men are able to accept responsibility, often for the first time in their lives. The dogs help them settle down and establish contact with the other residents, for they now have a common interest to share—their dogs.

A school in upstate New York cares for People in Need of Supervision (once called juvenile delinquents but now known as P.I.N.S.). The boys are given dogs to care for and, in fact, their campus is a haven for stray dogs who somehow learn that this is the place to come for food, safety, and lots of love.

All across the United States and in a number of European countries, research is under way to determine the values and the true nature of the man-nonhuman bond. It is highly unlikely that these are matters that occupied the minds of the early peoples who took the small wolf *Canis lupis pallipes* into their care and began the selective breeding that led, perhaps as long as 8,000 years ago, to recognizable breeds of dogs. The Sumerians had Salukis; the peoples of Siberia almost as long ago had Samoyeds. The Greyhound is of enormous antiquity, and so are the Afghan and other coursing hounds of the desert regions of the Middle East. Of great interest is the fact that the Maltese is also a very ancient breed. The Italian Greyhound, a toy breed, was in Pompeii when Vesuvius wiped out the city. There were also small companion dogs in Tibet and China about as long ago.

The presence of breeds like the Maltese, the Italian Greyhound, and various Chinese "sleeve dogs" suggests that although people thousands of years ago didn't understand the true character of strokes, the nature of heart attacks, or the predisposition of the stressed body to develop cancer, they somehow knew that their state of mind and probably state of health were improved by the companionship of the dog. When science has finished with all these deliberations, we may be forced to the astounding conclusion that the greatest use to which man has ever put the dog is to increase his own longevity and preserve his own peace of mind and, in some cases, his very sanity. It has taken us a long time to come to understand just what dogs really do mean in our lives.

12
Famous Dogs and Their People

Pat Beresford and Leonard Brumby, Jr.

All the world's a stage,
And all the men and women merely players.

As You Like It, WILLIAM SHAKESPEARE

Six dogs stand in the center of the Best in Show ring, and all you see is one tiny toy at the end of the line.

Stand at the breed ring where ten superbly conditioned terriers are competing for Best of Breed, and you can only see that third dog in line.

When a ring has keen competition and you can't take your eyes off one dog, that one dog has got to be great.

How do dogs achieve that greatness in the ring? Breeding and temperament, conditioning and presentation are a large part of the whole. And then there is that elusive, intangible, undefinable thing called showmanship.

Many great dogs had *it*, and *it* made them famous in their time and—for many dog people—for all time. The great Wire Fox Terrier bitch Wrangler's Peggy had *it*. In her star-dusted years of the twenties, a box was used for examination. If she thought she was a shoo-in for Best in Show, she would stand like a proper lady. Bring in another close contender and her handler could feel the vibration travel from her neck up the lead to his hand as she shifted her act into high gear.

Another showman with that certain something was Herman Rinkton. The red, smooth Dachshund was a showstopper with his no-nonsense march to his own music, tail wagging furiously as he outstepped his equally great handler, Hans Sacher. He was hard to beat.

In 1912, an examination block was *de rigueur* at dog shows.

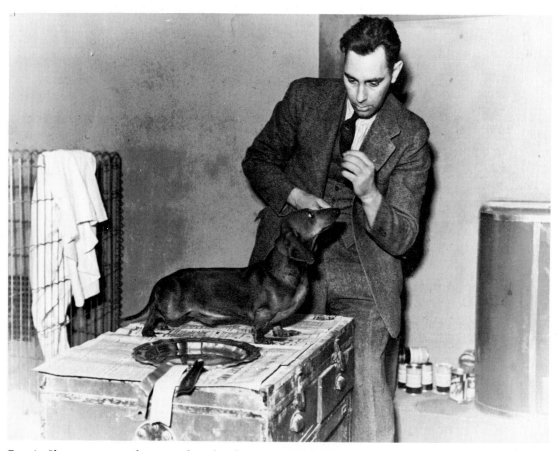

Best in Show meant another treat from handler Hans Sacher for Dachshund Ch. Herman Rinkton, 1939. *St. Louis Globe-Democrat*

Ch. Marjan II's fluid performance was almost eclipsed by his owner-handler's demonstration of the social graces. At the finish of each sweep of the ring, Mrs. Anna Marie Paterno curtsied to the judge, 1940.

Mrs. G. Winant's Scottish Terrier, Ch. Walsing Winning Trick of Edgerstoune, handled by Phil Prentice. Judge Joseph P. Sims awarded the Terrier Group at 1950 Westminster. *Evelyn Shafer*

Albert E. Van Court selects Bulldog Ch. Kippax Fearnaught for Best in Show at the 1955 Westminster Kennel Club Show. Westminster President, William A. Rockefeller, presented the silver bowl. *Evelyn Shafer*

All eyes were on the Non-Sporting ring when Harry Sangster led the Bulldog Kippax Fearnaught to first place more times than most can remember. And it was hard to see another dog when Mrs. Claude J. Fitzgerald was in competition with Mighty Sweet Regardless, her elegant Boston Terrier bitch, floating out on the end of the long ribbon of a lead.

And if the dogs lacked a bit of charisma on their own, who can erase the memory of their handlers who added the something special that put the pair in a class by themselves? Will anyone who was at the 1940 Westminster Show forget the sight of Anna Marie Paterno sweeping into a long bow at the feet of Hound judge Joseph Quirk as she finished her turn? Resplendent in formal military uniform, Judge Quirk returned the gesture in courtly fashion. She bowed again. Once again, he acknowledged her thanks. For all we know, had he not awarded the Group to her Saluki, Marjan II, they might still be down on the floor at the old Garden, complimenting each other.

Of course, no two dog people have ever been known to agree on what makes a dog "great," but when old-timers get together and talk about the glory days gone by, they often agree that the all-white Wire Fox Terrier Flornell Spicy Piece of Halleston, piloted by Percy Roberts, was a great one. Then you'd have to give equal time to Mrs. John G. Winant's Scottish Terrier Walsing Winning Trick of Edgerstoune. And if you were a Hound man, you might agree that the day in 1936 when Albert E. Smith showed Amory Haskell's Harrier Mr. Reynal's Monarch to Best in Show at Morris and Essex was one great day for a superlative specimen of the breed.

Can any chronicle be complete without mention of Louis Murr and his regal Borzoi Vigow of Romanoff or the phantom ballet choreographed by Sunny Shay and her Afghan Shirkhan of Grandeur? It was hard to see another Doberman in the ring when Peggy Adamson's dog Dictator v. Glenhugel—whose bearing fit his name—was putting on his show.

Could any Sporting Group be complete without mention of the Irish Water Spaniel Mahoney's O'Toole? Or Charlie Palmer and his Pointer Captain Speck? Setters were well represented in the golden era by Mrs. Cheever Porter's Irish Milson O'Boy, a crowd-pleaser who enjoyed every minute spent in the ring, while the English held their ground with Dr. A. A. Mitten's Blue Dan of Happy Valley and, in later years, Rock Fall's Colonel, who was campaigned to a staggering record by his proud owner and handler, William Holt.

The team of Blue Dan and his handler, Benny Lewis, was mesmerizing. Nattily attired in knickers, Lewis set a rhythmic pace that was poetry in motion. He "broke the barrier" for professional handlers; almost all prominent handlers had terrier backgrounds until this upstart appeared on the scene and, with his magic fingers, completely hand-stripped his string of Setters into top presentation.

The Sporting, Working, and Terrier Groups had many great professional handlers in those early years, while the owner-handlers appeared to dominate Hounds, Non-Sporting, and many Toys. Who could beat Mrs. Vincent Matta and her incredible string of Pomeranians, particularly Little Tim Stepper, or E. W. Tipton, Jr., and his mighty Min Pin, Little Daddy?

Conditioning a top show dog hasn't changed much over the years! Ch. Vigow of Romanoff has a good workout on the road with his breeder-owner Louis Murr, 1934.

One of the few breeder-owner-handler teams to win Westminster: Sunny Shay and her Afghan, Ch. Shirkhan of Grandeur, had broad smiles after the 1957 event. *Evelyn Shafer*

The "bit different dog," Ch. Mahoney's O'Toole, an Irish Water Spaniel owned by Mrs. Charles Wynns, came close to the top Westminster award in 1943 when he was awarded best American Bred Dog. *William Brown*

Winifred Heckmann awards Pointer, Ch. Captain Speck, the Group award at the International Kennel Club Show in Chicago, 1952. Handled by Charles Palmer. *Frasie*

The great Irish Setter, Ch. Milson O'Boy, owned by Mrs. Cheever Porter. By comparison with today's profusely coated Sporting dogs, this elegant Setter might look out of coat, but his bearing and dignity say "Champion" in any era, c. 1935. *Tauskey*

Ch. Rock Fall's Colonel, an orange belton English Setter, amassed a phenomenal record of wins, guided by his breeder-owner, William T. Holt. The Sporting Group at the Westchester Kennel Club show in 1952, under judge Neill P. Overman, was one more prestigious win in his career. *Evelyn Shafer*

Left: The mighty Min Pin, known affectionately as "Little Daddy," Ch. Rebel Roc's Casanova Kurt, was bred and owned by Mrs. E. W. Tipton, Jr., and handled by Mr. Tipton. Judge Percy Roberts officiated at this event in 1961. *Frasie. Right:* A dog's-eye view of the Winner's circle. Ch. Zeloy Mooremaide's Magic, a Wire Fox Terrier owned by Marion G. Bunker and handled by Jimmy Butler, took Best in Show at Westminster in 1966. *Gilbert; collection of John Marvin*

In 100 years of dog shows, it probably can be said without much dispute that the heyday of shows, handlers, and dogs was that lush period between the Depression and World War II, when the rich were truly different from you and me today. Great kennels flourished, and the magnitude of investment in money and management was in a class we will never experience again. Magnificent establishments such as "Salamagundi" and "Blakeen," with seemingly endless winning Poodles; "Chappaqua," where each of the dozen or so breeds raised had their own individual kennel buildings, all under the watchful eye of Leonard Brumby, Sr.; Leonard Buck's Spaniel kennels; Harry Peters's "Windholme" Greyhounds; Mrs. Richard Bondy's "Wildoaks" Kennel where some of the greatest American-bred Fox Terriers first saw the light of day; Mr. and Mrs. James A. Farrell's "Foxden," and the "Downsbragh" of the William Brainards, sheltering terriers as well as some of the great hounds of the day. Ohio was home to the T. H. Carruthers's "Hetherington" Kennels, and Mrs. Hartley Rockefeller Dodge's "Giralda" has become legend.

There was a high concentration of predominantly terrier establishments centered on Long Island, New York, and out of these kennels emerged not only the superstar dogs of that era but the managers who became the unbeatable handlers and, in later years, the distinguished all-breed judges. The list is a who's who of pure-bred dogs: Percy Roberts, Henry Stoecker, Billy Land, Johnny Murphy, Peter Knoop, Ed Bracy, Robert Braithwaite, and Howard Tyler, to name but a very few. Curiously enough, John Gowdy, the manager-handler of Mrs. Edward Alker's Twin Pond Kennels—considered by his peers to be the greatest of them all—only showed his employer's Welsh Terriers during his entire career.

No lineup of great dogs would be complete without some winners—and losers—of the biggest show of all, Westminster. On the night of February 9, 1960, when diminutive Clara Alford escorted the indomitable Pekingese Chik T'Sun of Caversham into the winners circle, it was the last jewel in the diadem of an extraordinary career. He had tried on two other occasions for the final nod, and on this, his last ring appearance, he added the Westminster rosette to 120 other Best in Show successes, to set an all-time record that wasn't challenged until the late 1970s.

More than half the Best in Show wins at Westminster have been awarded to a representative of the Terrier Group. But the one dog, almost universally acclaimed as the greatest Terrier of them all by custodians of the past and acolytes of the present, never won the Garden.

Winthrop Rutherford, a distinguished Terrier man of the period, reflected on the career of this Smooth Fox Terrier after the dog's lead had been hung up. "When the Fox Terrier Standard was drawn up in 1876," he said, "they closed their eyes and dreamed of Saddler."

Few dog people need to reminded of his full name, Nornay Saddler, and those that were spectators at his first show in this country, the February 9, 1937, Terrier Specialties at the old Grand Central Palace, recall him as an ignominius fourth in a class of four. Ask those same people who the winners were, and they will say all that anyone remembered afterward was the Smooth that lost.

He wasn't seen again until the following May when he came out at Morris and Essex under the firm hand of Leonard Brumby, Sr., to take Best of Breed. He was rarely defeated thereafter. His career was unique, for Brumby and his owner, James. M. Austin, tried to avoid taking him back to a show he had won or put him under a judge who had put him up. He never went out of the area of the big shows, and he was always shown again under judges who had defeated him.

As often happens, an equally great dog's career may be eclipsed because of the time frame in which he is shown. Such was the case with John Gan's magnificent German Shepherd Dog Pfeffer v. Bern, handled to perfection by Ernest Loeb. At the moment of truth, Loeb would drop the lead and walk away, leaving the dog posed as though cast in bronze. He won Group after Group only to walk into the final lineup to face Nornay Saddler.

Fame is a fleeting, euphoric thing, but in the world of pure-bred dogs we have a "hall of fame" in the records and accomplishments of hundreds of great dogs who are now behind the stars of today and the hopefuls of tomorrow. Their names are not soon forgotten.

One of the top-winning show dogs of all time, the Pekingese, Ch. Chik T'Sun of Caversham, owned by C. C. Venable and always beautifully presented by Clara Alford, 1957. *Tulsa Daily World*

Rin-Tin-Tin ponders his own portrait. *Warner Bros.*

Famous Dogs of Stage and Screen

Walt Disney's Pluto.
*The Museum of Modern Art/
Film Stills Archive*

Lady and the Tramp.

Old Yeller.

The Shaggy Dog with Fred MacMurray.

One Hundred and One Dalmations.

Broadway's Annie and Sandy.

William Powell, Myrna Loy, and Asta in *After the Thin Man*.
The Museum of Modern Art/Film Stills Archive

Hollywood's Annie and Sandy with admirer, First Lady Nancy Reagan.
New York Post photography by Norcia. © 1982, *News Group Publications, Inc.*

Lassie says good-bye at 1965 Golden Gate Kennel Club Show. *V. M. Hanks, Jr.*

Bebe Daniels with Strongheart, the first canine movie star. *The Museum of Modern Art/Film Stills Archive*

Roddy McDowell and Lassie in *Lassie Come Home*. *The Museum of Modern Art/Film Stills Archive*

13

Famous People and Their Dogs

Walter R. Fletcher

During the first century of the AKC many thousands of enthusiastic and colorful fanciers contributed to the sport of dogs—breeding, competing, and working actively in organization and club work and introducing new breeds to the United States. These fanciers came from all walks of life. Weekend after weekend, all year long, they joined the march to show grounds to compete in one of the very few sports in which the whole family can participate and have fun.

It is impossible to attempt to mention all who have played leading roles, but a handful of names will live long in the annals of the sport.

Born two years before the AKC came into being was the mistress of Giralda Farms, Geraldine Rockefeller Dodge, the niece of John D. Rockefeller and the wife of Marcellus Hartley Dodge, grandson of the founder of Remington Arms Company. Although she had dogs all of her life, she first showed in 1923 with a German Shepherd, one of more than 80 breeds she owned.

Mrs. Dodge's name is synonymous with Morris and Essex, by far the most opulent canine event ever staged in this country. Every May throngs of up to 50,000 made their way to her estate in Madison, New Jersey, for *the* dog show.

Although the Giralda Shepherds were almost unbeatable in the 1920s and 1930s, they never won the top award at Westminster, but Mrs. Dodge did win with a Pointer and a Doberman. In 1933 she became the first woman ever to judge Best in Show at Madison Square Garden.

When she died in 1973, it took an auction firm a year and a half to appraise and catalog all the works of dog art she had collected, and these works brought

214

Geraldine Rockefeller Dodge of Giralda Farms looks over one of her many Best in Show Winners, 1939.

the tidy sum of $7 million. Part of the proceeds from the sale were donated to St. Hubert's Giralda, an animal shelter Mrs. Dodge set up on her estate, which serves eight communities covering more than 90 square miles and handles some 3,000 dogs, cats, and other small animals annually. Paintings, sculptures, and books not included in the sale are displayed in a gallery at the shelter.

Mrs. Cheever Porter, who died in 1981 at the age of 93, was almost a contemporary of the AKC from its infancy. She was a figure skater and for five years she staged charity figure-skating carnivals at Madison Square Garden. She was also a fight fan who sat in the first row for all the Joe Louis bouts and an inveterate first-row theatergoer.

In the dog show world, this New Yorker remained a woman of mystery, even though she was a prominent Irish Setter fancier for more than 50 years. Of all her dogs, the only one she ever kept as a pet at her Manhattan townhouse was her first big winner in the twenties, a redcoat named Ch. St. Cloud's Fermanagh.

Her most famous dog was Ch. Milson O'Boy, first shown as a pup in 1933. He was retired after Westminster in 1938 and was considered by many the greatest Irish Setter of the century. O'Boy had a Pinkerton detective who guarded him on the bench and walked with him to and from the ring. The Irish Setter had a fan club, and Mrs. Porter received many cards on his birthday. One of his admirers was Gov. Alfred E. Smith of New York, who ran for president in 1928. One year the Westchester judging was delayed so that the popular

Governor Smith could have his picture taken with the Irish Setter from the sidewalks of New York.

Mrs. Porter had many other top-winning redcoats, as well as the number one Gordon Setter in the breed's history—Ch. Legend of Gael. She also had a multi-Best-in-Show English Setter, Afghan, Dobe, and Boxer. None of her dogs, however, ever took Westminster. Although she had some of the best known canines in America, she herself probably was the least known of the great fanciers.

The Poodle has been the country's top dog since 1960, and it was Hayes Blake Hoyt, a noted breeder, exhibitor, and judge, who did much to bring the breed to the fore. When the Poodle started to pay the price of being number one, suffering from indiscriminate backyard breeders out to make a fast dollar, Mrs. Hoyt, whose Blakeen Kennel produced more than 100 champions, was quick to say: "The tremendous popularity the Poodle is enjoying in America today is lamentable, not commendable. I should take my share of the blame. For years, I did my best to make the breed a favorite with the public."

The first Poodle ever to go Best in Show at Westminster was Mrs. Hoyt's white standard import, Ch. Nunsoe Duc de la Terrace, in 1935. Mrs. Hoyt's miniatures ran up tremendous records, and a dozen other breeds that came out of Blakeen Kennel did very well. "I've also had some mixed breeds and loved them," she said. "It's better to have a parti-colored pet than a splendid specimen who has to be given tranquilizers to be taken into a ring."

The late Alva Rosenberg was an 18-year-old youth when he had his first judging assignment in 1910. He was subsequently to rule at more than 1,000 shows over the next six decades as the most respected and sought-after arbiter in the land. A blue ribbon from Alva was treasured above all others by exhibitors. Several of our best known all-rounders told me they learned much about judging by stewarding for this gentle gentleman.

Rosenberg was born in Brooklyn and was taken to his first show—Westminster—by his mother when he was eight years old. Two judges, Dr. and Mrs. Edward Berendson, started Alva on his doggy career. After school the youngster would run to their home to help around the kennel. When he was a teenager, the Berendsons proposed him for membership in the Long Island Kennel Club.

What was his greatest thrill in the sport to which he gave so much? "Finding a good dog and starting it on a career," Alva said. "I've never hesitated to take a really good one out of the classes and put it over champions. It's been my good fortune to have given some great dogs their first Best in Show."

Alva was a most modest man. When interviewed for a column in *The New York Times*, as he sat on a sofa in front of a big fireplace at his home in Connecticut, one was struck with the kindness and humility that emanated from the great authority. And his one request was that he not be unduly praised. For years a dealer in antiques, Rosenberg possessed an understanding of quality and beauty that carried over to the show ring, where he ardently sought the same perfection.

Another great all-rounder was Percy Roberts, the "English Squire." Percy started in his native land as a kennel boy at 16 and came to this country in 1913. As a handler, Roberts was the only person to guide four dogs to Best in Show at Westminster. In 1948 he turned in his handler's license to judge, an assignment

Alva Rosenberg *(right)* presenting Best in Show ribbon to Walter Goodman, noted breeder and exhibitor of Skye Terriers, 1958. *Page of New York*

Percy Roberts. *Ritter*

he took very seriously. The wax-mustachioed man, who favored checkered vests, always said judges were the architects of a breed while breeders were the builders.

During the quarter-century when they worked shows, Major and Bea Godsol were among the most active judges in the country. They also did much to promote obedience training on the West Coast. The first match for the educated set held in California was on their ranch in Dixon. When the Godsols were married, Bea had 25 Newfoundlands, Sealyhams, and Beagles, while Major had about the same number of German Shepherds, all on 20 unfenced acres. As Bea told it, when the dogs took off in the morning, it was quite a sight. But when the "Godsol pack" started to roam off the ranch, the neighbors were not too happy. So up went a fence.

During World War II, Major was in charge of the War Dog Center at Fort Robinson, in Arkansas. "We had one thousand doghouses and an occupant for each one," he told me.

William Kendrick was a 20-year-old junior at Princeton when he first was called upon to judge in 1924. He's been a busy arbiter ever since. Wild Bill, as he is affectionately known, always calls them as he sees them and isn't influenced by dog ads or the animal rating systems conducted by canine publications. The silver-haired septuagenarian maintains that rating systems favor the wealthy exhibitor who repeatedly can send his dogs all over America with a capable handler.

"I think all rating systems should be relegated to the ash can," he said. Kendrick also is scornful of junior showmanship, declaring that it encourages overhandling and adding: "We should judge dogs, not kids."

There is almost no doggy household that doesn't have books about canines, whether they be volumes on training, grooming, judging, medical advice, or individual breeds. Howell Book House, which publishes the official AKC *The Complete Dog Book*, the best-selling dog opus in publishing history, was founded by Elsworth Howell.

The tall, well-groomed, articulate man started as a youngster at Grolier, Inc., publishers of *The Book of Knowledge* and other encyclopedias, and rose to become its vice-president and a director. His love of the sport came naturally, since his father was a Schipperke breeder, exhibitor, and arbiter. Howell's judging began when he was 22, in 1938, when he ruled on Schipperkes at Morris and Essex. In addition to his publishing career, he's best known in dogs for his English Setters, and he's been the national club's AKC delegate since 1958.

August Belmont, a former AKC board chairman and grandson of the fourth AKC President, made a mark for himself with Chesapeake and Labrador Retrievers. Belmont not only proved proficient in running his dogs in the field but also won in the breed and obedience rings. His Bo-Marc of South Bay made Chesapeake history by earning a C.D. obedience degree when he was a six-month-old pup and then gaining a breed Championship and finally an amateur field title. But it was a Lab named Super Chief who really makes Belmont's eyes sparkle. Soupy, whom he called a "once in a lifetime dog," won the National Amateur and National Open Retriever Championships in 1968, the only time this has ever been accomplished. Mrs. Belmont is also a Retriever trial

All-Breed Judge William Kendrick, at left. *William Brown*

Evelyn Monte Van Horn, noted authority on Field Trials for English Springer Spaniels. *Herb Levart*

August Belmont gives hand signal to one of his Retrievers.

enthusiast. Indeed, her husband once said, "Louise does a much better job than I. She's run several dogs to both Field and Amateur Championships."

John Olin, a sportsman from Illinois famous for his gundogs, was the founder of the Orthopedic Foundation for Animals, which has the largest collection of radiographs of dogs' hips in the world. OFA deals principally with hip dysplasia, striving to prevent this skeletal abnormality in dogs and at the same time applying the knowledge to man. "A dog's life is said to be seven times as rapid as a human's," Olin said. "So by studying skeletal problems in canines, we have a speed-up laboratory. Our work should unravel a great many skeletal problems in man."

Although Olin's Nilo Kennel (*Olin* spelled backward) was famous for its Labrador Retrievers, Pointers, English Springers, and Brittanys, the Lab was the breed that Olin favored. His Nilo's King Buck, the national open winner in 1952 and 1953, was the model for the United States duck stamp in 1959, the only dog thus far to be so honored.

On the sled-dog trail, few could match the peerless driving of Eva Seeley. More familiarly known as Short because of her diminutive size, she was a pioneer in the sport, having started to drive in 1929. On her eightieth birthday, in 1971, tributes poured in from all over the country, including a telegram from President Nixon.

Short always stressed the dual-purpose dog who could both win ribbons in the ring and pull a sled. To prove her point, she often used champions on her sled teams. She did much to get the Alaskan Malamute registered with the AKC and was named honorary life president of the Siberian Husky Club of America. Sled dogs for World War II were trained at her Chinook Kennels, and she also supplied dogs for the Navy's Operation Deepfreeze in Antarctica.

Most people remember Herbert H. Lehman as the governor and U. S. senator from New York State, but only a few will recall that he and his wife established the Boxer breed in this country. In 1912 the Lehmans bought one in Switzerland for a house pet. Two years later they imported several more, including the Sieger, Dampf von Dam, who was shown by Mrs. Lehman and made Boxer history when he took the Best of Breed at Westminster and two months later became the country's first Boxer champion. Years later, the Lehmans had 150 Boxers in their Park Avenue "kennel," with nary a complaint from the neighbors—all the dogs were ceramic or bronze statues.

"WHY DIDN'T HE WIN FIRST PLACE?"

Lyndon Johnson's White House Beagles Him and Her were dead. Sensing LBJ's loss, FBI boss J. Edgar Hoover gave the president a new Beagle. Johnson right away dubbed the dog J. Edgar, although its registered name was Greeson's Chum.

When Willard Deason, a close family friend of the Johnsons, found out that J. Edgar had some field trial talent, he borrowed the dog to take with him to the Chambersburg Beagle Club trial in Chambersburg, Pennsylvania, on September 25, 1966. Deason, an expert Beagler, put himself down as handler and the owner as L. B. Johnson, Stonewall, Texas, thinking that it wouldn't be quite fair to the judges if they were aware that they were judging the president's dog; but the secret didn't last very long.

J. Edgar was awarded second place to become the first and only White House dog to gain admission to the AKC's record books.

Deason felt sure that LBJ would be pleased about J. Edgar's success. In the Oval Office on Monday, LBJ read the inscription on the red rosette and then peering over his glasses at Deason he said, "Why didn't he win first place?"

The late John Olin (*at left*) with Retriever field trialers Bing Gruenwald (*center*) and Andrieus A. "Pete" Jones. *Evelyn Shafer*

Nilo's King Buck, the first dog ever to appear on a Federal Duck Stamp. *Olin Conservation Dept.*

Famous Dog Show Superintendent, George Foley *(left)* with Superintendents Helen Seder, A. Dowell Mansfield, and Thomas J. Crowe. *William Brown*

Mr. Dog Show—George Francis Foley—was the holder of the AKC number one superintendent's license. His first job was to put on a show for the Chester County (Pa.) Agricultural Fair Association in 1908. He worked two days and a night writing the catalog and then attended to the many details that go with running a show. His fee was $100. Fifty years later he was doing a little better financially, getting $2,500 for a small fixture and $75,000 for one of the biggies. In its heyday, the Foley Dog Show Organization handled 150 events annually. Rarely seen without his milk chocolate buds, this little man was responsible for many of the changes in shows, such as eliminating sawdust in the aisles, replacing the shoulder-high fences around the rings, and making the events more attractive for exhibitors and spectators.

Without those unsung heroes and heroines of the rings—the stewards—there would be problems galore. These devoted men and women give exhibitors their armbands, check dogs into the ring, make certain the winners receive the proper ribbons and prizes, and serve as secretaries for the judges. When Morris and Essex was in full swing, there were 100 to 150 stewards at work.

Robert Griffing for several years had assembled the needed personnel for the prestigious Morris and Essex event. He felt it was a waste of training and ability for the group to serve at just one show. So in 1948 he founded the Stewards Club of America, which supplies ring aides to clubs that ask for them. For the most part, the stewards' daylong toil is rewarded only with a free admission ticket, a catalog, and a lunch. These truly dedicated men and women serve mainly for the love and satisfaction they derive from the sport.

More Famous People and Their Dogs

"Irresponsible critics are a disturbing element!" was the caption for this cartoon, which portrays President Franklin D. Roosevelt and Fala, his Scottish Terrier. *Allen Foster, Courtesy of Franklin D. Roosevelt Library*

President and Mrs. Herbert C. Hoover accompanied by their White House pet, Pat. *Wide World Photo*

General of the Army Dwight D. Eisenhower and wife, Mamie, at Potomac Boxer Club Specialty Show. 1948. *William Brown*

Mme. Wellington Koo, wife of the former
Chinese Ambassador to the U.S., holds
two Pekingese at a Dog Show
during World War II. *Percy T. Jones*

Pee Wee Reese of Brooklyn Dodgers fame
rounds second base with Toy Manchester
Terrier, 1951. *Acme Photo*

President Lyndon B. Johnson enters the Oval Office and responds to his Beagles' joyful greeting.

The Duke and Duchess of Windsor, Pug enthusiasts, presenting trophies at the Pug Dog Club of America Specialty Show. 1958.

Gayelord Hauser on an early television show shares the spotlight with Sealyham Terrier.

AMERICAN
Kennel Register

Copyright, 1884. Entered at the Post Office as Second Class Matter.

PUBLISHED BY THE FOREST AND STREAM PUBLISHING CO., 39 & 40 PARK ROW.

P. O. Box 2832.   **New York, August, 1884.**   VOL. II—No. 8.

SCOTCH TERRIERS.
Miss Mary Laing's "Foxie" and Mr. J. A. Adamson's "Roger Rough."

14
The Early Sporting Press

Herm David

The organized showing and handling of dogs in America did not begin overnight with the first meetings of the AKC in the fall of 1884. Those meetings were a natural culmination of more than a century of building American interest in dogs.

The establishment of canine competitions was, in retrospect, inevitable. First, however, America had to experience important economic and societal changes. We needed a leisure class with the means to support the sport. We had to consolidate some of our growth and recover from a terrible Civil War. Unlike compact, homogeneous Great Britain, the United States (and Canada, which was a full partner in the formation of the AKC) had to develop transportation and communication. In this respect it also had to develop a sporting press.

Through the Civil War period American newspapers were filled with politics, foreign dispatches, ship sailings, religion, agriculture, and obituaries. They had no sporting pages. We had to wait until a specialized, sporting press could facilitate communication before pure-bred dogs could even be discussed among those with serious interest in the subject. This press was the only way early enthusiasts could identify each other. Its columns carried descriptions of the British breeds, announcements of what few books there were, and veterinary advice. Eventually they became a forum for public debates about dogs and, later, the need for dog organizations—and the forms they should take.

Public competitions could not take place without organizers. These people met through the sporting press. When they required public announcements for their public competitions they relied on the sporting press of the day. We still do. When the call went out for the formation of local clubs it was through the columns of our sporting journals. When leadership was needed it frequently came from the editors, or kennel editors, of sporting publications.

227

Opposite: The cover of the *American Kennel Register* in which an editorial first called for the formation of an American Kennel Club.

Much of the leadership, the public discussion, and the public notices of the first AKC meetings were products of our sporting periodicals.

When we needed a national sporting ethic, when we first had to become conscious of the need for conservation, these came to us in columns and books written by a man with a strange and tragic genius.

North Americans did not have to be taught to appreciate pure-bred dogs. They had long imported the best they could afford in horses, beef and dairy cattle, sheep and swine. Dogs were not, of course, the same sort of cash crop. Except in affluent areas, dogs had to earn their keep. Most were all-purpose types—herders, protectors, assets to the hunter's gun, and family companions.

America's first book on hunting—which could also be considered our first dog book, since two-thirds of it is about dogs—was *The Sportsman's Companion*, first published in New York in 1783. Its anonymous author is believed to have been a former British officer who grew fond of the country he had been sent to subjugate. He decided to remain. Although three editions of the book were issued, it had only sparse circulation and carried no lasting influence. The same can be said of a translation of an Italian treatise, *A Method of Raising and Training Pointers*, published in Charleston, South Carolina, in 1799.

The first of what could genuinely be termed the sporting press in America was launched in 1829 by John Stuart Skinner in Baltimore. It was called the *American Turf Register and Sporting Magazine. The Register* regularly ran articles on various field sports and occasionally on dogs.

The American Turf Register's contributions were many, but by far its greatest was the introduction to print of "Frank Forester" and its encouragement of the author, Henry William Herbert. Herbert's impact on North American field sports and their practice, mores, and conservation has been greater and more enduring than that of any other man. Many generations of American boys had their imaginations fired and their tastes refined by this prolific genius, who long hid behind his pseudonym because he felt it was beneath the dignity of a scholar and serious author to be identified with such a relatively inconsequential subject as outdoor sports.

A member of one of England's greatest families, Herbert was banished from England at the age of 24. Researchers have never uncovered either the cause or the source of the order of exile. Herbert was prolific almost beyond belief, pouring out translations of French, Latin, and Greek classics, poetry, histories, historical novels, theatrical criticism—and the sporting works of Frank Forester. His friend Edgar Allan Poe entreated him to polish his literary efforts, but ever needful of the publisher's next check, he was never known to have written more than a first draft.

Herbert drew an uncompromising line between pot hunting and sport. The latter, he insisted, demanded the company of a dog of quality and good training. He further insisted that a dog should be treated sympathetically and with respect.

Herbert went much further in his self-appointed mission to popularize quality dogs with American hunters. He shepherded *The Sportsman's Vade Mecum*, written by his Canadian friend, Jonathan Peel, through publication in 1850 by illustrating it and lending it his name as editor. Issued under Peel's pseudonym, "Dinks," it was the second important American book on the dog.

Henry William Herbert, "Frank Forester," in a portrait from *Wildwood's Magazine*, June 1888.

Frank Forester in shooting costume.

Herbert also fostered the American publications of Edward Mayhew, the veterinarian, and Gen. W. N. Hutchinson, who was the first to publish a system of relatively gentle dog training.

Herbert was an extreme romanticist to the end. When his wife abandoned him in 1858, he wrote two suicide notes, which must be among the longest on record. One, to the coroner, was 635 words long; another, of 750 words, was addressed to the American press. The wonder is that a man could sustain such an outpouring without changing his mind—but Herbert invited friends to a gathering in a New York hotel and, with his scene set, went into an adjoining room and fatally shot himself.

It is probably through his influence on his successors that Herbert had his greatest impact. I have seen worn copies of his books in the libraries of M. C. Campbell, Horace Lytle, Nash Buckingham, and Hobart Ames. Henry P. Davis and McDowell Lyon told me of their reverence for Herbert's teachings and talents. It would be safe to say that among the founders of both the National American Kennel Club and the American Kennel Club, every man among them had read at least one of Herbert's works and had been influenced by it.

Late in 1830, a year after the founding of *The American Turf Register*, there appeared a publication wondrous for its time. Called *The Cabinet of Natural History*, its format was that of a book, but it was issued in parts, usually monthly. It was first published by brothers John and Thomas Doughty in Philadelphia, with Thomas serving as writer and illustrator and John as businessman. Its text is nearly as valid and entertaining now as when it was published. But *The Cabinet* is most celebrated for its 54 colored stone-lithograph plates. These were the first colored American sporting—and dog—plates. Dogs are featured in several of the hunting scenes, and there are two dog portraits, one of a Newfoundland, the other of an "Exquimaux Dog." Perhaps because it was too far ahead of its time, however, the project failed in 1834 after 30 parts were issued.

It would be difficult to overestimate the importance of America's printmakers in building a base of support for the ownership of quality dogs. Their art form, published at popular prices, found permanent and prominent placement in homes across the land. Daily exposure of American youth to depictions of dogs in happy, even idealized settings built a demand for pure-bred dogs as several generations matured and established households of their own. Among the "sporting prints" of Currier & Ives alone, I have counted 92 that feature dogs in a flattering way. Of these, 22 are portraits of pure-breds.

By mid-nineteenth century our struggling sporting publications were getting some help from such national illustrated weeklies as *Gleason's Pictorial* and *Harper's Weekly*. There was widespread borrowing from British publications, most of which was not authorized. As time went on more and more Americans could afford to subscribe to English periodicals. Great Britain, with a much larger leisure class and a more compact geography, was generally well ahead of us in developing organized sports.

The American Turf Register passed from the hands of Skinner in 1835 to an intermediate owner and was then purchased by William T. Porter, who moved it to New York and continued its publication through 1844. The sporting department of *The Spirit of the Times*, founded in 1831, had been edited by Porter. There followed a confusing series of ownerships and title changes, but this *Spirit* continued through June 22, 1861. *Porter's Spirit of the Times* was launched on September 6, 1856, and continued until December 28, 1861, when it apparently became a casualty of the Civil War. *Wilkes Spirit of the Times* was founded and edited by George Wilkes in September 1859. In 1868 it took sole possession of the honored name *Spirit of the Times* and continued publication through 1902. The true heir of *Porter's Spirit*, however, was *Turf, Field and Farm*, a weekly founded in April 1865, which purchased the *Spirit*'s library, engravings, and files. It ran until 1903, when it was absorbed by *Sports of the Times*.

The "Esquimaux Dog," from *The Cabinet of Natural History,* 1833. *Herm David*

The oldest known drawings of an Old English Sheepdog, by Robert Hills, London 1811.

HARPER'S WEEKLY.

JOURNAL OF CIVILIZATION.

VOL. XXVI.—No. 1323.
Copyright, 1882, by HARPER & BROTHERS.

NEW YORK, SATURDAY, APRIL 29, 1882.

TEN CENTS A COPY.
$4.00 PER YEAR, IN ADVANCE.

Harper's Weekly cover, 1882, showing miscellaneous sketches by Paul
Frenzeny of the Westminster Kennel Club Dog Show. *Herm David*

HARPER'S WEEKLY.
JOURNAL OF CIVILIZATION.

VOL. XXVII.—No. 1377.
Copyright, 1883, by HARPER & BROTHERS.

NEW YORK, SATURDAY, MAY 12, 1883.

TEN CENTS A COPY.
$4.00 PER YEAR, IN ADVANCE.

Sketches from the seventh Westminster Dog Show, 1883. The dogs are identified as *(beginning at lower left)*: (1) Longhaired St. Bernard Dog; (2) English Mastiff; (3) Irish Water Spaniel; (4) Clumber Spaniels; (5) Bulldog; (6) English Beagle; (7) Irish Terrier; (8) Pug Dog; (9) Blenheim Spaniel; (10) Red Irish Setter. *Herm David*

Other American sporting periodicals that carried meaningful information about dogs prior to the first generally recorded competitions in 1874—and that helped make them possible—were *The Chicago Field* (weekly from February 21, 1874), *The Canadian Sportsman* (weekly from 1874), *Forest and Stream* (weekly from August 1873), *Fur, Fin and Feather* (bimonthly from 1868), and *Dramatic News and Sporting Age* (weekly from 1874). All of these carried articles on dogs, and most had kennel departments. An early kennel editor of *Forest and Stream*, perhaps its first, was Maj. J. M. Taylor, a Kentuckian who eventually became the first AKC President. *Forest and Stream* had a succession of kennel editors who were seldom identified in its columns. They included Col. William M. Tileston, the prime mover in the formation of the Westminster group and its first show chairman. He relinquished the Westminster and *Forest and Stream* posts to found his own weekly, *The Country*, which lasted only two years.

THE CHAMPION IRISH SETTER, "TIM."

THE CHAMPION ENGLISH SETTER "ROCKINGHAM."

THE FIRST PRIZE MASTIFF, "MINTING."

THE ENGLISH BLOOD-HOUND, "BARNABY"

THE BLACK POODLE, "STYX"

THE CHAMPION POINTER, "BRACKETT."

THE FIELD SPANIEL, "COMPTON BANDIT."

PRIZE DOGS FROM THE BENCH SHOW AT MADISON SQUARE GARDEN.—From Photographs by Pach Brothers.

Dogs from "The Bench Show at Madison Square Garden," 1888, pictured in *Harper's Weekly*. Herm David

1. "Cardinal" (Fox-hound). 2. "Irish Chief" (Irish Water-Spaniel). 3. "Nemours" (Basset Hound). 4. "Jack" (Irish Setter). 5. "Gretchen" (Dachshund). 6. "Foreman" English Setter.
7. "Meteor" (Pointer). 8. "Ursula" (St. Bernard). 9. "Bruce" (Deer-hound). 10. "Bengonia" (Black Greyhound). 11. "Black Tournie" (Black Cocker Spaniel). 12. "Dan" (Mastiff).

SCENES AT THE BENCH SHOW, MADISON SQUARE GARDEN.—DRAWN BY A. BERGHAUS.—[SEE PAGE 315.]

Scenes from the 1884 Westminster Show. *Herm David*

"**Ruffed Grouse Shooting in Pennsylvania—A Chance for a Double**," *Harper's Weekly*, 1881. *Herm David*

In order to record entries in the stud registry it had launched, *Forest and Stream* published what is now a treasure house of American dog history, *The American Kennel Register*, which ran as a monthly from April 1883 through October 1888. Although *Forest and Stream* came out of New York, the AKR was headquartered in Philadelphia. From the AKR's location and the terrier raspishness of its editorial tone, its anonymous editor was probably the fiesty Scotsman James Watson, who lived in Philadelphia and may have been the most dog-knowledgeable man in America. The first stud registry was published in 1878 by the National American Kennel Club, having been motivated by the club's founder, Dr. Nicholas Rowe, and was kept by Arnold Burges, one-time kennel editor of *Forest and Stream*. Because the NAKC was not a strong organization, the years mounted before its second volume appeared in 1884, and Rowe was constantly taunted by both *Forest and Stream* and the *American Kennel Register* for this deficiency. In the end Rowe had to produce volumes two and three at his own expense.

The American Kennel Register is the first American periodical that I have been able to find that was exclusively devoted to dogs. Early on, the AKC made overtures to *Forest and Stream* to purchase the *Register*, but the Club was rejected—after all, the AKR was a going proposition and the AKC was an untested, fledgling organization. The AKC turned to Dr. Rowe, who gave it his second and third volumes and persuaded the NAKC to give volume one to its onetime rival. The acquisition of these books, which were the beginning volumes of the AKC Stud Registry, marked a turning point for the AKC.

An early Field Trial, prior to the founding of the AKC, as shown in *Harper's Weekly*, October 5, 1878. The man with the flag is Nicholas Rowe. *Herm David*

Two of the sporting periodicals that had sprung up in the late nineteenth century emerged as powerhouses. The New York–based *Forest and Stream* was soon engaged in a continuing battle with *The Chicago Field*, which had a rocky start as *The Field*. *The Chicago Field* was bought in 1876 by Dr. Rowe, who gave it a fresh vitality that brought it enduring life. It became *The American Field* in July 1881 and continues under that name as America's oldest continuous sporting institution. *Forest and Stream* was absorbed by *Field and Stream*, the popular contemporary magazine, in 1932.

15

The Dog In Art

Shirlee Kalstone

Dogs have been represented in art from the time man began to carve and to draw. The dog is found on canvas; in marble, bronze, wood, stone, terra cotta, ivory, jade, pottery, and porcelain; in engravings, drawings, and prints; in tapestry, heraldry, and illuminated manuscripts; and in photography. We see the dog on coins, on stamps, tombs, and even in churches. Dogs appear in cartoons and often assume satirical roles. He has been represented as watchdog, guardian, hunter, companion of royalty and aristocracy, pampered pet of great ladies, playmate of children, friend of the poor, comrade of famous authors, and colleague of knights. No period of history is without him. Indeed, we encounter the dog in art in so many manifestations throughout so many centuries that the subject can barely be covered in one chapter.

Early Drawings and Carvings

An overview of the dog in art must begin with the starting point of all art, for animals first inspired man's artistic abilities. As far back as prehistoric times, primitive man attempted to reproduce doglike creatures and other animals in hunting scenes on the walls and ceilings of caves in the late Upper Paleolithic period. Most of these drawings appear rather childlike, but a close study reveals prehistoric man's ability to depict animal life with exacting realism and great simplicity of form.

Next comes the art of ancient Egypt. Much is known about the dogs of ancient Egypt through picture writing, or hieroglyphics, for a variety of breeds are represented on tombs of the various empires, some separated by a time span of hundreds or even thousands of years. The domesticated dog had developed into a number of different types by this time, some of them ancestors of present-day breeds.

239

The Vision of St. Eustace by Pisanello (Antonio Pisano, *c.* 1395–*c.* 1455). *The National Gallery, London*

Egyptian artists were greatly concerned with the decoration of tombs, and one of the first dogs to appear on a monument was the "Khufu," a Spitz- or Chow-like breed, depicted as a house dog on the tomb of King Cheops, or Khufu, who began building the Great Pyramid of Ghizeh in 3733 B.C. A millennium later, about 2650 B.C., four distinct types of dogs appeared on the tomb of King Antefaa II in the valley of El Assasif. One of these, named "Bahakaa," alias "Mahut," wears a narrow collar around his neck with a bow or bell in front. Nearby hieroglyphics indicate "white gazelle," possibly referring to the dog's color and swiftness. The second dog is called "Abakaru," or "Abaker," and wears a broad collar with a bow in front. He resembles a gazehound with his pointed muzzle, erect ears, and tail. The third dog, called "Pahates," alias "Kami," is heavy and Mastiff-like. He is shown seated, possibly to indicate that his function was not to hunt but to keep watch. Nearby hieroglyphics, translated as "black," probably refer to his color. The fourth dog, named "Tekar" or "Tekal," walks between the Pharaoh's legs. Some authorities think Tekar looks like a Dalmatian, but others believe he is more like a Terrier-type house dog.

The Dog in Painting and Engravings

Many of the world's famous artists have put dogs into their compositions. With the possible exception of the horse, the dog has been portrayed on canvas more than any other animal in existence.

Italian Art

Italian art was greatly influenced by St. Francis of Assisi, who was a passionate animal lover. Thus it is not surprising to see dogs in so many great religious paintings. Duccio (Duccio di Buoninsegna, c. 1260–1319) and Giotto (Giotto di Bondone, c. 1267–1337) painted dogs in early religious frescos. A dog accompanies a shepherd and his flock in Duccio's *Nativity and Prophets*, and a Greyhound appears in Giotto's famous fresco cycle, *Joachim with the Shepherd*, covering the interior of the Arena Chapel at Padua. The first real *animalier*, Antonio Pisano—called Pisanello—(c. 1395–1455) painted the *Vision of St. Eustace* (National Gallery, London), a magnificent work often compared to a mille-fleurs tapestry with its flecks of bright crimson and gold. Pisanello possessed an excellent knowledge of dog anatomy, and he was able to portray the dog's sensitivity and warmth. In the picture, St. Eustace, on horseback, and nine splendid dogs are startled at the sight of a great crucifix-crowned stag.

Florentines Fra Angelico (1417–1455) and Fra Filippo Lippi (c. 1406–1469) chose a short-haired dog with cropped ears to guard the Christ child in their *Adoration of the Magi* (National Gallery, Washington), and Piero di Cosimo (1462–1521) was inspired by mythology in his tender scene of *The Death of Procris* (National Gallery, London), showing Lelaps, a dog created by the god Vulcan in his forge, watching over a dead body. Wealthy merchants and the aristocracy of sixteenth-century Venice liked to have their portraits painted, and artists of the Venetian School often painted the sitter with his or her favorite dog. Titian (c. 1487–1576) dominated Venetian art at the time, and he became the favorite portrait painter of Italian nobility. Dogs appear prominently in

Titian's portraits *Charles V.* (Prado, Madrid), *Duke Federigo Gonzaga of Mantua* (Prado), and *Giovanni Francesco Acquaviva*. Titian's famous *Venus of Urbino* (Uffizi, Florence) possibly shows the first red-and-white toy Spaniel to appear on a canvas. Titian frequently introduced dogs into religious and mythological themes, and some dramatic examples include the hounds of *Venus and Adonis*, *The Death of Actaeon*, and *Bacchus and Ariadne*; the Spaniel of *Tobias and the Angel*; the shaggy Bichon-like dog of *Venus and Cupid*; and the Terrier-type of *The Last Supper*, gnawing a bone under the table.

Paolo Caliari (1528–1588), known as Veronese, included many dogs in his paintings. Veronese reproduced a variety of breeds and probably was the first artist to paint the Saluki. He must have admired Salukis immensely for they appear in some 30 paintings between 1559 and 1585, including the magnificent *Christ in the House of Simon the Pharisee*. Wonderful toy Spaniels appear in *Madonna of the Cuccina Family*, *The Queen of Sheba Before Solomon*, and *Incognita*. Veronese's version of *Venus and Adonis* shows Venus holding the sleeping Adonis in her arms and looking angrily at Cupid who is trying to stop his restless hound from barking. One of Veronese's most ambitious and beautiful paintings is the immense religious scene *The Marriage Feast at Cana* (Louvre). The entire canvas is alive with people and dogs, and leashed together in the foreground are two hounds that are believed to be a satire on the institution of marriage.

The most brilliant and sought after painter in the eighteenth century was Giovanni Battista Tiepolo (1696–1770). His delightful painting *The Dancing Dogs* shows four spirited mixed-breed dogs—three dressed in little coats—dancing on their hind legs to a tambourine and pipes. Beautiful Pointers appear in Tiepolo's *Ecce Homo* and *Le Cene* (both at the Louvre). Tiepolo's son, Domenico (1727–1804), was famous for his engraved and etched caricatures. Domenico's dancing dogs in the *Punchinello* series of *Divertimento per li Regazzi* ("Diversions for the Children") are entertaining and delightful creatures. And there was Giuseppi Crespi (1665–1747), who placed a little Spaniel on a pillow, watching his mistress scratching herself in *The Flea* (Louvre).

Spanish Art

Although the artists of Spain were not famous for painting animals, dogs do appear often in the work of Diego Rodriguez de Silva y Velazquez (1599–1660). One of Velazquez's most famous works, the large *Las Meninas* in Madrid's Prado Museum, shows the Infanta Dona Margarita, daughter of Philip IV, her attendants, and two dwarfs watching a sitting for a double portrait of the King and Queen. In the foreground, a large brindled Mastiff, lying half asleep, is being poked by one of the dwarfs. Spanish royalty of the seventeenth century seemed fascinated with large breeds, and Velazquez often used them for dramatic effect in his pictures. This is evident in *Don Antonio el Inglese* (Prado), a dwarf in the King's service, who holds the leash of a huge black-and-white dog that stands almost as high as the little man's shoulders. Velazquez gives us another large black-and-white dog wearing a wide fancy collar in his portrait of the King's son, *Prince Baltasar Carlos in Hunting Dress* (Prado). Bartolome Esteban Murillo (1617–82) seems to have been a dog lover, too, for different breeds appear in many of his paintings. One lovely picture of the *Holy Family* (Prado) shows the Christ child playing with a little dog that raises its front leg to be patted. Other Murillo works with dogs are *Don Justino de Neve* (National Gallery, London), in which a charming Spaniel wears a bow on its collar; *The Birth of the Blessed Virgin* (Louvre), with a white dog resembling a Maltese; *Children Eating* and *Children Playing Dice*; and the portrait of the handsome Marshall of Seville Cathedral, *Don Andres de Andrade y la Cal* (Metropolitan), accompanied by his huge dog wearing a thick, wide leather collar. In the eighteenth century, Francisco de Goya y Lucientes (1746–1828) often introduced dogs into his portraits and genre subjects. One Goya painting, *The Marquesa de Pontejos*, now part of the Andrew Mellon Collection of the National Gallery of Art in Washington, D.C., is said to be the most beautiful work portraying a Pug.

Dutch, Flemish, and German Art

Artists of the low countries of northern Europe stressed landscapes and the daily home lives of people rather than religious or mythological themes. The Church influenced early painting to a degree, but it was not as dominating a control as in Italy. Suddenly, the dogs on canvases did *not* belong to the nobility but were instead the dogs of the bourgeoisie, and the artists took great pleasure in emphasizing their canine qualities. We see the overindulged pets of the middle class, the dogs of peasants, and even the undernourished mongrels of the street. They are suddenly natural—they fight, they growl, they play, they even relieve themselves!

Almost as many Dutch painters honored the dog as did the Italians. An early Dutchman, Jeronen Anthoniszoon van Aken (1450–1516), better known by the pseudonym Hieronymus Bosch, painted dogs in dreamlike allegorical fantasies. Bosch, often called the "Ancestor of Surrealism," was essentially a religious painter, and his complex symbolic and often bizarre works are psychological enigmas even today. Examples of his early style include *The Adoration of the Magi* (Metropolitan), in which a white Greyhound sits prominently in the foreground, and *The Seven Deadly Sins* (Prado), in which dogs appear in several scenes. Perhaps Bosch's best known painting is *The Garden of Earthy Delights* (Prado), a strangely modern tryptich, populated with hundreds of grotesque humans, dogs, and other bizarre animals.

Anthonie Mor (1512–76), who painted under a latinized version of his name, Antonio Moro, was one of the best known portraitists of the sixteenth century. *The Dwarf of Cardinal Grandville* (Louvre) shows the dramatic contrast between large dog and small human that fascinated many painters, including the Spanish master Velazquez. Cardinal Grandville's dwarf is posing with an enormous dog said to be a Great Dane that nearly reaches his shoulders and accentuates his small stature. The dog wears an immense collar decorated with studs and shields bearing the Cardinal's coat-of-arms.

Gerard Ter Borch (1617–81) and Jan Steen (1626–69) have given us numerous genre paintings in which charming and colorful dogs appear. Ter Borch's scene in a Dutch room, *The Music Lesson: A Young Woman Playing the*

Theorbo (National Gallery), shows a comely girl playing a lute for two men while, nearby, her black-and-white Spaniel listens to the music. Another delightful Ter Borch canvas is *Young Boy with a Dog*, in which a determined lad on his knees picks fleas from a shaggy Spaniel's coat. Jan Steen delighted in painting ordinary people enjoying life. In some of his gentle scenes, we see a child saying grace while underneath the table a dog overturns a soup tureen on the floor; a dog sleeping while pipers and fiddlers play; a dog and a cat sitting together listening to music; and a dog sniffing the aroma of an orange on a chair. Steen, who at times managed a brewery while he was actively painting, delighted in picturing the high spirits and merrymaking of the working class. *Merry Company on a Terrace* (Metropolitan) shows a lovely liver-and-white Spaniel being led into a courtyard by a dwarf. The dog is pulling a toy horse, to the elation of the exuberant onlookers. The toy horse is attached to his collar by a red cord.

One can see some of the most exquisite red-and-white Spaniels in the world of art in Dutch paintings, notably *Domestic Scene* by Eglon van der Neer (1634–1703); *The Happy Mother* by William van Mieris (1662–1747) and *The Musicians* by Jacob Ochtervelt (1634–1708), in the collection of the Art Institute of Chicago; and Gabriel Metsu's *The Sleeping Sportsman* in the Wallace Collection, London. Other Dutch artists who honored the dog were Jan Vermeer, Pieter de Hooch, Nicholas Maes, Albert Cuyp, Lucas van Leyden, Adrian van Ostade, and Cornelius Dusart.

A masterpiece of Flemish painter Jan van Eyck (c. 1385–1441)—the bridal portrait *Giovanni Arnolfini and Giovanna Cenani* (National Gallery, London)—shows a Griffon-Terrier, one of the most famous rough-coated little dogs in art, standing in the foreground.

Peter Paul Rubens (1577–1640), one of the greatest painters of his age, seems to have adored dogs. Described by Delacroix as the "Homer of Painting," Rubens was famous all over Europe in his day, and his work was in demand at every court. Rubens painted dogs with great joie de vivre and, like his horses and his women, they were massive and fleshy. Superb dogs appear in many compositions: scenes of the chase, landscapes, battle scenes, clashes between nymphs and satyrs, and other mythological tableaux. A few outstanding works include the hounds of the colorful *Venus and Adonis* (Metropolitan), and the magnificent *Diana and her Nymphs*, and the noble black-and-white mongrel in *The Judgement of Paris* (National Gallery). Between 1615 and 1621, Rubens produced a series of monumental hunting scenes, one of which, *Wolf and Dog Hunt* (Metropolitan), shows a number of large breeds savagely attacking wolves. One is fascinated, almost against one's will, with the passionate movements and the rippling muscles of the animals, yet the painting is filled with the most violent conflict. Rubens also produced a series of 20 huge paintings representing a tableau of the life of Marie de Medicis, now in the *Salle Rubens* of the Louvre, in which many hounds and toy breeds are prominent.

The aristocratic canvases of the supreme Flemish portraitist Sir Anthony van Dyck (1599–1641) conveyed the devotion between dog and master in a number of pictures of noblemen, most clearly *James Stuart, Duke of Richmond and Lennox* (Metropolitan) and *Philippe LeRoy, Seigneur de Ravels* (Wallace Collection). Both show slim and elegant Greyhounds staring adoringly at their masters. In 1632 van Dyck was summoned to England by Charles I to become the principal court painter. While there, he painted a number of studies of the royal family children with their dogs.

Some of the earliest and best examples of the dog in German art appear in the works of Albrecht Durer (1471–1528), a painter, engraver, and woodcutter. His famous *St. Eustace* shows a pack of hunting dogs, drawn with great care, gathered around their master who kneels in prayer. Wonderful-looking rough-haired Griffons appear in Durer's *The Knight and Man of Arms* and *The Visitation*.

Lucas Cranach the Elder (1472–1553) painted many scenes of hunters and dogs. It is said that his paintings were "so realistic that hounds bayed at his representation of a stag and birds tried to nest in the pictured antlers." Classic portraits were stylish during Cranach's time, and the rich and the nobility, attired in splendid garments, often sat for portraits along with their favorite dogs. Two of Cranach's most celebrated and colorful portraits are *Henry the Pious* and *Katharina of Mecklenberg* (Staatliche Kunstsammlungen, Dresden). Henry, richly dressed in black, crimson, and gold, poses with his sword, while his dog stands behind his legs and seems to be snarling. Katharina, also regally costumed with three jewelled necklaces and eight rings on her fingers, poses beside her little Lion Dog.

French Art

French artists of the sixteenth century returned to the classically elaborate and sumptious Italian type of art and emphasized mythological and legendary subjects. The stimulus for the classical revival was the reconstruction of the old Louvre and the palace of Fontainebleau by Francis I, crowned in 1515. Francis, an enthusiast of Italian art, was the patron of the Fontainebleau School, and the royal residence quickly became the foremost artistic salon of its day. Around the same time, an artistic cult began to emerge about Diana, Roman goddess of the chase, and one of the loveliest mythological paintings from the Fontainebleau School appeared—*Diana the Huntress* (Louvre)—with the sensuous goddess in the nude, running with a white Greyhound. The goddess's face is believed to be a portrait of Diane de Poitiers, mistress of Henri II.

Dwarf Spaniels (now known as Papillons) appear frequently in seventeenth-century portraits of French life. A fine example is found in *Louis XIV and His Heirs* by Nicolas de Largillière (1656–1746), now in the Wallace Collection. Simon Vouet (1590–1649), the most important influence in French painting in the first half of the seventeenth century, painted a study of the goddess Diana lying on the ground next to two Greyhounds.

Painters of the eighteenth century turned their attention to genre subjects—indoor and outdoor scenes—in which dogs played a prominent role. Jean Honore Fragonard (1732–1806) was one of the most important artists to portray French life with lightness and grace, and his canvases are filled with dogs. Fragonard's exquisite *The Love Letter* (Metropolitan) shows a shaggy King Charles Spaniel sitting on a stool next to an attractive lady who is writing a letter. *The Souvenir* (Wallace Collection) shows a Spaniel sitting on a stone bench watching his fashionable mistress carve the letter *S* on a tree. Another Fragonard canvas shows two small dogs, dressed as humans, standing on their hind legs, with one holding a flag. Jean-Baptiste Greuze (1725–1805) gives us many dogs. *The Broken Mirror* (Wallace Collection) shows a delightful little dog examining pieces of broken glass with his owner, and *The Boy with a Dog* (Wallace Collection) gives prominence to a black-and-white Spaniel. The dazzling Diana and her hounds appear once again in *The Bath of Diana* (Louvre) by Francois Boucher (1702–70). Boucher's *Le Chien Savant* shows a little white Poodle, in lion trim, dancing before his splendidly attired mistress. Francois-Hubert Drouais (1727–75) shows a lovely toy Spaniel in *Boy with a Black Spaniel* (Metropolitan) and a vivacious little dog in *Madame de Pompadour* (National Gallery, London). Pompadour, mistress of Louis XV, owned two favorite Spaniels named Inez and Mimi, and one of them appears in this portrait, standing with her hind legs on a brocade chair, front paws resting on an ornate table. She is looking affectionately at her mistress.

Alexandre-François Desportes (1661–1743) and Jean Baptiste Oudry (1686–1755) qualify as two of the most famous animal painters in the world of art. Desportes, a great favorite of Louis XIV, was designated official *peintre de la venerie du Roi* ("painter of the King's Hunt"). In the days of Louis XIV, it was said that "the *Grand Veneur* had as his hunt staff two equerries, 14 lieutenants, 24 captains, five valets for the Bloodhounds, and 70 grooms. In the stables were as many as 250 horses, and in the kennels 200 couples of hounds."

What bliss for a sporting painter!

Desportes painted many still life compositions and portraits, but he is best known for his picturesque hunting scenes. One of Desportes's most enchanting pictures—*Self-Portrait as a Huntsman* (Louvre)—shows a Greyhound and a Pointer looking adoringly into the artist's face.

Oudry, a pupil of Nicolas de Largillière, became the leading French artist of this genre. As a student, Oudry painted a portrait of a hunter with his dog. Largillière (who disliked the image of the hunter) predicted: "You will never be anything but a painter of dogs." Oudry was idolized by Louis XV; in fact, the King set Oudry up in sumptious rooms at the Louvre and had him paint several dogs in his presence. Oudry produced hundreds of paintings of dogs and hunting scenes, and he also acted as director of the Beauvais and Gobelins Tapestry works, for which he designed *The Hunts of Louis XV* series of gorgeous tapestries of hunting scenes that took place at Fontainebleau, Rambouillet, and Chantilly.

The dog was a bit neglected when painters of the Impressionist School began to see things differently in the last half of the nineteenth century and established a new art style. They ignored the conventional themes of the past and began to celebrate the lighter side of life. Gone were the dark colors of their predecessors. In their place appeared sensuously appealing portraits, landscapes, and other outdoor scenes, painted both in brilliant colors and delicate pastels. Among the Impressionists, Pierre Bonnard, Gustave Courbet, Paul Gauguin, Edouard Manet, Henri Matisse, Pierre Auguste Renoir, Henri Rousseau, and Georges-Pierre Seurat painted dogs, but the dogs were usually of incidental interest to the composition. Seurat's huge pointillist canvas—*Sunday Afternoon on the Island of La Grand Jatte* (Art Institute of Chicago)—is a good case in point because the scene includes two dogs in the foreground, although

Diana the Huntress, a French mythological painting from the Fontainebleau School, sixteenth century. *The Louvre Museum*

Above: Alexandre Francois Desportes: *Dogs, Dead Game and Fruit,* dated 1715. *Trustees of the Wallace Collection, London. Below:* Jean Baptiste Oudry: *Wild Duck Hunting. Trustees of the Wallace Collection, London.*

A Gallery of the Dog in Art

FROM THE COLLECTIONS OF THE AKC AND THE DOG MUSEUM OF AMERICA

RICHARD ANSDELL, R.A. "Highland Tod (Fox) Hunter" (1859).
Oil on canvas. 29 x 63½ inches. *AKC Collection*

EDMUND H. OSTHAUS. English Setter, "Toledo Blade".
Oil on canvas. 15¾ x 23½ inches. *AKC Collection*

GEORGE EARL.
White English Terrier (sic), "Prince"
(c. 1856). Oil on oval canvas.
14½ x 16 inches.
AKC Collection

GEORGE EARL.
Scotch (sic) Deer Hound, "Warrior" (c. 1856).
Oil on oval wood.
20 x 18½ inches. *AKC Collection*

J.S. NOBLE. Bloodhounds (late 19th Century). Oil on canvas.
54 x 43 inches. *Promised Gift The Dog Museum of America.*
Collection Mr. & Mrs. Robert V. Lindsay.

Photo by Grant Taylor.

PERCIVAL L. ROSSEAU. English Setter, "Leda" (1906).
Oil on canvas. 57 x 36½ inches. *AKC Collection*

G. MUSS-ARNOLT. English Setter, "Real English".
Oil on canvas. 10 x 8 inches. *AKC Collection*

G. MUSS-ARNOLT. Pointer.
Oil on canvas. 9 x 7 inches. *AKC Collection*

G. MUSS-ARNOLT. Setter and Pointer. Oil on canvas. 9¾ x 15½ inches.
AKC Collection

ARTHUR WARDLE. Dandie Dinmont Terriers.
Oil on canvas. 21¾ x 13¾ inches.
AKC Collection

ARTHUR WARDLE. Detail of Smooth Fox Terriers (1936).
Oil on canvas. 15¾ x 21¾ inches. *AKC Collection*

ARTHUR WARDLE. Smooth Fox Terriers, "The Totteridge XI".
Oil on canvas. 28 x 35½ inches. *AKC Collection*

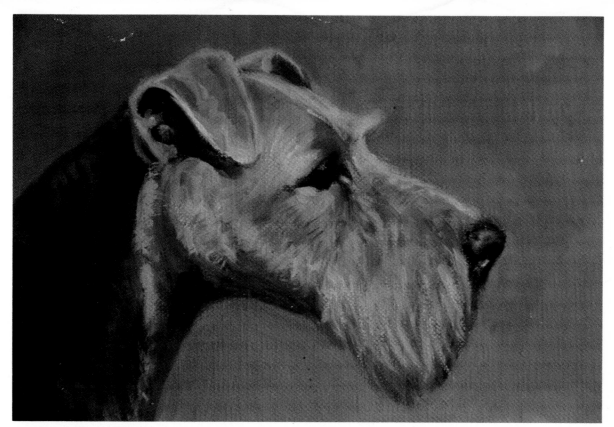

EDWIN MEGARGEE.
Detail of Welsh Terrier, "Ch. Twin Ponds Belle".
Oil on canvas. 19½ x 23½ inches.
AKC Collection

JOHN EMMS. Fox Terrier, "Richmond Jock" (1881).
Oil on canvas. 13¾ x 16 inches. *AKC Collection*

PIERRE JULES MENE. Terriers (c. 1851).
Parian figurine. 7 x 13 inches.
AKC Collection

JUNE HARRAH. Poodle, "Ch. Duc de la Terrace of Blakeen".
Cast Bronze sculpture. 5½ x 5 inches.
Collection The Dog Museum of America. Gift of Mr. Frank T. Sabella.

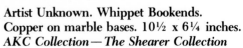

Artist Unknown. Whippet Bookends.
Copper on marble bases. 10½ x 6¼ inches.
AKC Collection — The Shearer Collection

FRATIN. Whippet and rabbit.
Cast bronze sculpture. 10 x 15 inches.
AKC Collection — The Shearer Collection

JUNE HARRAH. Borzoi, "Ch. Vigow of Romanoff".
Cast bronze sculpture. 6¼ x 8 inches.
Collection The Dog Museum of America.
Gift of Mr. Frank T. Sabella

CHAMBERLAIN-WORCESTER. Mastiff — Inkwell (18th Century English).
Porcelain. 9 x 11 inches. *AKC Collection*

W.E. TURNER. Spaniels (1868).
Oil on canvas. 23 x 29¾ inches. *AKC Collection*

HECTOR

W.R. NOBLE. Greyhound, "Hector" (1835). Oil on canvas.
21¼ x 17¼ inches. *AKC Collection—The Shearer Collection*

GEORGE FENN.
Greyhounds (1833).
Oil on canvas.
18½ x 24 inches.
AKC Collection

P. REINAGLE, A.R.A. English Setter (1804). Oil on canvas.
11½ x 13½ inches. *AKC Collection*

ABRAHAM COOPER, R.A. Bulldogs, "Crib and Rosa" (1817).
Oil on wood. 9½ x 12 inches. *AKC Collection*

A. POPE, JR. Foxhounds and Black & Tan Coonhound.
Print. 15½ x 20 inches. *AKC Collection*

SIR EDWIN A. LANDSEER. "Alexander and Diogenes".
Oil on canvas. 43½ x 54 inches. *AKC Collection*

This painting by Sir Edwin H. Landseer is a parody on the story of Alexander the Great and the cynical and eccentric philosopher, Diogenes.

It is said that Diogenes, who carried a lantern through the streets of Corinth seeking an honest man, was very humble and chose to live in a tub.

Alexander admired the cynic and called upon him with his court followers. He expressed this admiration and said he would be glad to grant any wish that Diogenes could make. The request of Diogenes, according to the legend, was that Alexander "get out of my sunlight." Following the abrupt and audacious reply, Alexander declared, "If I weren't Alexander I would be Diogenes." The painting depicts the scene when the two met.

MAUD EARL. "Silent Sorrow" — King Edward VII's favorite Terrier,
"Caesar", mourns his master (1910).
Oil on canvas. 35½ x 27½ inches.
AKC Collection

EDWIN MEGARGEE.
Harrier, "Mr. Reynal's Monarch" (1937).
Oil on canvas. 23¾ x 31 inches.
AKC Collection

EDWIN MEGARGEE.
Smooth Fox Terrier, "Ch. Nornay Saddler" (1940).
Oil on canvas. 17½ x 23½ inches.
AKC Collection

EDWIN MEGARGEE. Bedlington Terriers.
Oil on canvas. 18 x 24 inches.
Collection The Dog Museum of America.
Gift of Mrs. Miles McMillin, Frederick Rockefeller
and William Rockefeller

MAUD EARL. Yorkshire Terrier (c. 1884).
Oil on canvas. 13½ x 15½ inches.
AKC Collection

MAUD EARL. Detail of Pointers on a moor (1905).
Oil on canvas. 25½ x 45¾ inches. *AKC Collection*

Edouard Manet: *A King
Charles Spaniel, c. 1866.
Ailsa Mellon Bruce
Collection, National Gallery
of Art, Washington*

they are merely part of a large crowd on a Sunday outing, doing all the things
people and animals are supposed to do on Sunday. Rare exceptions, where dogs
are given considerable prominence, are Matisse's *The Blue Dog* and Renoir's
Madame Charpentier and Her Children (Metropolitan), in which an exquisite
little girl sits on a black-and-white Newfoundland that is lying on the floor in the
foreground.

In the post-Impressionistic period, Henri de Toulouse-Lautrec (1864–1901)
placed dogs in a few paintings, but they appear more often in his posters and
lithographs. Lautrec took his inspiration from the music halls, cabarets, and
circuses of Paris. One of his favorite Montmartre haunts was La Souris, a bar
owned by Madame Armande Palmyre. Lautrec painted and sketched many
studies of Bouboule, Palmyre's Bulldog, which are now in the Musee d'Albi
near Nice. Lautrec loved animals, especially dogs and horses, and he used many
Collies, Poodles, Terriers, Bulldogs, and mongrels in his works.

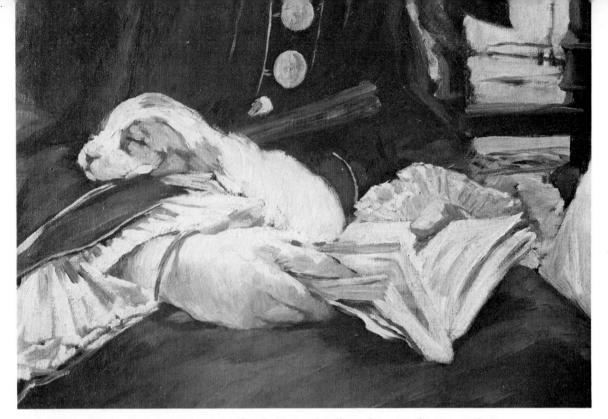

Above: Edouard Manet: Gare Saint-Lazare (detail). National Gallery of Art, Washington. Gift of Horace Havemeyer in memory of his mother, Louisine W. Havemeyer. Below: Pierre Auguste Renoir: Madame Charpentier and Her Children. The Metropolitan Museum of Art, Wolfe Fund, 1907.

British Art

The English, of all the artists in the world, are renowned for their portrayal of man's best friend. The great portraitists Sir Joshua Reynolds (1723–1792) and Thomas Gainsborough (1727–88) placed scores of dogs in their works. Reynolds, first president of the Royal Academy, painted what is thought to be the first black Cocker Spaniel to appear on canvas, *The Earl of Dalkeith* (Tate Gallery), as well as the first known British representation of a Maltese, *Nelly O'Brien* (Wallace Collection). Reynolds also painted a number of adorable children and their dogs, and the love between them is clearly evident in his pictures of *The Brummel Children* playing with their puppies and *Miss Jane Bowles* (originally titled *Love Me, Love My Dog*), an absolutely angelic child who is sitting and hugging her Spaniel.

Gainsborough added an air of gracefulness and breeding to the dogs he painted, as well as to his human subjects. His portrait *Perdita* shows a lovely dog, which has been identified as a Pomeranian or Spitz, walking by a stylish lady's side. Similar dogs appear in Gainsborough's *The Morning Walk* (National Gallery), *Pomeranian Bitch and Puppy* (Tate), and *The Mall in St. James Park* (Frick Collection), while Setters, Spaniels, Pointers, Hounds, and Collies appear prominently in other portraits. Gainsborough's stirring life-size portrayal of *Greyhounds Coursing a Fox* is thought to be based on an earlier hunt painting which he owned, by the seventeenth-century Flemish artist Frans Snyders.

While the relationship between sport and art has existed from primitive times, sporting art reached its pinnacle during eighteenth- and nineteenth-century England, when many artists specialized in brilliantly colored pictures of horses and dogs and scenes of hunting, shooting, coursing, racing, and coaching. Outstanding examples are to be found in the works of Henry Alken, Sr., Francis Barlow, William and Henry Barraud, Henry B. Chalon, John Ferneley, George Garrard, Sawrey Gilpin, John Frederick Herring, Sr., Samuel Howitt, Benjamin Marshall, George Morland, Philip Reinagle, John Sartorius and his equally famous son, Francis, James Seymour, George Stubbs, James Ward, and John Wootton.

Although George Stubbs (1724–1806) is best known for his anatomical studies and portraits of horses, he also painted dogs, notably the many studies of Fino, the black-and-white Spitz owned by the Prince of Wales (later George IV); *A Hound and a Bitch in Landscape* (Tate Gallery); *Five Foxhounds in a Landscape*; and perhaps Stubbs's greatest dog painting, *Ringwood, a Foxhound*, created for the famous Foxhound breeder Charles Pelham and his Brocklesby pack.

Philip Reinagle (1749–1833) began as a portrait painter, but when he reached his early thirties, the love of dogs, horses, and the outdoors made him turn to sporting subjects. A Reinagle oil painting, *Sportsman with Setter and Pheasant*, hangs in the AKC offices, as does a pair of Reinagle engravings, *Greyhound with Rabbit* and *Italian Greyhounds*. A great deal of Reinagle's work was engraved and can be found in volumes of *The Sporting Magazine* and *The New Sporting Magazine* and also in *The Annals of Sport* and *The Sportsman's Repository*. He also painted, with uncanny perception, studies of 24 breeds expressly for the book *The Sportsman's Cabinet*, published in 1803.

Sir Joshua Reynolds: *Miss Jane Bowles. Trustees of the Wallace Collection, London*

George Stubbs: *A Hound and a Bitch in Landscape. Tate Gallery, London*

Sir Edwin Landseer: *King Charles Spaniels. Tate Gallery, London*

Sir Edwin Landseer: *Dignity and Impudence. Tate Gallery, London*

Sir Edwin Landseer (1802–1873), probably the best known of all animal painters, portrayed dogs with almost human qualities in his touching canvases. An infant prodigy, Landseer began drawing dogs when he was five, and when he was admitted to the Academy School at the age of 12, its Director called him "the little dog boy." Landseer became a great favorite of Queen Victoria and Prince Albert and often painted the royal family and their dogs, including many studies of Eos the Prince's favorite Greyhound bitch. The charming *Windsor Castle in Modern Times* (now in the Royal Collection) shows the happy royal family surrounded by three delightful Terriers, with Eos at her master's knee.

Landseer's anthropomorphic version of a well-known incident taken from Plutarch's life of Alexander the Great demonstrates his great talent in associating man's affectations with animals. Alexander appears as a well-fed Bull Terrier wearing an ornate bronze collar. He stands imperiously in the center of the picture, surrounded by fawning courtiers and is admonished by the "snarlish and currish" philosopher, changed by Landseer's brush into the form of a scraggy Terrier. The painting was such a great success that Landseer painted the same topic several times—*Alexander and Diogenes* hangs in the Tate Gallery as well as in the reception room of the AKC offices.

In another cleverly satirical work—*Laying Down the Law*—a dignified white Standard Poodle sitting in a red chair rests its front paw on one page of a book, while its spectacles lie on the other. An inkwell with quill pens, sealing wax, and legal documents are scattered about the desk. Richard Ormond describes the scene in his book *Sir Edwin Landseer* and adds: "The dog's floppy ears and fluffy front parody the judge's full-bottomed wig, ruffles and ermine, while the red chair and cushion suggest the scarlet robes of the bench. . . . Squashed in on each side of the poodle is a variety of dogs, which ape lawyers, court officials and jurors. . . ."

The sentimental Landseer was frequently criticized for giving his paintings soft-hearted titles, such as *A Distinguished Member of the Humane Society*, in which a black-and-white Newfoundland sits proudly by the water's edge and waits for someone to rescue; and *Dignity and Impudence*, where a Bloodhound, Grafton, and a wheaten Scotch Terrier, Scratch, look out from the same kennel as someone apparently is approaching. Grafton sits calm and dignified, but one can see that the impudent Scratch is waiting for the right moment to leap out.

Richard Ansdell (1815–85), a serious rival to Landseer in his time, was born in Liverpool in the west of England but was famous for producing lush sporting scenes in the highlands of Scotland. His painting *Highland Tod*, dated 1859, which hangs in the reception room of the AKC, portrays the end of a successful fox hunt in the Aberdeenshire mountains and is a superb example of Ansdell's mastery in informally placing groups of figures in dramatic settings.

John Emms (1843–1912) was both a recognized dog authority and an artist who could paint Terriers and Foxhounds with remarkable skill. His paintings *Two Foxhounds and a Fox Terrier on a Kennel Bench* and several studies of Fox Terriers—*Richmond Jack* (1881), *Brown Ruby* (1882), and *Ch. Briggs* (1883)—are part of the collection of the AKC.

In 1855 a painter named R. Marshall produced a composition of historical significance to dog fanciers in that it is the earliest known painting of a dog show, held almost 20 years before the formation of the Kennel Club of England.

The dog show, or "match," took place at Jemmy Shaw's public house, The Queen's Head Tavern, in London, where on the walls are pictures of prize-fighters and rat-killing contests, including the famous 1843 engraving *Jem Burn's Four Pets*. The painting shows many dog fanciers of over 100 years ago sitting around tables with their prize dogs. Most of the animals are leashed to table legs, although a few small dogs are sitting on the tops of the tables.

The names of George Earl and his daughter Maud are renowned to most connoisseurs of dog art. George Earl (b. 1800), descended from ancient Worcestershire and Gloucestershire sporting families, was one of the early members of the Kennel Club of England. He, too, was a sportsman and a student of dogs from the practical as well as the artistic standpoint. A reviewer commented in *The American Field* magazine in 1925 that "the chief qualities of the George Earl paintings are their mellow coloring, their soft hazy atmosphere, their airial perspective or depth. These, together with an evenness of impasto, an absence of crude color, and a fidelity to subject, place George Earl among the conspicuous English painters of the last half of the Victorian Age." George Earl painted many breeds, and he also drew on wood. He is represented at the AKC by several paintings: a magnificent head study of the Scottish Deerhound *Warrior*; a large oil of a Dachshund named *Judy*, standing with her front paws on a rabbit; a portrait of a white English Terrier, *Prince*; and a head study of a Mastiff, *Barry*, whose collar is dated 1886.

One of the most fascinating pieces at the AKC is a print titled *The Field Trial Meet*, an illustration of an early British field trial made around 1870 after a George Earl painting. The busy picture is a wonderful presentation of the outstanding figures and well-known dogs of that early period of field trials. Accompanying the print is a key that makes it possible to identify every person and every dog. Today, many of the names read like a Who's Who of Dogdom: Vero Shaw, one of the most prominent dog writers of the last century; W. Brailsford, Sr., "the father of field trials"; Edward Laverack, founder of the Laverack strain of English Setters; William Arkwright, Pointer breeder and author of the now-classic *The Pointer and His Predecessors*; J. H. Walsh, editor of the *British Field* magazine and known to the dog world as "Stonehenge," author of *The Dogs of the British Islands* and other classic works; P. L. Purcell-Llewellin, founder of the Llewellin strain of English Setters, and many, many more, including one woman, Mrs. Richard Lloyd Price, the owner of the property.

Maud Earl was born in London's West End, and even her good friends did not know how old she was. Her paintings, with few exceptions, were brilliant delineations of dogs that existed from late Victorian times through the first part of the twentieth century, and they were produced in England, France, Belgium, and the United States (Miss Earl moved to this country in 1916). In an interview in the December 1931 *Gazette*, Miss Earl commented prophetically:

> I suppose that all of my sporting and artistic tastes come from the old Earls. As an only child, I was brought up by my father, and as a very small girl instructed to draw from the skeleton figures of a man, a horse and a dog. It is for that reason I have been able to hold my place among the best dog painters; no one has ever touched me in my knowledge of anatomy.

Art critics and dog fanciers praised her work in the early 1880s, and she quickly won the patronage of royalty when Queen Victoria commissioned her to paint a favorite Collie. King Edward VII and Queen Alexandra also commanded Miss Earl to paint many of their favorite dogs. In the same *Gazette* interview, Maud Earl describes the painting of the first portrait of Caesar, the King's favorite Wire Fox Terrier, and tells how it was executed under the constant and direct supervision of the monarch. She was given a room in Buckingham Palace near the King's private apartments, and as the work progressed, one or the other of the royal couple would interrupt to ask questions. Miss Earl again painted Caesar after Edward's death. "This was called *Silent Sorrow*," commented Miss Earl. "It was a study of the dog with his head resting on the seat of a large easy chair, that of his dead master." The picture was used as a double-page supplement to the *Illustrated London News* in their Memorial Number after the funeral. Today the poignant *Silent Sorrow* hangs in the office of William Stifel, President of the American Kennel Club. Several other Maud Earl works are part of the AKC's collection of canine art, among them, paintings of a Yorkshire Terrier; the Cocker Spaniel *Ch. Lucknow Creme de la Creme*; a Pekingese; the Poodle *Duke de la Terace*, and the magnificent *Two Pointers on Point in a Field*, as well as a lithograph of a head study of two Clumber Spaniels. Miss Earl's illustrations appear in many books, notably *The Sportsman's Year* and *The Power of the Dog*, a volume of colored plates of 20 breeds, with descriptions by Arthur Croxton-Smith. Maud Earl died in New York City in 1943.

During the 1890s, London photographer-turned-painter Francis Barraud (1856–1924) created a dog painting that would become one of the world's most famous trademarks. Inspired by his brother's black-and-white Terrier, Nipper, peering quizzically into the horn of a phonograph, Barraud called the composition *His Master's Voice* and later sold it to the Gramophone Company Limited of London. The American rights to the famous dog and phonograph trademark were acquired by the Victor Talking Machine Company shortly after the turn of the century and then in 1929 by RCA.

Francis Barraud: *His Master's Voice*, the painting that became the familiar trademark of RCA.

Arthur Wardle (1864–1949), a self-taught painter and draughtsman, is another artist who is renowned for his glorious portraits of pure-bred dogs and for sporting art. Wardle lived, painted, and exhibited in London, and for over 75 years his portraits and sketches had been exhibited at the Royal Academy. Among the many Wardle compositions at the AKC are a study of two Airedale Terriers, *Ch. Mistress Royal and Ch. Master Royal*; exquisite head studies of Dandie Dinmont Terriers and Spaniels; a portrait of a Newfoundland; and an exciting canvas filled with Fox Terriers, *The Totteridge XI*, as well as many lithographs and photogravures.

The many other compositions at the AKC by English artists include Ward Binks's gouaches of German Shepherds, *Ch. Eli and Ch. Cito von der Markfeste*, and of a Pointer *Ch. Nancolleth Markable*; dogs from Geraldine Rockefeller Dodge's Giralda kennels; Lilian Cheviot's painting of two Sealyham Terriers, *Ch. Pinegrade Scotia Swell and Pinegrade Perfection*, which became two of the breed's all-time greats; James Lambert's painting of a Mastiff, *Lion*, dated 1778; John Sargent Noble's oil of a Pug and a Welsh Terrier; Frank Patton's Bulldog bitch, *Salvo*, dated 1892; Kole Sowerby's portrait of the Bulldog, *Don Leon*, dated 1894; Henry Stull's splendid corded Poodle, *Styx*, an 1883 winner at the Crystal Palace dog show; Steven Taylor's portrait of an orange-and-white English Setter, dated 1820; Waller's corded Poodle, *Ch. Joe II*, dated 1869; and the many beautiful engravings of Greyhounds and Whippets of the Shearer Collection.

American Art

Many native American artists have portrayed the dog magnificently as have others who were born in foreign lands and achieved fame in the United States.

John James Audubon (1785–1851), the American naturalist who is famous for his writings and pictures of the birds of North America, painted a self-portrait that is of significance to dog historians. Audubon depicted himself as a young man in a hunting scene in which a liver-colored Cocker Spaniel and a Terrier attack a wounded bittern. The painting is the first known portrayal of a working Cocker Spaniel as it existed about 140 years ago in this country.

Another brilliant figure in the world of animal and sporting art is Arthur Fitzwilliam Tait (1819–1905), born near Liverpool, England. When he was 15 years old, Tait went to work for a firm of art dealers. He was so determined to study art that after working a 12-hour day, he attended night classes at the Royal Institute in Manchester. Tait settled in the United States in 1850, where over the years he became one of America's greatest sporting artists, painting dogs, game birds, and animals and hunting and fishing scenes with vivid perception. Tait was an accomplished angler, hunter, and woodsman, and he loved the Adirondacks. He had a camp on Long Lake and sketched there almost every year for three decades beginning in 1852. Then the drawings were converted into paintings at his Manhattan studio.

Tait's works have been exhibited at the Metropolitan Museum of Art, the Whitney Museum of American Art, and the Baltimore Museum of Art. Many of his paintings were lithographed by Currier and Ives, and because of Tait's fame they were reproduced with great care and precision. Four splendid shooting pictures with dogs, *On a Point, Flush'd, Chance for Both Barrels*, and *Retrieving*, were published by Currier and Ives in 1857 as a series of lithographs under the title *American Field Sports*. An oil painting of *Two Spaniels*, one black and one spotted, by Tait is part of the AKC's art collection.

Then we have the splendid work of Jonathan M. Tracy (1844–93), who was born near Rochester, Ohio, and descended from early American pioneers, some of whom came to this country on the *Mayflower*. After a term at L'Ecole des Beaux Arts in Paris, Tracy returned to the United States and began to paint portraits of women and children, but he soon switched exclusively to dogs and men in hunting scenes. Tracy was once called the American Landseer, and his fame as an animal painter was both instantaneous and enduring. As a dog show and field trial judge, Tracy was something of an anatomist. His compositions were not just sporting pictures; they were miniature likenesses of a particular living dog or living man, and they were painted with great vigor and brilliance. Tracy's oil paintings of the English Setter, *Petrel*, and Gordon Setter, *Bob*, and his etching of two Pointers, *Rip-Rap and Ch. King of Kent*, are in the collection of the AKC.

America can be justly proud of German-born Gustave Muss-Arnolt (1858–1927), who painted spirited and energetic studies of many different breeds but had a special fondness for gundogs. As an all-round dog show judge, Muss-Arnolt was greatly concerned with depicting the particular show points and characteristics of the breeds he painted. He was commissioned by many famous and wealthy owners of gundogs to paint the top American-bred and imported Pointers and Setters of the time. Muss-Arnolt possessed the rare ability to catch small individual qualities, the indefinable "something" that distinguishes one dog from another as it does one person from another. The AKC's art collection contains many paintings by Muss-Arnolt, among them the breathtaking *Setter and Pointer on Point*; a Pointer in a field, *Beaufort*; portraits of the Boston Terrier, *Ch. Arroyo Anarchist*, the Airedale, *Champion the New King*, the smooth Fox Terrier, *Blemton Vindex*, and the Chow Chow, *Wan Lung*, as well as several head studies of English Setters, Gordon Setters, and Pointers.

Few artists have been able to equal Edmund H. Osthaus (1858–1928) in the painting of hunting dogs. Born in Germany, Osthaus came to the United States in the early 1880s. He served as Director of the Toledo Academy of Fine Arts in Toledo, Ohio, from 1886 to 1893 and then resigned to devote his life to painting, shooting, and following field trials. Osthaus was a great sportsman. He entered his Pointers and Setters in national field trials and was considered an outstanding field-trial judge as well. He became famous for his superbly colored portrayals of gundogs in realistic settings. Osthaus painted some of the most famous Setters and Pointers in America, including Count Gladstone, with great vigor and brilliance. A connoisseur of his paintings wrote: "Edmund Osthaus who trained and shot over his own Setters and Pointers, transformed oil paint into dog flesh quivering under the stress of a point." His sketch book was with him when he died in 1928 at his Florida hunting lodge. One of the best known of his paintings, the English Setter, *Toledo Blade*, hangs in the office of the President of the AKC.

Percival Rosseau (1859–1937) was one of America's greatest dog painters. Rosseau, the son of a plantation owner, was born near New Orleans, Louisiana.

After his father died of wounds inflicted in the Civil War, the young Percival was raised by friends of the family. He was a hunter from boyhood and was intimately acquainted with hunting country life. A successful businessman by the age of 35, Rosseau decided to retire from business and devote his life to travel and the knowledge of art. He studied at the Academie Julian in Paris and attracted much attention shortly after the turn of the century with a painting titled *Diana Hunting*, in which a dog was accorded as much prominence as the subject.

Rosseau painted and sketched unsurpassed hounds and sporting dogs in authentic hunt country settings. One has only to look at a Rosseau painting to perceive that this was an artist who knew his gundogs and hounds. The viewer senses immediately that Rosseau was a real sportsman who was as intimately acquainted with the dogs as with the terrain that fitted them. In addition to Rosseau's ability to portray living and breathing dogs on canvas, he was a superb colorist. A large Rosseau painting is part of the collection of the AKC—a portrait of the English Setter, *Leda*, dated 1906.

Edwin Megargee (1883–1958), a native of Philadelphia, Pennsylvania, was another brilliant artist who specialized in dogs and horses. And like Tracy, Muss-Arnolt, Osthaus, and Rosseau, he not only drew accurate physical likenesses of his subjects but was able to portray their character as well. Megargee painted portraits of many well-known dogs and also did drypoints and aquatints. Many of his paintings appeared on magazine covers, while others were exhibited in leading galleries. He illustrated a number of dog books, *Dogs*; *Dogs from A–Z*, and *The Dog Dictionary* to name a few. In 1946 Mr. Megargee painted 26 panels of head studies of famous dogs for the kennels aboard the United States Line's *America*. These included dogs owned by Mr. and Mrs. Sherman Hoyt, Mrs. William du Pont, Mr. and Mrs. M. Hartley Dodge, and other sportsmen and society leaders. Today, hand-colored photographs of the originals are part of the art collection of the American Kennel Club. The talented Mr. Megargee designed the Greyhound Bus logo and combined the American Foxhound, Newfoundland, and Chesapeake Bay Retriever breeds into the bookplate of the American Kennel Club. The original pen-and-ink drawing for the bookplate now hangs in the AKC Library.

Mr. Megargee was known as an ardent sportsman and an accredited dog show judge. He served as President of the Scottish Terrier Club of America and the Associated Terrier Clubs and was a director of the American Kennel Club. He headed the AKC Library Committee almost from that group's inception.

Megargee compositions at the American Kennel Club include oil paintings of the renowned Smooth Fox Terrier *Ch. Nornay Saddler*; the Harrier *Ch. Reynal's Monarch*; the Welsh Terrier *Ch. Twin Ponds Belle*; the Clumber Spaniel *Royaline White Foam*; the Fox Terrier *Ch. Spicy Bit of Halleston*; and a specially mounted plaque of a dog genealogy chart, which appeared in the January 31, 1949 issue of *Life* magazine. The plaque was presented to Mr. Megargee by *Life* upon his completion of the work.

Another artist whose work is unusually delightful is Marguerite Kirmse (1885–1935), who was born in England and studied at the Royal Academy of Music. She came to vacation in America as a young woman and liked the country so much that she decided to stay and seek her fortune. The versatile Marguerite Kirmse worked with pencil, pen and ink, pastels, and oils, but after

Six of Megargee's S. S. *America* head studies.

the appearance of her drypoint of a Scottish Terrier puppy, *The Brushwood Boy*, in 1921, the majority of her efforts were devoted to etchings. Marguerite Kirmse produced hundreds of etchings, pastels, and illustrations for books and magazine covers depicting Terriers, gundogs, Hounds, and many other breeds, and she even sculpted and produced a few dog bronzes. Some of her most beautiful work appears in the Derrydale Press books *Dogs* and *Dogs in the Field*. Few artists were better qualified for their work than Marguerite Kirmse, for she bred Scottish Terriers under the "Tobermory" prefix and also kept Pointers, Setters, Spaniels, Airedales, and Irish Terriers at her kennels. She is represented in the collection of the AKC by the pastels of Sealyham Terriers, *Hemlock Hill Ivo Clyde*, dated 1917, and *Hemlock Hill Boy Scout*, dated 1918; a white chalk-and-crayon drawing of a Bulldog head, *King Orry*; a pair of prints, *The Fox* and *The Hound*, dated 1933; and a pastel and oil, *Under Mistletoe*, of a Scottish Terrier and Welsh Terrier, dated 1935.

The subject of the dog in art would not be complete without a brief mention of Frederick Machetanz (1908–), who lives in Alaska and specializes in painting the natural beauty of the far North and the working relationship between sled dogs and men.

Some other works by well-known American artists in the collection of the AKC are Terri Bresnahan's paintings of the Dachshund, *Ch. Heidi-Flottenberg*; the Scottish Terrier, *Ch. Laindon Lawds*; and the Pekingese, *Fuh Sam*; F. C. Clifton's beautiful portraits of the white Bull Terriers, *Fire Chief* and *Ch. Yorkville Belle*; Bert Cobb's etching of a German Shepherd Dog, *Ch. Giralda's Cito V.D. Markfeste*; Gladys Brown Edwards's oil painting of five Lakeland Terriers; C. C. Fawcett's pastel of the Wire Fox Terrier, *Ch. Hetherington Model Rhythm*; George Fenn's lovely oil of two Greyhounds, dated 1833; Elizabeth M. Harvey's pastel of a Pomeranian; Gilman Low's exquisite portrait of the Sealyham Terrier, *Ch. Barberryhill Bootlegger*; Phyllis Mackenzie's oil painting of three Shih Tzu; William Mangford's head study of the St. Bernard *Odin*; George Ford Morris's 1910 lithograph of a Pointer on a blue background; prints by Alexander A. Pope, Jr., from his *Celebrated Dogs of America* series (these were collected by Theodore Roosevelt when he was a student at Harvard in 1879); lovely oils, pastels, and charcoals of Whippets by Jill Rich; William Schnelle's Wire Fox Terrier portrait, *Ch. Halleston Wyche Wondrous*, and his portrait of the Sealyham terrier *Bootlegger*. Helen Sherman Wilson's pastel of three wheaten Scottish Terriers; F. H. Stoll's oil of the Japanese Spaniel *Ch. Kowanna Fumi Konoye*; and P. Stretton's painting of two Airedale Terriers, *Boxwood Barkentine and Boxwood Bashful*.

The Dog in Caricatures, Satire, and Cartoons

A look at the dog in art must also include a brief mention of caricatures, satire, and cartoon dogs. Amusing portrayals of canines date back to the New Kingdom of Egypt (1580–1085 B.C.), and the British Museum's extensive Egyptian collection includes a strip of satirical drawings, inspired by tomb paintings of the period, in which dogs and other animals take the place of human beings and perform humanlike activities.

The English painter and engraver William Hogarth (1697–1764) produced some of the most satirical engravings of dogs and even involved his favorite Pug,

William Hogarth: *The Painter and His Pug.* Hogarth owned two Pugs, one called Pugg, which he had in 1730, and another called Trump, which by 1740 had replaced the older dog. The self-portrait shows the dog Trump. *Tate Gallery, London*

Trump, in a bit of mockery. Hogarth painted a self-portrait in 1745 and placed Trump prominently in the foreground. When the painting was first exhibited, the resemblance between Trump and his master did not go unnoticed by Hogarth's enemies, and the work evoked amusing reviews about the "two inseparable companions . . . cheek by jowl." Hogarth's bitter enemy, Charles Churchill, published a sarcastic pamphlet, *Epistle to William Hogarth*, several years later. An enraged Hogarth made some changes in his self-portrait shortly thereafter and produced a satirical engraving entitled *The Bruiser*, in which he substituted a menacing-looking bear in place of his own image to represent Churchill but left the long-faced Trump still in foreground, urinating over Churchill's pamphlet.

Dogs appear in Hogarth's *Marriage à la Mode, Beer Street and Gin Lane,* and *The Rake's Progress,* and they are sadistically pictured in *The Four Stages of Cruelty* series. *The First Stage of Cruelty* is an especially grisly scene. It shows a group of cheering children torturing and maiming dogs and other animals. In the center of the engraving, three boys plunge an arrow into the anus of a howling dog, while another youth sets his dog savagely upon a frightened cat. Hogarth, a true animal lover, produced the series "to prevent in some degree the cruel treatment of animals which makes the streets of London more disagreeable to the human mind, than anything whatever, the very describing of which gives me pain."

English cartoonists Thomas Rowlandson (1756–1827) and George Cruikshank (1792–1878), were gifted with amazing eyes for comic incident and created ribald and spirited drawings. Both artists tucked all sorts of dogs into their drawings at every opportunity.

J. J. Grandville (Jean-Ignace Isidore Gerard, 1803–1847), the famous French illustrator, portrayed human pretentions with anthropomorphic mockery. Grandville specialized in ridiculing society by using animals in human situations and clothing to condemn man's affectations. No one escaped Grandville's satire—he knocked the rich and the poor, the stylish and the shabby, the literate and the illiterate, the liberals and the conservatives. Grandville became famous in the middle of the nineteenth century when his illustrations appeared in *Les Animaux*. The work consisted of short stories by some of the most renowned writers of the day accompanied by Grandville's drawings. In one tale, "Animals as Doctors," by Pierre Bernard, a group of animals are tired of being treated by veterinarians. They learn medicine themselves, positive that they can do better than the veterinarians, and then practically kill a poor dog with a broken paw. Another story, "Journey of an African Lion to Paris," by Honoré de Balzac, tells about an African lion that comes to France to see what Parisian lions are like. He is shown around Paris by an overbearing dog in top hat and costume. The dog takes the lion to a café for ice cream and then to a carnival ball where "animal passions break out." In a third tale, the pet dog of a famous drama critic dies of boredom after adopting the profession of a reviewer.

In modern times, James Thurber drew some of the most poignant and hilarious sketches of real and imaginary dogs in *Dogs, Women and Men*; *The Hound and the Bug*; *The Hound and the Hare*; *The Hound and the Hat*, and other works. Thurber usually was more sympathetic to animals than to humans. And who can forget such canine cartoon stars as Harold Gray's Sandy, Little Orphan Annie's faithful companion; Brad Anderson's Marmaduke; Chick Young's Daisy, Dagwood Bumstead's dog; Walt Disney's Pluto and Goofy; and Disney's *Lady and the Tramp* and the *101 Dalmatians*—characters with loyal followings for generations. The AKC is the proud possessor of an original Walt Disney Donald Duck sketch, in which the world's best known web-footed creature stands under an AKC sign that cautions "No people allowed."

Saul Steinberg, Roy McKie, and Eric Gurney have created wonderfully humorous dogs, too. Charles Schulz's Snoopy, an enchanting black-and-white Beagle, is adored by both young and old. Snoopy made his first newspaper appearance in 1950 and has since become the most celebrated dog in the world. His capers entertain millions of daily and Sunday readers who glance at "Peanuts" before reading the news of the day. Snoopy has starred in more than 25 television specials, a few television extravaganzas, a full-length film, and a long-running Broadway musical. He has been the subject of several books and has even authored a few of his own, including the best-selling *It Was a Dark and Stormy Night*. The intrepid Beagle has even skated in the *Ice Follies* and has gone to the moon with the astronauts.

"There go the most intelligent of all animals." *James Thurber*

"Other end, Mr. Pemberton." *James Thurber*

Donald Duck, by Walt Disney. Disney gave the AKC the original, which now hangs in its offices. © *Walt Disney Productions*

© 1981 United Feature Syndicate, Inc.

"So you're not pedigreed! My ancestors didn't come over on the Mayflower, either!"

Marmaduke, by Brad Anderson. © 1981 *United Features Syndicate, Inc.*

"On my way home today on the bus, a lone grape rolled down the aisle and came to rest near my foot. It was pale green and looked to be of the seedless variety." Drawing by Booth; © 1974 *The New Yorker Magazine, Inc.*

"Write about dogs!"

Babylonian terra-cotta plaque showing a dog accompanied by a man. *c.* 1900–1700 B.C. *British Museum*

The Dog in Sculpture, Carvings, Pottery, and Porcelain

Since the beginnings of civilization, dogs have appeared as subjects of sculpture, statuary, carvings, pottery, and porcelains. Sculptors generally depicted the dog as they saw him, and from these works of art of so many styles and throughout so many centuries, it is possible to a degree to trace the dog's development, as well as to learn much about the preferences of the times.

Some of the earliest known examples of dog carvings are terra-cotta plaques from Babylonia, dating from 1900–1700 B.C., which show huge Mastiff-like dogs. In one scene, a man has wrapped two lengths of heavy rope around a dog's neck to use as a lead. Tutankhamen, the Egyptian boy-king, was undoubtedly a dog lover, for many works of art depicting dogs are among the fantastic treasures found in his tomb. There were a magnificently carved and decorated dog coffin and an exquisite stuccoed wood chest with vivid hunting scenes, one panel showing the king in his chariot accompanied by hunting hounds wearing broad gold collars. Tutankhamen's tomb contained several tributes to the dog-god, Anubis, including a life-size effigy made of black lacquered wood. Its eyes were obsidian and alabaster and rimmed with gold, as were the insides of its erect ears. Its nails were made of silver, and around Anubis's neck was a golden collar and, below, golden ribbons with ends falling to its forelegs.

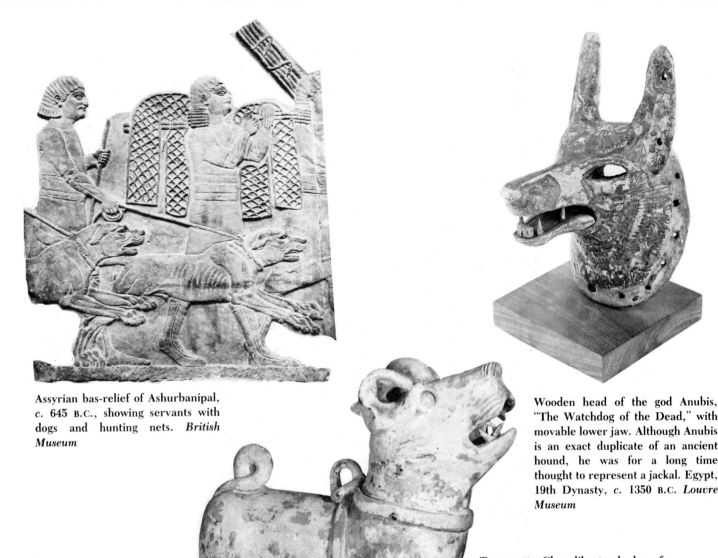

Assyrian bas-relief of Ashurbanipal, *c.* 645 B.C., showing servants with dogs and hunting nets. *British Museum*

Wooden head of the god Anubis, "The Watchdog of the Dead," with movable lower jaw. Although Anubis is an exact duplicate of an ancient hound, he was for a long time thought to represent a jackal. Egypt, 19th Dynasty, *c.* 1350 B.C. *Louvre Museum*

Terra-cotta Chow-like tomb dog of the Han Dynasty (China, 206 B.C.–A.D. 220). The dog's harness is similar to those of the present day. *Victoria and Albert Museum*

The Assyrian Kings Ashurnasirpal II, who reigned from 883 to 859 B.C., and Ashurbanipal, 668–626 B.C., maintained large kennels of Molossians, huge Mastiff-like dogs that were used for hunting and for war. Many of the kings' dogs appear on dramatic bas-reliefs in which they are hunting lions. The dogs were trained to pursue the most savage of beasts and would drive them into nets stretched across a path by the kings' servants.

Carvings believed to be the progenitor of the Akita appear on tombs of early Japanese people. The first pieces from China are bronzes of the Chow Dynasty (1122–206 B.C.), which show two or possibly three different types of dogs. Pottery figures, bas-reliefs, and tomb tiles of the Han Dynasty (206 B.C.–A.D. 220) depict Greyhounds, other hunting dogs, and Chow-like guard dogs. It is interesting to note that the harnesses carved on many terra-cotta dogs of the Han period are much the same as present-day styles.

Dogs appear in Roman statuary, most notably the marble figure of the enormous Mastiff owned by the Grand Duke of Tuscany, attributed to Myron, one of the most famous artists of the day; the "Marble Dogs" from the villa of the Roman Emperor Antonius, now in the Vatican Museum; and the exquisitely modeled pair of Greyhounds—a dog holding a bitch's ear—uncovered at Monte Cagnolo. The Greeks, Romans, and peoples of other Mediterranean cultures portrayed dogs on vases, ewers, drinking horns, and other pottery and on mosaics and bas-reliefs on sarcophagi.

In the Middle Ages, the canine race had its patron saints, and St. Hubert (patron of northern Europe), St. Eustace (religious protector of southern Europe), and St. Roch and their dogs were popular statuary themes. St. Roch, one of the four patron saints of the sick, traveled through the countryside helping peasants and, according to legend, contracted the plague while helping the afflicted. St. Roch could not heal himself and went off into the depths of the forest to die. Miraculously, a dog belonging to a neighboring lord appeared with a loaf of bread in its mouth and remained by the saint's side, tenderly licking his wounds. A dog with bread in its mouth frequently appears beside St. Roch in Medieval sculpture. One of the finest examples is a polychromed oak piece thought to have come from the Cherbourg Cathedral in France about 1530, which is now a part of the Cloisters of the Metropolitan Museum of Art.

Dogs also appear in stone scenes and designs on the facades of cathedrals and large estates, burial vaults, and other statuary of the Middle Ages. They are carved of wood on bench ends, fonts, and misericords in churches in most European countries, and they appear on roundels and medallions accompanying secular figures. Tomb effigies of the period show knights and crusaders with dogs at their feet in heavenly repose, a symbol of their faithfulness to God.

During the Renaissance, artists and craftsmen were mainly concerned with men and women, and dogs often accompany humans in that period's statuary. A dog frequently appeared at a woman's feet to symbolize affection and fidelity, while a lion generally sat at a man's feet to denote manliness and bravery. We are indebted to Benvenuto Cellini (1500–1572) for four magnificently detailed dogs in his bronze *The Nymph of Fontainebleau* (now in the Louvre).

From 1830 to the beginning of the nineteenth century, bronze sculpture reached its pinnacle with the establishment of the Animalier School. The best pieces were fashioned in France, while others came from Germany, Austria, and Russia. At the time, people began to think that animals were capable of feelings, and the Animalier sculptors stressed the emotions and realistic physical characteristics of their subjects. Bronzes suddenly became exciting. The lovely patinas, the beauty of muscular power, the actions and vitality of the Animalier animals have not since been equaled. Foremost of the sculptors who produced Animalier bronzes are Antoine-Louis Barye (known as the "Supreme Animalier" and the "Michelangelo of animal sculptors"), Pierre Jules Mene (best known of the Animaliers), Emanuel Fremiet, Jules Moigniez, Christophe Fratin, Rosa and Isidor Bonheur, Paul Colomera, P. E. Delabierre, Alfred Dubucand, Georges Gardet, Ferdinand Pautrot, and a sculptor of the German School who signed his bronzes "Waagen." The Animaliers modeled many different breeds, particularly the Greyhound, a dog that holds a unique position among pure-breds, for no other canine has so influenced artists and sculptors.

Tin-glazed earthenware plate from Italy, *c. 1600. Victoria and Albert Museum*

The Animaliers are represented at the AKC by Barye's *Lying Deer* and Fratin's *Whippet and Rabbit* and a plaque, *Whippets and Rabbit*.

Among the outstanding American sculptors in the field of dogs today are June Harrah, Kay Finch, Damara Bolte, and Richard Chashoudian. Some of the distinguished works on exhibition at the AKC are H. R. D.'s *Three Terriers Wrestling*; Diller's *German Shepherd*; Charles Disioia's *Basset Hounds*; R. Fath's Great Pyrenees, *Ch. Estat d'Argeles of Basquarie*; B. Froaman's *Two Whippet Dogs Running*; Gorham's Whippet, *Noble*; and Kathy Lyon's *Miniature Schnauzer*, *Whippet with Rabbit*, and *Yorkshire Terrier*; Mackarness's Cocker Spaniel, *Ch. Baby Ruth*, Fox Terriers *Ch. Sabine Rarebit* and *Ch. Sabine Result*, a bronze plaque, *Spaniels*, and Scottish Terrier, *Gorham et cie*; Joe Mercer's Whippet, *Ch. Mica of Meander*; Gary Weisman's *German Shepherd Dog* (head), and the many bronze and brass Greyhounds and Whippets of the Shearer Collection.

The dog has been a favorite subject for modelers of earthenware, stoneware, and porcelain, either as a primary subject or accompanying figures of humans. Outstanding likenesses of dogs have been produced by Staffordshire, Worcester, Chelsea, Lowestoft, Royal Doulton, and Rockingham of England; Meissen, Dresden, Nymphenburg, Nuremburg, and Rosenthal of Germany; Vincennes, Sevres, Strasbourg, and Faience (tin-glazed earthenware) of France; Delft of Holland; Royal Copenhagen and Bing & Groendahl of Denmark; and Bennington of the United States. Tin-glazed earthenware platters and dishes of the seventeenth and eighteenth centuries were often painted with dogs in hunting scenes. The porcelain collection at the Metropolitan Museum of Art contains several boxes and *bonbonnieres* in the shapes of various breeds of dogs and snuffboxes painted with dogs. One dazzling nineteenth-century Meissen snuffbox, made of hand-paste porcelain with jewelled gold and silver mounts, is painted inside and out with Pugs and a Spaniel.

Today, bronze and porcelain figures of dogs are among the most collectible *objets d'art*. Pieces by the American artist Edward Marshall Boehm are cherished by collectors because they are the only exceptional porcelain dogs made in the United States. Boehm figures are on exhibition at the White House, the Elysee Palace in Paris, Buckingham Palace in London, and many major American and foreign museums.

The Dog in Heraldry

Heraldry, or the science of armorial bearings, might also be defined as a pictorial language that reveals a bearer's identity as well as other significant information. The use of animals in heraldry became popular in the fifteenth and sixteenth centuries. Dogs and other heraldic animals are portrayed in either natural or stylized form.

Various breeds of dogs appear on English, Scottish, and European heraldic devices, with the Greyhound being the most popular, followed by the Talbot Hound (a descendant of the St. Hubert Hound brought to Britain by William the Conqueror, and now extinct), the Bloodhound, the Mastiff, the Foxhound, and the Water Spaniel. In general, dogs serve as decorative and artistic appendages and are most often placed at one or both sides of armorial shields as supporters. The idea of having two beasts support an armorial shield probably was conceived by engravers of the day, who wanted artistically to fill in the space left when a shield was enclosed in a circular seal.

The Dog in Tapestry

Tapestry is one of the oldest forms of woven art and was known in the ancient Middle East, Asia, and pre-Columbian America. The first mention of tapestry in Europe dates from around the end of the eighth century, during the early Middle Ages. One of the earliest woven pieces to portray dogs is the Bayeux tapestry, commissioned by Bishop Odo of Bayeux, half-brother of William the Conqueror, and probably produced shortly after 1066. Although this early piece is called a tapestry, it is actually an embroidered linen hanging, 19 inches wide and over 230 feet long. This remarkable secular work is a visual record of the events that preceded the invasion of England by William the Conqueror, the invasion itself, and King Harold's defeat at the Battle of Hastings in 1066.

Dogs appear on sections of the border and in several scenes in the tapestry. One tableau shows King Harold leading a hunting party. The king is on horseback, holding a hawk on his left wrist, while hawking hounds and other large dogs wearing collars with leash rings run ahead. Dr. R. H. A. Merlin, author of *De Canibus—Dog and Hound in Antiquity*, believes that the hawking dogs probably were the ancestors of today's Spaniels and Poodles. Their jobs were to flush game for the falconers to fly hawks at and probably to retrieve after the kill. The larger dogs in the Bayeux tapestry closely resemble the strong and

English heraldry: Collared Greyhounds supporting the arms of the Earl of Ashburnham.

LE ROY ET L'ESTAT

Ashburnham Earl of Ashburnham

PREST
PLIR
D'ACCOM

Talbot Earl of Shrewsbury

The now-extinct Talbot Hound *rampant* on the coats of arms of the families of Talbot, Earl of Shrewsbury.

Hunter Blair

Greyhound *sejant* atop the Hunter Blair crest, with Talbot Hounds "in full course."

The White Greyhound of Richmond, one of the ten heraldic beasts to stand outside Westminster Abbey during the coronation of Queen Elizabeth II in 1953. Drawing by Edward Bawden from the sculpture by James Woodford. *British Crown Copyright. By Permission of the Controller of Her Britannic Majesty's Stationery office.*

ferocious Alaunt, a long-extinct breed that, according to cynologists, combined the qualities of the Mastiff and Greyhound. It is believed that the Alaunts became the bull- and bear-baiters of later years and that they are the ancestors of Bulldogs. Another scene from the Bayeux tapestry shows a hunting party wading out to double-ended Viking-type ships, while the hawk and hawking hounds are being carried on board. Later, on shore, the Alaunts follow horsemen holding swords and shields.

Dogs appear in a considerable number of Medieval and Renaissance tapestries, most often in scenes of the chase. Venery, an ancient term meaning the art of hunting, and hawking were the sports of royalty, nobility, and religious men at the time. In fact, many kings and clergymen became prominent not because of their royal power or religious observances but for their passion for hunting or hawking.

Because of royal patronage, artists of the Middle Ages were able to immortalize the chase in tapestries. A few of the most beautiful examples include:

The Chatsworth Hunts, also known as *The Devonshire Hunting Tapestries*—four pieces, woven about the middle of the fifteenth century at the Tournai or Arras workshops in France and now part of the Victoria and Albert Museum collection in London. Practically every kind of chase is depicted in the four huge panels. One elaborate scene, with both men and ladies on the hunting field, depicts the old ritual of the "dogdraw," in which relay teams of Greyhounds chase a deer to exhaustion.

The Lady with the Unicorn—six pieces, woven in France about 1500, presumably for the LeViste family, and now in the Cluny Museum in Paris. The magnificent "millefleurs" tapestries, on a background of vivid red, are decorated with flowers, plants, trees, birds, small animals, various hounds, the lion, and the unicorn. In the sixth piece a dog described as a *Bichon Maltais* sits on a brocade cushion next to a sumptuously dressed lady who is inspecting her jewels, probably as a symbol of fidelity.

The Hunts of the Unicorn—seven pieces, woven in France or Flanders about 1500 and now hanging in the Cloisters of the Metropolitan Museum of Art in New York. Unquestionably, the Hunts of the Unicorn pieces are the most magnificent representations of the dog in tapestry. Greyhounds and other sight- and scent-hounds play an important role in the symbolism and story of the unicorn hunt, and they prominently appear in six of the seven pieces. In *The Start of the Hunt*, handsomely dressed noblemen and hunters venture forth in a forest to find the unicorn. The men hold three Greyhounds and two scent-hounds on leash. In the second tapestry, *The Unicorn Dips His Horn into the Stream*, hunters and hounds have tracked the unicorn and pause to watch the beast purify the water. The third tapestry, *The Unicorn Leaps into the Stream*, shows the scent-hounds following the fabulous beast into the water while the sight-hounds anxiously await their chance to give chase. In the fourth tapestry, *The Unicorn Defends Himself*, the unicorn gores a Greyhound with his horn while he kicks a hunter with his hind legs. The wound doesn't deter the rest of the pack, which seems anxious to close in on the beast. A huntsman sounds his horn in the fifth tapestry, *The Unicorn Is Tamed by the Maiden*, in the presence of the sight- and scent-hounds. In the sixth tapestry, *The Unicorn Is Killed and Brought to the Castle*, the returning hunters and hounds are greeted by the lord and lady of the castle. Two of the hunters pierce the unicorn with their swords

Detail from *A Mon Suel Desir*, "The Lady With the Unicorn Tapestries." A Bichon Maltais sits on a brocade cushion. *Cluny Museum, Paris*

while a hound sinks his teeth into the beast's flesh. Another dog bears his teeth, and two Greyhounds anxiously leap forward, eager to participate in the kill. Kenneth Clark, commenting on Medieval hunting and symbolism in *Animals and Men*, writes that the Unicorn may well symbolize Christ in this tapestry.

The Hunts of the Emperor Maximillian—12 pieces, woven in Brussels in the sixteenth century from cartoons by Bernard van Orley and now in the Louvre Museum in Paris. Dogs hunt wild boars in scenes inspired by illuminations from *Livre de Chasse du Roi Modus*, a fourteenth-century hunting treatise.

Scene from *The Hunts of the Emperor Maximillian* tapestries, showing one of the hounds wearing a quilted jerkin, or *jacque*, as protection against the bites of wild animals. *Louvre, Paris*

The Kings of Denmark—Woven in Denmark about the end of the sixteenth century and now part of the collection of the National Museum of Denmark. The pieces depict Danish kings who ruled at that time, including Frederick II with his faithful dog Wildbrat.

The Hunts of Louis XV—Nine pieces, woven at the Gobelins workshop in France, 1743, from cartoons by Jean-Baptiste Oudry and now in the Uffizi Gallery in Italy. The most beautiful tapestry, *The Pack*, shows huntsmen and whippers-in blowing hunting horns in the Forest of Fontainebleau as a pack of baying hounds gathers.

16

The Dog In Prose

Dogs make good reading. A fascination with their spirit and their relationship to man has spawned an impressive body of first-rate literature. Though the selections included here are by American authors, which meant that such favorites as Flush and Lassie had to be passed by, there are plenty of worthy American representatives to take up the slack. Some, like Albert Payson Terhune's "Lad," John Steinbeck's traveling companion, "Charley," and Jack London's courageous "Buck," will be old friends. Others may be less familiar, but no less deserving: John Graves' "Blue," Eugene O'Neill's "Blemie," Gene Hill's "Fred."

There are dogs of all kinds to be found here, both pure-bred and not. Dogs, like people, are not perfect, as "Muggs" in "The Dog That Bit People" will plainly show. But whether they are funny, or tragic, or inspiring, all the dogs represented in this sampler have been included because there is something about them, that ring of dog-truth, that reminds us of dogs we have known well, or would very much like to have known well—and now do.

Memoirs of a Yellow Dog

O. Henry

I don't suppose it will knock any of you people off your perch to read a contribution from an animal. Mr. Kipling and a good many others have demonstrated the fact that animals can express themselves in remunerative English, and no magazine goes to press nowadays without an animal story in it, except the old-style monthlies that are still running pictures of Bryan and the Mont Pelée horror.

But you needn't look for any stuck-up literature in my piece, such as Bearoo, the bear, and Snakoo, the snake, and Tammanoo, the tiger, talk in the jungle books. A yellow dog that's spent most of his life in a cheap New York flat, sleeping in a corner on an old sateen underskirt (the one she spilled port wine on at the Lady Longshoremen's banquet), mustn't be expected to perform any tricks with the art of speech.

I was born a yellow pup; date, locality, pedigree and weight unknown. The first thing I can recollect, an old woman had me in a basket at Broadway and Twenty-third trying to sell me to a fat lady. Old Mother Hubbard was boosting me to beat the band as a genuine Pomeranian-Hambletonian-Red-Irish-Cochin-China-Stoke-Poges fox terrier. The fat lady chased a V around among the samples of grosgrain flannelette in her shopping bag till she cornered it, and gave up. From that moment I was a pet—a mamma's own wootsey squidlums. Say, gentle reader, did you ever have a 200-pound woman breathing a flavor of Camembert cheese and Peau d'Espagne pick you up and wallop her nose all over you, remarking all the time in an Emma Eames tone of voice: "Oh, oo's um oodlum, doodlum, woodlum, toodlum, bitsy-witsy skoodlums?"

From pedigreed yellow pup I grew up to be an anonymous yellow cur looking like a cross between an Angora cat and a box of lemons. But my mistress never tumbled. She thought that the two primeval pups that Noah chased into the ark were but a collateral branch of my ancestors. It took two policemen to keep her from entering me at the Madison Square Garden for the Siberian bloodhound prize.

I'll tell you about that flat. The house was the ordinary thing in New York, paved with Parian marble in the entrance hall and cobblestones above the first floor. Our flat was three—well, not flights—climbs up. My mistress rented it unfurnished, and put in the regular things—1903 antique upholstered parlor set, oil chromo of geishas in a Harlem tea house, rubber plant and husband.

By Sirius! there was a biped I felt sorry for. He was a little man with sandy hair and whiskers a good deal like mine. Henpecked?—well, toucans and flamingoes and pelicans all had their bills in him. He wiped the dishes and listened to my mistress tell about the cheap, ragged things the lady with the squirrel-skin coat on the second floor hung out on her line to dry. And every evening while she was getting supper she made him take me out on the end of a string for a walk.

If men knew how women pass the time when they are alone they'd never marry. Laura Lean Jibbey, peanut brittle, a little almond cream on the neck muscles, dishes unwashed, half an hour's talk with the iceman, reading a package of old letters, a couple of pickles and two bottles of malt extract, one hour peeking through a hole in the window shade into the flat across the airshaft—that's about all there is to it. Twenty minutes before time for him to come home from work she straightens up the house, fixes her rat so it won't show, and gets out a lot of sewing for a ten-minute bluff.

I led a dog's life in that flat. 'Most all day I lay there in my corner watching that fat woman kill time. I slept sometimes and had pipe dreams about being out chasing cats into basements and growling at old ladies with black mittens, as a dog was intended to do. Then she would pounce upon me with a lot of that drivelling poodle palaver and kiss me on the nose—but what could I do? A dog can't chew cloves.

I began to feel sorry for Hubby, dog my cats if I didn't. We looked so much alike that people noticed it when we went out; so we shook the streets that Morgan's cab drives down, and took to climbing the piles of last December's snow on the streets where cheap people live.

One evening when we were thus promenading, and I was trying to look like a prize St.

Bernard, and the old man was trying to look like he wouldn't have murdered the first organ-grinder he heard play Mendelssohn's wedding-march, I looked up at him and said, in my way:

"What are you looking so sour about, you oakum trimmed lobster? She don't kiss you. You don't have to sit on her lap and listen to talk that would make the book of a musical comedy sound like the maxims of Epictetus. You ought to be thankful you're not a dog. Brace up, Benedick, and bid the blues begone."

The matrimonial mishap looked down at me with almost canine intelligence in his face.

"Why, doggie," says he, "good doggie. You almost look like you could speak. What is it, doggie—Cats."

Cats! Could speak!

But, of course, he couldn't understand. Humans were denied the speech of animals. The only common ground of communication upon which dogs and men can get together is in fiction.

In the flat across the hall from us lived a lady with a black-and-tan terrier. Her husband strung it and took it out every evening, but he always came home cheerful and whistling. One day I touched noses with the black-and-tan in the hall, and I struck him for an elucidation.

"See here, Wiggle-and-Skip," I says, "you know that it ain't the nature of a real man to play dry nurse to a dog in public. I never saw one leashed to a bow-wow yet that didn't look like he'd like to lick every other man that looked at him. But your boss comes in every day as perky and set up as an amateur prestidigitator doing the egg trick. How does he do it? Don't tell me he likes it."

"Him?" says the black-and-tan. "Why, he uses Nature's Own Remedy. He gets spifflicated. At first when we go out he's as shy as the man on the steamer who would rather play pedro when they make 'em all jackpots. By the time we've been in eight saloons he don't care whether the thing on the end of his line is a dog or a catfish. I've lost two inches of my tail trying to sidestep those swinging doors."

The pointer I got from that terrier—vaudeville please copy—set me to thinking.

One evening about 6 o'clock my mistress ordered him to get busy and do the ozone act for

Lovey. I have concealed it until now, but that is what she called me. The black-and-tan was called "Tweetness." I consider that I have the bulge on him as far as you could chase a rabbit. Still "Lovey" is something of a nomenclatural tin can on the tail of one's self-respect.

At a quiet place on a safe street I tightened the line of my custodian in front of an attractive, refined saloon. I made a dead-ahead scramble for the doors, whining like a dog in the press despatches that lets the family know that little Alice is bogged while gathering lilies in the brook.

"Why, darn my eyes," says the old man, with a grin; "darn my eyes if the saffron-colored son of a seltzer lemonade ain't asking me in to take a drink. Lemme see—how long's it been since I saved shoe leather by keeping one foot on the foot-rest? I believe I'll——"

I knew I had him. Hot Scotches he took, sitting at a table. For an hour he kept the Campbells coming. I sat by his side rapping for the waiter with my tail, and eating free lunch such as mamma in her flat never equalled with her homemade truck bought at a delicatessen store eight minutes before papa comes home.

When the products of Scotland were all exhausted except the rye bread the old man unwound me from the table leg and played me outside like a fisherman plays a salmon. Out there he took off my collar and threw it into the street.

"Poor doggie," says he; "good doggie. She shan't kiss you any more. 'S a darned shame. Good doggie, go away and get run over by a street car and be happy."

I refused to leave. I leaped and frisked around the old man's legs happy as a pug on a rug.

"You old flea-headed woodchuck-chaser," I said to him—"you moon-baying, rabbit-pointing, egg-stealing old beagle, can't you see that I don't want to leave you? Can't you see that we're both Pups in the Wood and the missis is the cruel uncle after you with the dish towel and me with the flea liniment and pink bow to tie on my tail. Why not cut that all out and be pards forever more?"

Maybe you'll say he didn't understand—maybe he didn't. But he kind of got a grip on the

Hot Scotches, and stood still for a minute, thinking.

"Doggie," says he, finally, "we don't live more than a dozen lives on this earth, and very few of us live more than 300. If I ever see that flat any more I'm a flat, and if you do you're flatter; and that's no flattery. I'm offering 60 to 1 that Westward Ho wins out by the length of a dachshund."

There was no string, but I frolicked along with my master to the Twenty-third Street ferry. And the cats on the route saw reason to give thanks that prehensile claws had been given to them.

On the Jersey side my master said to a stranger who stood eating a currant bun:

"Me and my doggie, we are bound for the Rocky Mountains."

But what pleased me most was when my old man pulled both of my ears until I howled, and said:

"You common, monkey-headed, rat-tailed, sulphur-colored son of a door mat, do you know what I'm going to call you?"

I thought of "Lovey," and I whined dolefully.

"I'm going to call you 'Pete,' " says my master; and if I'd had five tails I couldn't have done enough wagging to do justice to the occasion.

LOST!

(from Lad: A Dog)

Albert Payson Terhune

Four of us were discussing abstract themes, idly, as men will, after a good dinner and in front of a country-house fire. Someone asked:

"What is the saddest sight in everyday life? I don't mean the most gloomily tragic, but the saddest?"

A frivolous member of the fireside group cited a helpless man between two quarreling women. A sentimentalist said:

"A lost child in a city street."

The Dog-Master contradicted:

"A lost *dog* in a city street."

Nobody agreed with him of course; but that was because none of the others chanced to know dogs—to know their psychology—their souls, if you prefer. The dog-man was right. A lost dog in a city street is the very saddest and most hopeless sight in all a city street's abounding everyday sadness.

A man between two quarreling women is an object piteous enough, heaven knows. Yet his plight verges too much on the grotesque to be called sad.

A lost child?—No. Let a child stand in the middle of a crowded sidewalk and begin to cry.

In one minute fifty amateur and professional rescuers have flocked to the Lost One's aid. An hour, at most, suffices to bring it in touch with its frenzied guardians.

A lost dog?—Yes. No succoring cohort surges to the relief. A gang of boys, perhaps, may give chase, but assuredly not in kindness. A policeman seeking a record for "mad dog" shooting—a professional dog-catcher in quest of his dirty fee—these will show marked attention to the wanderer. But, again, not in kindness.

A dog, at some turn in the street, misses his master—doubles back to where the human demigod was last seen—darts ahead once more to find him, through the press of other human folk—halts, hesitates, begins the same maneuvers all over again; then stands, shaking in panic at his utter aloneness.

Get the look in his eyes, then—you who do not mind seeing such things—and answer, honestly: Is there anything sadder on earth? All this, before the pursuit of boys and the fever of thirst and the final knowledge of desolation have turned him from a handsome and prideful pet into a slinking outcast.

Yes, a lost dog is the saddest thing that can meet the gaze of a man or woman who understands dogs. As perhaps my story may help to show—or perhaps not.

Lad had been brushed and bathed, daily, for a week, until his mahogany-and-snow coat shone. All this, at The Place, far up in the North Jersey hinterland and all to make him presentable for the Westminster Kennel Show at New York's Madison Square Garden. After which, his two gods, the Mistress and the Master took him for a thirty-mile ride in The Place's only car, one morning.

The drive began at The Place—the domain where Lad had ruled as King among the lesser folk for so many years. It ended at Madison Square Garden, where the annual four-day dog show was in progress.

You have read how Lad fared at that show—how, at the close of the first day, when he had two victories to his credit, the Mistress had taken pity on his misery and had decreed that he should be taken home, without waiting out the remaining three days of torture-ordeal.

The Master went out first, to get the car and bring it around to the side exit of the Garden. The Mistress gathered up Lad's belongings—his brush, his dog biscuits, etc., and followed, with Lad himself.

Out of the huge building, with its reverberating barks and yells from two thousand canine throats, she went. Lad paced, happy and majestic, at her side. He knew he was going home, and the unhappiness of the hideous day dropped from him.

At the exit, the Mistress was forced to leave a deposit of five dollars, "to insure the return of the dog to his bench" (to which bench of agony she vowed, secretly, Lad should never return). Then she was told the law demands that all dogs in New York City streets shall be muzzled.

In vain she explained that Lad would be in the streets only for such brief time as the car would require to journey to the One Hundred and Thirtieth Street ferry. The door attendant insisted that the law was inexorable. So, lest a policeman hold up the car for such disobedience to the city statutes, the Mistress reluctantly bought a muzzle.

It was a big, awkward thing, made of steel, and bound on with leather straps. It looked like a rat-trap. And it fenced in the nose and mouth of its owner with a wicked criss-cross of shiny metal bars.

Never in all his years had Lad worn a muzzle. Never, until to-day, had he been chained. The splendid eighty-pound collie had been as free of The Place and of the forests as any human; and with no worse restrictions than his own soul and conscience put upon him.

To him this muzzle was a horror. Not even the loved touch of the Mistress' dear fingers, as she adjusted the thing to his beautiful head, could lessen the degradation. And the discomfort of it—a discomfort that amounted to actual pain—was almost as bad as the humiliation.

With his absurdly tiny white forepaws, the huge dog sought to dislodge the torture-implement. He strove to rub it off against the Mistress' skirt. But beyond shifting it so that the forehead strap covered one of his eyes, he could not budge it.

Lad looked up at the Mistress in wretched appeal. His look held no resentment, nothing but sad entreaty. She was his deity. All his life she had given him of her gentleness, her affection, her sweet understanding. Yet, to-day, she had brought him to this abode of noisy torment, and had kept him there from morning to dusk. And now—just as the vigil seemed ended—she was tormenting him, to nerve-rack, by this contraption she had fastened over his nose. Lad did not rebel. But he besought. And the Mistress understood.

"Laddie, dear!" she whispered, as she led him across the sidewalk to the curb where the Master waited for the car. "Laddie, old friend, I'm just as sorry about it as you are. But it's only for a few minutes. Just as soon as we get to the ferry, we'll take it off and throw it into the river. And we'll never bring you again where dogs have to wear such things. I promise. It's only for a few minutes."

The Mistress, for once, was mistaken. Lad was to wear the accursed muzzle for much, *much* longer than "a few minutes."

"Give him the back seat to himself, and come in front here with me," suggested the Master, as the Mistress and Lad arrived alongside the car. "The poor old chap has been so cramped up and pestered all day that he'll like to have a whole seat to stretch out on."

Accordingly, the Mistress opened the door and motioned Lad to the back seat. At a bound the collie was on the cushion, and proceeded to curl up thereon. The Mistress got into the front seat with the Master. The car set forth on its six-mile run to the ferry.

Now that his face was turned homeward, Lad might have found vast interest in his new surroundings had not the horrible muzzle absorbed all his powers of emotion. The Milan Cathedral, the Taj Mahal, the Valley of the Arno at sunset—these be sights to dream of for years. But show them to a man who has an ulcerated tooth, or whose tight, new shoes pinch his soft corn, and he will probably regard them as Lad just then viewed the twilight New York streets.

He was a dog of forest and lake and hill, this giant collie with his mighty shoulders and tiny white feet and shaggy burnished coat and mournful eyes. Never before had he been in a city. The myriad blended noises confused and deafened him. The myriad blended smells assailed his keen nostrils. The swirl of countless multicolored lights stung and blurred his vision. Noises, smells and lights were all jarringly new to him. So were the jostling masses of people on the sidewalk and the tangle and hustle of vehicular traffic through which the Master was threading the car's way with such difficulty.

But, newest and most sickening of all the day's novelties was the muzzle.

Lad was quite certain the Mistress did not realize how the muzzle was hurting him nor how he detested it. In all her dealings with him—or with anyone or anything else—the Mistress had never been unkind; and most assuredly not cruel. It must be she did not understand. At all events, she had not scolded or forbidden, when he had tried to rub the muzzle off. So the wearing of this new torture was apparently no part of the law. And Lad felt justified in striving again to remove it.

In vain he pawed the thing, first with one foot, then with both. He could joggle it from side to side, but that was all. And each shift of the steel bars hurt his tender nose and tenderer sensibilities worse than the one before. He tried to rub it off against the seat cushion—with the same distressing result.

Lad looked up at the backs of his gods, and whined very softly. The sound went unheard, in the babel of noise all around him. Nor did the Mistress, or the Master turn around, on general principles, to speak a word of cheer to the sufferer. They were in a mixup of crossways traffic that called for every atom of their attention, if they were to avoid collision. It was no time for conversation or for dog-patting.

Lad got to his feet and stood, uncertainly, on the slippery leather cushion, seeking to maintain his balance, while he rubbed a corner of the muzzle against one of the supports of the car's lowered top. Working away with all his might, he sought to get leverage that would pry loose the muzzle.

Just then there was a brief gap in the traffic. The Master put on speed, and, darting ahead of a delivery truck, sharply rounded the corner into a side street.

The car's sudden twist threw Lad clean off his precarious balance on the seat, and hurled him against one of the rear doors.

The door, insecurely shut, could not withstand the eighty-pound impact. It burst open. And Lad was flung out onto the greasy asphalt of the avenue.

He landed full on his side, in the muck of the roadway, with a force that shook the breath clean out of him. Directly above his head glared the twin lights of the delivery truck the Master had just shot past. The truck was going at a good twelve miles an hour. And the dog had fallen within six feet of its fat front wheels.

Now, a collie is like no other animal on earth. He is, at worst, more wolf than dog. And, at best, he has more of the wolf's lightning-swift instinct than has any other breed of canine. For which reason Lad was not, then and there, smashed, flat and dead, under the fore-wheels of a three-ton truck.

Even as the tires grazed his fur, Lad gathered himself compactly together, his feet well under him, and sprang far to one side. The lumbering truck missed him by less than six inches. But it missed him.

His leap brought him scramblingly down on all fours, out of the truck's way, but on the wrong side of the thoroughfare. It brought him under the very fender of a touring car that was going at a good pace in the opposite direction. And again, a leap that was inspired by quick instinct alone, lifted the dog free of this newest death-menace.

He halted and stared piteously around in search of his deities. But in that glare and swelter of traffic, a trained human eye could not have recognized any particular car. Moreover, the Mistress and Master were a full half-block away, down the less crowded side street, and were making up for lost time by putting on all the speed they dared, before turning into the next westward traffic-artery. They did not look back, for there was a car directly in front of them, whose driver seemed uncertain as to his wheel control, and the Master was maneuvering to pass it in safety.

Not until they had reached the lower end of Riverside Drive, nearly a mile to the north, did either the Master or Mistress turn around for a word with the dog they loved.

Meantime, Lad was standing, irresolute and panting, in the middle of Columbus Circle. Cars of a million types, from flivver to trolley, seemed to be whizzing directly at him from every direction at once.

A bound, a dodge, or a deft shrinking back would carry him out of one such peril—barely out of it—when another, or fifty others, beset him.

And, all the time, even while he was trying to duck out of danger, his frightened eyes and his pulsing nostrils sought the Mistress and the Master.

His eyes, in that mixture of flare and dusk, told him nothing except that a host of motors were likely to kill him. But his nose told him what it had not been able to tell him since morning—namely, that, through the reek of gasoline and horse-flesh and countless human scents, there was a nearness of fields and woods and water. And, toward that blessed mingling of familiar odors he dodged his threatened way.

By a miracle of luck and skill he crossed Columbus Circle, and came to a standstill on a sidewalk, beside a low gray stone wall. Behind the wall, his nose taught him, lay miles of meadow and wood and lake—Central Park. But the smell of the Park brought him no scent of the Mistress nor of the Master. And it was they—infinitely more than his beloved countryside—that he craved. He ran up the street, on the sidewalk, for a few rods, hesitant, alert, watching in every direction. Then, perhaps seeing a figure, in the other direction, that looked familiar, he dashed at top speed, eastward, for half a block. Then he made a peril-fraught sortie out into the middle of the traffic-humming street, deceived by the look of a passing car.

The car was traveling at twenty miles an hour. But, in less than a block, Lad caught up with it. And this, in spite of the many things he had to dodge, and the greasy slipperiness of the unfamiliar roadway. An upward glance, as he came alongside the car, told him his chase was in vain. And he made his precarious way to the sidewalk once more.

There he stood, bewildered, heartsick—lost!

Yes, he was lost. And he realized it—realized it as fully as would a city-dweller snatched up by magic and set down amid the trackless Himalayas. He was lost. And Horror bit deep into his soul.

The average dog might have continued to waste energy and risk life by galloping aimlessly back and forth, running hopefully up to every stranger he met; then slinking off in scared disappointment and searching afresh.

Lad was too wise for that. He was lost. His adored Mistress had somehow left him; as had the Master; in this bedlam place—all alone. He stood there, hopeless, head and tail adroop, his great heart dead within him.

Presently he became aware once more that he was still wearing his abominable muzzle. In the stress of the past few minutes Lad had actually forgotten the pain and vexation of the thing. Now, the memory of it came back, to add to his despair.

And, as a sick animal will ever creep to the woods and the waste places for solitude, so the soul-sick Lad now turned from the clangor and evil odors of the street to seek the stretch of country-land he had scented.

Over the gray wall he sprang, and came earthward with a crash among the leafless shrubs that edged the south boundary of Central Park.

Here in the Park there were people and lights and motor-cars, too, but they were few, and they were far off. Around the dog was a grateful darkness and aloneness. He lay down on the dead grass and panted.

The time was late February. The weather of the past day or two had been mild. The brown-gray earth and the black trees had a faint odor of slow-coming spring, though no nostrils less acute than a dog's could have noted it.

Through the misery at his heart and the carking pain from his muzzle, Lad began to realize that he was tired, also that he was hollow from lack of food. The long day's ordeal of the dog show had wearied him and had worn down his nerves more than could a fifty-mile run. The nasty thrills of the past half-hour had completed his fatigue. He had eaten nothing all day. Like most high-strung dogs at a show, he had drunk a great deal of water and had refused to touch a morsel of food.

He was not hungry even now for, in a dog, hunger goes only with peace of mind, but he was cruelly thirsty. He got up from his slushy couch on the dead turf and trotted wearily toward the nearest branch of the Central Park lake. At the brink he stooped to drink.

Soggy ice still covered the lake, but the mild weather had left a half-inch skim of water over it. Lad tried to lap up enough of this water to allay his craving thirst. He could not.

The muzzle protruded nearly an inch beyond his nose. Either through faulty adjustment or from his own futile efforts to scrape it off, the awkward steel hinge had become jammed and would not open. Lad could not get his teeth a half-inch apart.

After much effort he managed to protrude the end of his pink tongue and to touch the water with it, but it was a painful and drearily slow process absorbing water drop by drop in this way. More through fatigue than because his thirst was slaked, he stopped at last and turned away from the lake.

The next half-hour was spent in a diligent and torturing and wholly useless attempt to rid himself of his muzzle.

After which the dog lay panting and athirst once more; his tender nose sore and bruised and bleeding; the muzzle as firmly fixed in place as ever. Another journey to the lake and another Tantalus-effort to drink—and the pitifully harassed dog's uncanny brain began to work.

He no longer let himself heed the muzzle. Experience of the most painful sort had told him

he could not dislodge it nor, in that clamorous and ill-smelling city beyond the park wall, could he hope to find the Mistress and the Master. These things being certain, his mind went on to the next step, and the next step was—Home!

Home! The Place where his happy, beautiful life had been spent, where his two gods abode, where there were no clang and reek and peril as here in New York. Home!—The House of Peace!

Lad stood up. He drew in great breaths of the muggy air, and he turned slowly about two or three times, head up, nostrils aquiver. For a full minute he stood thus. Then he lowered his head and trotted westward. No longer he moved uncertainly, but with as much sureness as if he were traversing the forest behind The Place—the forest that had been his roaming-ground since puppyhood.

(Now, this is not a fairy story, nor any other type of fanciful yarn, so I do not pretend to account for Lad's heading unswervingly toward the northwest in the exact direction of The Place, thirty miles distant, any more than I can account for the authenticated case of a collie who, in 1917, made his way four hundred miles from the home of a new owner in southern Georgia to the doorstep of his former and better loved master in the mountains of North Carolina; any more than I can account for the flight of a homing pigeon or for that of the northbound duck in Spring. God gives to certain animals a whole set of mystic traits which He withholds utterly from humans. No dog-student can doubt that, and no dog-student or deep-delving psychologist can explain it.)

Northwestward jogged Lad, and in half a mile he came to the low western wall of Central Park. Without turning aside to seek a gateway, he cleared the wall and found himself on Eighth Avenue in the very middle of a block.

Keeping on the sidewalk and paying no heed to the few pedestrians, he moved along to the next westward street and turned down it toward the Hudson River. So calmly and certainly did he move that none would have taken him for a lost dog.

Under the roaring elevated road at Columbus Avenue, he trotted; his ears tormented by the racket of a train that reverberated above him; his sense so blurred by the sound that he all but forgot to dodge a southbound trolley car.

Down the cross street to Amsterdam Avenue he bore. A patrolman on his way to the West Sixty-ninth Street police station to report for night duty, was so taken up by his own lofty thoughts that he quite forgot to glance at the big mud-spattered dog that padded past him.

For this lack of observation the patrolman was destined to lose a good opportunity for fattening his monthly pay. Because, on reaching the station, he learned that a distressed man and woman had just been there in a car to offer a fifty-dollar reward for the finding of a big mahogany-and-white collie, answering to the name of "Lad."

As the dog reached Amsterdam Avenue a high little voice squealed delightedly at him. A three-year-old baby—a mere fluff of gold and white and pink—was crossing the avenue convoyed by a fat woman in black. Lad was jogging by the mother and child when the latter discovered the passing dog.

With a shriek of joyous friendliness the baby flung herself upon Lad and wrapped both arms about his shaggy neck.

"Why *doggie!*" she shrilled, ecstatically. "Why, dear, *dear* doggie!"

Now Lad was in dire haste to get home, and Lad was in dire misery of mind and body, but his big heart went out in eagerly loving answer to the impulsive caress. He worshipped children, and would cheerfully endure from them any amount of mauling.

At the baby embrace and the baby voice, he stopped short in his progress. His plumy tail wagged in glad friendliness; his muzzled nose sought wistfully to kiss the pink little face on a level with his own. The baby tightened her hug, and laid her rose leaf cheek close to his own.

"I love you, Miss Doggie!" she whispered in Lad's ear.

Then the fat woman in black bore down upon them. Fiercely, she yanked the baby away from the dog. Then, seeing that the mud on Lad's shoulder had soiled the child's white coat, she whirled a string-fastened bundle aloft and brought it down with a resounding thwack over the dog's head.

Lad winched under the heavy blow, then hot resentment blazed through his first instant of grieved astonishment. This unpleasant fat creature in black was not a man, wherefore Lad contented himself by baring his white teeth, and with growling deep menace far down in his throat.

The woman shrank back scared, and she screamed loudly. On the instant the station-bound patrolman was beside her.

"What's wrong, ma'am?" asked the bluecoat.

The woman pointed a wobbly and fat forefinger at Lad, who had taken up his westward journey again and was halfway across the street.

"Mad dog!" she sputtered, hysterically. "He—he bit me! Bit *at* me, anyhow!"

Without waiting to hear the last qualifying sentence, the patrolman gave chase. Here was a chance for honorable blotter-mention at the very least. As he ran he drew his pistol.

Lad had reached the westward pavement of Amsterdam Avenue and was in the side street beyond. He was not hurrying, but his short wolf-trot ate up ground in deceptively quick time.

By the time the policeman had reached the west corner of street and avenue the dog was nearly a half-block ahead. The officer, still running, leveled his pistol and fired.

Now, anyone (but a very newly-appointed patrolman or a movie-hero) knows that to fire a shot when running is worse than fatal to any chance of accuracy. No marksman—no one who has the remotest knowledge of marksmanship—will do such a thing. The very best pistol-expert cannot hope to hit his target if he is joggling his own arm and his whole body by the motion of running.

The bullet flew high and to the right, smashing a second-story window and making the echoes resound deafeningly through the narrow street.

"What's up?" excitedly asked a boy, who stood beside a barrel bonfire with a group of chums.

"Mad dog!" puffed the policeman as he sped past.

At once the boys joined gleesomely in the chase, outdistancing the officer, just as the latter fired a second shot.

Lad felt a white-hot ridge of pain cut along his left flank like a whip-lash. He wheeled to face his invisible foe, and he found himself looking at a half-dozen boys who charged whoopingly down on him. Behind the boys clumped a man in blue flourishing something bright.

Lad had no taste for this sort of attention. Always he had loathed strangers, and these new strangers seemed bent on catching him—on barring his homeward way.

He wheeled around again and continued his westward journey at a faster pace. The hue-and-cry broke into louder yells and three or four new recruits joined the pursuers. The yap of "Mad dog! *Mad dog!*" filled the air.

Not one of these people—not even the policeman himself—had any evidence that the collie was mad. There are not two really rabid dogs seen at large in New York or in any other city in the course of a year. Yet, at the back of the human throat ever lurks that fool-cry of "Mad dog!"—ever ready to leap forth into shouted words at the faintest provocation.

One wonders, disgustedly, how many thousand luckless and totally harmless pet dogs in the course of a year are thus hunted down and shot or kicked or stoned to death in the sacred name of Humanity, just because some idiot mistakes a hanging tongue or an uncertainty of direction for signs of that semi-phantom malady known as "rabies."

A dog is lost. He wanders to and fro in bewilderment. Boys pelt or chase him. His tongue lolls and his eyes glaze with fear. Then, ever, rises the yell of "Mad Dog!" And a friendly, lovable pet is joyfully done to death.

Lad crossed Broadway, threading his way through the trolley-and-taxi procession, and galloped down the hill toward Riverside Park. Close always at his heels followed the shouting crowd. Twice, by sprinting, the patrolman gained the front rank of the hunt, and twice he fired—both bullets going wide. Across West End Avenue and across Riverside Drive went Lad, hard-pressed and fleeing at top speed. The cross-street ran directly down to a pier that jutted a hundred feet out into the Hudson River.

Along this pier flew Lad, not in panic terror, but none the less resolved that these howling New Yorkers should not catch him and prevent his going home.

Onto the pier the clattering hue-and-cry followed. A dock watchman, as Lad flashed by, hurled a heavy joist of wood at the dog. It whizzed past the flying hind legs, scoring the barest of misses.

And now Lad was at the pier end. Behind him the crowd raced; sure it had the dangerous brute cornered at last.

On the stringpiece the collie paused for the briefest of moments glancing to north and to south. Everywhere the wide river stretched away, unbridged. It must be crossed if he would continue his homeward course, and there was but one way for him to cross it.

The watchman, hard at his heels, swung upward the club he carried. Down came the club with murderous force—upon the stringpiece where Lad had been standing.

Lad was no longer there. One great bound had carried him over the edge and into the black water below.

Down he plunged into the river and far, far under it, fighting his way gaspingly to the surface. The water that gushed into his mouth and nostrils was salty and foul, not at all like the water of the lake at the edge of The Place. It sickened him. And the February chill of the river cut into him like a million ice-needles.

To the surface he came, and struck out valorously for the opposite shore much more than a mile away. As his beautiful head appeared, a yell went up from the clustering riff-raff at the pier end. Bits of wood and coal began to shower the water all around him. A pistol shot plopped into the river a bare six inches away from him.

But the light was bad and the stream was a tossing mass of blackness and of light-blurs, and presently the dog swam, unscathed, beyond the range of missiles.

Now a swim of a mile or of two miles was no special exploit for Lad—even in ice-cold water, but this water was not like any he had swum in. The tide was at the turn for one thing, and while, in a way, this helped him, yet the myriad eddies and cross-currents engendered by it turned and jostled and buffeted him in a most perplexing way. And there were spars and barrels and other obstacles that were forever looming up just in front of him or else banging against his heaving sides.

Once a revenue cutter passed not thirty feet ahead of him. Its wake caught the dog and sucked him under and spun his body around and around before he could fight clear of it.

His lungs were bursting. He was worn out. He felt as sore as if he had been kicked for an hour. The bullet-graze along his flank was hurting him as the salt water bit into it, and the muzzle half-blinded, half-smothered him.

But, because of his hero heart rather than through his splendid strength and wisdom, he kept on.

For an hour or more he swam until at last his body and brain were numb, and only the mechanical action of his wrenched muscles held him in motion. Twice tugs narrowly escaped running him down, and in the wake of each he waged a fearful fight for life.

After a century of effort his groping forepaws felt the impact of a submerged rock, then of another, and with his last vestige of strength Lad crawled feebly ashore on a narrow sandspit at the base of the elephant-gray Palisades. There, he collapsed and lay shivering, panting, struggling for breath.

Long he lay there, letting Nature bring back some of his wind and his motive-power, his shaggy body one huge pulsing ache.

When he was able to move, he took up his journey. Sometimes swimming, sometimes on ground, he skirted the Palisades-foot to northward, until he found one of the several precipice-paths that Sunday picnickers love to climb. Up this he made his tottering way, slowly; conserving his strength as best he could.

On the summit he lay down again to rest. Behind him, across the stretch of black and lamp-flecked water, rose the inky skyline of the city with a lurid furnace-glow between its crevices that smote the sky. Ahead was a plateau with a downward slope beyond it.

Once more, getting to his feet, Lad stood and sniffed, turning his head from side to side, muzzled nose aloft. Then, his bearings taken, he set off again, but this time his jog-trot was slower and his light step was growing heavier. The terrible strain of his swim was passing from his mighty sinews, but it was passing slowly because he was so tired and empty and in such pain of body and mind. He saved his energies until he should have more of them to save.

Across the plateau, down the slope, and then across the interminable salt meadows to westward he traveled; sometimes on road or path, sometimes across field or hill, but always in an unswerving straight line.

It was a little before midnight that he breasted the first rise of Jersey hills above Hackensack. Through a lightless one-street village he went, head low, stride lumbering, the muzzle weighing a ton and composed of molten iron and hornet stings.

It was the muzzle—now his first fatigue had slackened—that galled him worst. Its torture was beginning to do queer things to his nerves and brain. Even a stolid, nerveless dog hates a muzzle. More than one sensitive dog has been driven crazy by it.

Thirst—intolerable thirst—was torturing Lad. He could not drink at the pools and brooks he crossed. So tight-jammed was the steel jaw-hinge now that he could not even open his mouth to pant, which is the cruelest deprivation a dog can suffer.

Out of the shadows of a ramshackle hovel's front yard dived a monstrous shape that hurled itself ferociously on the passing collie.

A mongrel watchdog—part mastiff, part hound, part anything you choose—had been dozing on his squatter-owner's doorstep when the pad-pad-pad of Lad's wearily-jogging feet had sounded on the road.

Other dogs, more than one of them, during the journey had run out to yap or growl at the wanderer, but as Lad had been big and had followed an unhesitant course they had not gone to the length of actual attack.

This mongrel, however, was less prudent. Or, perhaps, dog-fashion, he realized that the muzzle rendered Lad powerless and therefore saw every prospect of a safe and easy victory. At all events, he gave no warning bark or growl as he shot forward to the attack.

Lad—his eyes dim with fatigue and road dust, his ears dulled by water and by noise—did not hear nor see the foe. His first notice of the attack was a flying weight of seventy-odd pounds that crashed against his flank. A double set of fangs in the same instant, sank into his shoulder.

Under the onslaught Lad fell sprawlingly

into the road on his left side, his enemy upon him.

As Lad went down the mongrel deftly shifted his unprofitable shoulder grip to a far more promisingly murderous hold on his fallen victim's throat.

A cat has five sets of deadly weapons—its four feet and its jaws. So has every animal on earth—human and otherwise—except a dog. A dog is terrible by reason of its teeth. Encase the mouth in a muzzle and a dog is as helpless for offensive warfare as is a newborn baby.

And Lad was thus pitiably impotent to return his foe's attack. Exhausted, flung prone to earth, his mighty jaws muzzled, he seemed as good as dead.

But a collie down is not a collie beaten. The wolf-strain provides against that. Even as he fell Lad instinctively gathered his legs under him as he had done when he tumbled from the car.

And, almost at once, he was on his feet again, snarling horribly and lunging to break the mongrel's throat-grip. His weariness was forgotten and his wondrous reserve strength leaped into play. Which was all the good it did him; for he knew as well as the mongrel that he was powerless to use his teeth.

The throat of a collie—except in one small vulnerable spot—is armored by a veritable mattress of hair. Into this hair the mongrel had driven his teeth. The hair filled his mouth, but his grinding jaws encountered little else to close on.

A lurching jerk of Lad's strong frame tore loose the savagely inefficient hold. The mongrel sprang at him for a fresh grip. Lad reared to meet him, opposing his mighty chest to the charge and snapping powerlessly with his close-locked mouth.

The force of Lad's rearing leap sent the mongrel spinning back by sheer weight, but at once he drove in again to the assault. This time he did not give his muzzled antagonist a chance to rear, but sprang at Lad's flank. Lad wheeled to meet the rush and, opposing his shoulder to it, broke its force.

Seeing himself so helpless, this was of course the time for Lad to take to his heels and try to outrun the enemy he could not outfight.

To stand his ground was to be torn, eventually, to death. Being anything but a fool Lad knew that; yet he ignored the chance of safety and continued to fight the worse-than-hopeless battle.

Twice and thrice his wit and uncanny swiftness enabled him to block the big mongrel's rushes. The fourth time, as he sought to rear, his hind foot slipped on a skim of puddle-ice.

Down went Lad in a heap, and the mongrel struck.

Before the collie could regain his feet the mongrel's teeth had found a hold on the side of Lad's throat. Pinning down the muzzled dog, the mongrel proceeded to improve his hold by grinding his way toward the jugular. Now his teeth encountered something more solid than mere hair. They met upon a thin leather strap.

Fiercely the mongrel gnawed at this solid obstacle, his rage-hot brain possibly mistaking it for flesh. Lad writhed to free himself and to regain his feet, but seventy-five pounds of fighting weight were holding his neck to the ground.

Of a sudden, the mongrel growled in savage triumph. The strap was bitten through!

Clinging to the broken end of the leather the victor gave one final tug. The pull drove the steel bars excruciatingly deep into Lad's bruised nose for a moment. Then, by magic, the torture-implement was no longer on his head but was dangling by one strap between the muzzled mongrel's jaws.

With a motion so swift that the eye could not follow it, Lad was on his feet and plunging deliriously into the fray. Through a miracle, his jaws were free; his torment was over. The joy of deliverance sent a glow of Berserk vigor sweeping through him.

The mongrel dropped the muzzle and came eagerly to the battle. To his dismay he found himself fighting not a helpless dog, but a maniac wolf. Lad sought no permanent hold. With dizzying quickness his head and body moved—and kept moving, and every motion meant a deep slash or a ragged tear in his enemy's short-coated hide.

With ridiculous ease the collie eluded the mongrel's awkward counter-attacks, and ever kept boring in. To the quivering bone his short front teeth sank. Deep and bloodily his curved tusks slashed—as the wolf and the collie alone can slash.

The mongrel, swept off his feet, rolled howling into the road; and Lad tore grimly at the exposed under-body.

Up went a window in the hovel. A man's voice shouted. A woman in a house across the way screamed. Lad glanced up to note this new diversion. The stricken mongrel yelping in terror and agony seized the second respite to scamper back to the doorstep, howling at every jump.

Lad did not pursue him, but jogged along on his journey without one backward look.

At a rivulet, a mile beyond, he stopped to drink. And he drank for ten minutes. Then he went on. Unmuzzled and with his thirst slaked, he forgot his pain, his fatigue, his muddy and blood-caked and abraded coat, and the memory of his nightmare day.

He was going home!

At gray dawn the Mistress and the Master turned in at the gateway of The Place. All night they had sought Lad; from one end of Manhattan Island to the other—from Police Headquarters to dog pound—they had driven. And now the Master was bringing his tired and heartsore wife home to rest, while he himself should return to town and to the search.

The car chugged dispiritedly down the driveway to the house, but before it had traversed half the distance the dawn-hush was shattered by a thundrous bark of challenge to the invaders.

Lad, from his post of guard on the veranda, ran stiffly forward to bar the way. Then as he ran his eyes and nose suddenly told him these mysterious newcomers were his gods.

The Mistress, with a gasp of rapturous unbelief, was jumping down from the car before it came to a halt. On her knees, she caught Lad's muddy and bloody head tight in her arms.

"Oh, Lad," she sobbed incoherently. "Laddie! *Laddie!*"

Whereat, by another miracle, Lad's stiffness and hurts and weariness were gone. He strove to lick the dear face bending so tearfully above him. Then, with an abandon of puppylike joy, he rolled on the ground waving all four soiled little feet in the air and playfully pretending to snap at the loving hands that caressed him.

Which was ridiculous conduct for a stately and full-grown collie. But Lad didn't care, because it made the Mistress stop crying and laugh. And that was what Lad most wanted her to do.

For the Love of a Man
(from The Call of the Wild)

Jack London

When John Thornton froze his feet in the previous December, his partners had made him comfortable and left him to get well, going on themselves up the river to get out a raft of saw-logs for Dawson. He was still limping slightly at the time he rescued Buck, but with the continued warm weather even the slight limp left him. And here, lying by the river bank through the long spring days, watching the running water, listening lazily to the songs of birds and the hum of nature, Buck slowly won back his strength.

A rest comes very good after one has traveled three thousand miles, and it must be confessed that Buck waxed lazy as his wounds healed, his muscles swelled out, and the flesh came back to cover his bones. For that matter, they were all loafing,—Buck, John Thornton, and Skeet and Nig—waiting for the raft to come that was to carry them down to Dawson. Skeet was a little Irish setter who early made friends with Buck, who, in a dying condition, was unable to resent her first advances. She had the doctor trait which some dogs possess; and as a mother cat washes her kittens, so she washed and cleansed Buck's wounds. Regularly, each morning after he had finished his breakfast, she performed her self-appointed task, till he came to look for her ministrations as much as he did for Thornton's. Nig, equally friendly though less demonstrative, was a huge black dog, half-bloodhound and half-deerhound, with eyes that laughed and a boundless good nature.

To Buck's surprise these dogs manifested no jealousy toward him. They seemed to share the kindliness and largeness of John Thornton. As Buck grew stronger they enticed him into all sorts of ridiculous games, in which Thornton himself could not forbear to join; and in this fashion Buck romped through his convalescence and into a new existence. Love, genuine passionate love, was his for the first time. This he had never experienced at Judge Miller's down in the sun-kissed Santa Clara Valley. With the Judge's sons, hunting and tramping, it had been a working partnership; with the Judge's grandsons, a sort of pompous guardianship; and with the Judge himself, a stately and dignified friendship. But love that was feverish and burning, that was adoration, that was madness, it had taken John Thornton to arouse.

This man had saved his life, which was something; but, further, he was the ideal master. Other men saw to the welfare of their dogs from a sense of duty and business expediency; he saw to the welfare of his as if they were his own children, because he could not help it. And he saw further. He never forgot a kindly greeting or a cheering word, and to sit down for a long talk with them ("gas" he called it) was as much his delight as theirs. He had a way of taking Buck's head roughly between his hands, and resting his own head upon Buck's, of shaking him back and forth, the while calling him ill names that to Buck were love names. Buck knew no greater joy than that rough embrace and the sound of murmured oaths, and at each jerk back and forth it seemed that his heart would be shaken out of his body, so great was its ecstasy. And when, released, he sprang to his feet, his mouth laughing, his eyes eloquent, his throat vibrant with unuttered sound, and in that fashion remained without movement, John Thornton would reve-

rently exclaim, "God! you can all but speak!"

Buck had a trick of love expression that was akin to hurt. He would often seize Thornton's hand in his mouth and close so fiercely that the flesh bore the impress of his teeth for some time afterward. And as Buck understood the oaths to be love words, so the man understood this feigned bite for a caress.

For the most part, however, Buck's love was expressed in adoration. While he went wild with happiness when Thornton touched him or spoke to him, he did not seek these tokens. Unlike Skeet, who was wont to shove her nose under Thornton's hand and nudge and nudge till petted, or Nig, who would stalk up and rest his great head on Thornton's knee, Buck was content to adore at a distance. He would lie by the hour, eager, alert, at Thornton's feet, looking up into his face, dwelling upon it, studying it, following with keenest interest each fleeting expression, every movement or change of feature. Or, as chance might have it, he would lie farther away, to the side or rear, watching the outlines of the man and the occasional movements of his body. And often, such was the communion in which they lived, the strength of Buck's gaze would draw John Thornton's head around, and he would return the gaze, without speech, his heart shining out of his eyes as Buck's heart shone out.

For a long time after his rescue, Buck did not like Thornton to get out of his sight. From the moment he left the tent to when he entered it again, Buck would follow at his heels. His transient masters since he had come into the Northland had bred in him a fear that no master could be permanent. He was afraid that Thornton would pass out of his life as Perrault and François and the Scotch half-breed had passed out. Even in the night, in his dreams, he was haunted by this fear. At such times he would shake off sleep and creep through the chill to the flap of the tent, where he would stand and listen to the sound of his master's breathing.

But in spite of this great love he bore John Thornton, which seemed to bespeak the soft civilizing influence, the strain of the primitive, which the Northland had aroused in him, remained alive and active. Faithfulness and devotion, things born of fire and roof, were his;

yet he retained his wildness and wiliness. He was a thing of the wild, come in from the wild to sit by John Thornton's fire, rather than a dog of the soft Southland stamped with the marks of generations of civilization. Because of his very great love, he could not steal from this man, but from any other man, in any other camp, he did not hesitate an instant; while the cunning with which he stole enabled him to escape detection.

His face and body were scored by the teeth of many dogs, and he fought as fiercely as ever and more shrewdly. Skeet and Nig were too good-natured for quarreling—besides, they belonged to John Thornton; but the strange dog, no matter what the breed or valor, swiftly acknowledged Buck's supremacy or found himself struggling for life with a terrible antagonist. And Buck was merciless. He had learned well the law of club and fang, and he never forewent an advantage or drew back from a foe he had started on the way to death. He had lessoned from Spitz, and from the chief fighting dogs of the police and mail, and knew there was no middle course. He must master or be mastered; while to show mercy was a weakness. Mercy did not exist in the primordial life. It was misunderstood for fear, and such misunderstandings made for death. Kill or be killed, eat or be eaten, was the law; and this mandate, down out of the depths of Time, he obeyed.

He was older than the days he had seen and the breaths he had drawn. He linked the past with the present, and the eternity behind him throbbed through him in a mighty rhythm to which he swayed as the tides and seasons swayed. He sat by John Thornton's fire, a broad-breasted dog, white-fanged and long-furred; but behind him were the shades of all manner of dogs, half-wolves and wild wolves, urgent and prompting, tasting the savor of the meat he ate, thirsting for the water he drank, scenting the wind with him, listening with him and telling him the sounds made by the wild life in the forest; dictating his moods, directing his actions, lying down to sleep with him when he lay down, and dreaming with him and beyond him and becoming themselves the stuff of his dreams.

So peremptorily did these shades beckon him, that each day mankind and the claims of mankind slipped farther from him. Deep in the forest a call was sounding, and as often as he heard this call, mysteriously thrilling and luring, he felt compelled to turn his back upon the fire and the beaten earth around it, and to plunge into the forest, and on and on, he knew not where or why; nor did he wonder where or why, the call sounding imperiously, deep in the forest. But as often as he gained the soft unbroken earth and the green shade, the love for John Thornton drew him back to the fire again.

Thornton alone held him. The rest of mankind was as nothing. Chance travelers might praise or pet him; but he was cold under it all, and from a too demonstrative man he would get up and walk away. When Thornton's partners, Hans and Pete, arrived on the long-expected raft, Buck refused to notice them till he learned they were close to Thornton; after that he tolerated them in a passive sort of way, accepting favors from them as though he favored them by accepting. They were of the same large type as Thornton, living close to the earth, thinking simply and seeing clearly; and ere they swung the raft into the big eddy by the saw-mill at Dawson, they understood Buck and his ways, and did not insist upon an intimacy such as obtained with Skeet and Nig.

For Thornton, however, his love seemed to grow and grow. He, alone among men, could put a pack upon Buck's back in the summer traveling. Nothing was too great for Buck to do, when Thornton commanded. One day (they had grub-staked themselves from the proceeds of the raft and left Dawson for the head-waters of the Tanana) the men and dogs were sitting on the crest of a cliff which fell away, straight down, to naked bed-rock three hundred feet below. John Thornton was sitting near the edge, Buck at his shoulder. A thoughtless whim seized Thornton, and he drew the attention of Hans and Pete to the experiment he had in mind. "Jump, Buck!" he commanded, sweeping his arm out and over the chasm. The next instant he was grappling with Buck on the extreme edge, while Hans and Pete were dragging them back into safety.

"It's uncanny," Pete said, after it was over and they had caught their speech.

Thornton shook his head. "No, it is splendid, and it is terrible, too. Do you know, it sometimes makes me afraid."

"I'm not hankering to be the man that lays hands on you while he's around," Pete announced conclusively, nodding his head toward Buck.

"Py Jingo!" was Hans's contribution. "Not mineself either."

It was at Circle City, ere the year was out, that Pete's apprehensions were realized. "Black" Burton, a man evil-tempered and malicious, had been picking a quarrel with a tenderfoot at the bar, when Thornton stepped good-naturedly between. Buck, as was his custom, was lying in a corner, head on paws, watching his master's every action. Burton struck out, without warning, straight from the shoulder. Thornton was sent spinning, and saved himself from falling only by clutching the rail of the bar.

Those who were looking on heard what was neither bark nor yelp, but a something which is best described as a roar, and they saw Buck's body rise up in the air as he left the floor for Burton's throat. The man saved his life by instinctively throwing out his arm, but was hurled backward to the floor with Buck on top of him. Buck loosed his teeth from the flesh of the arm and drove in again for the throat. This time the man succeeded only in partly blocking, and his throat was torn open. Then the crowd was upon Buck, and he was driven off; but while a surgeon checked the bleeding, he prowled up and down, growling furiously, attempting to rush in, and being forced back by an array of hostile clubs. A "miners' meeting" called on the spot, decided that the dog had sufficient provocation, and Buck was discharged. But his reputation was made, and from that day his name spread through every camp in Alaska.

Later on, in the fall of the year, he saved John Thornton's life in quite another fashion. The three partners were lining a long and narrow poling-boat down a bad stretch of rapids on the Forty Mile Creek. Hans and Pete moved along the bank, snubbing with a thin Manila rope from tree to tree, while Thornton remained in the boat, helping its descent by means of a pole, and shouting directions to the shore. Buck, on the bank, worried and anxious, kept abreast of the boat, his eyes never off his master.

At a particularly bad spot, where a ledge of barely submerged rocks jutted out into the river,

Hans cast off the rope, and, while Thornton poled the boat out into the stream, ran down the bank with the end in his hand to snub the boat when it had cleared the ledge. This it did, and was flying down-stream in a current as swift as a mill-race, when Hans checked it with the rope and checked too suddenly. The boat flirted over and snubbed in to the bank bottom up, while Thornton, flung sheer out of it, was carried down-stream toward the worst part of the rapids, a stretch of wild water in which no swimmer could live.

Buck had sprung in on the instant; and at the end of three hundred yards, amid a mad swirl of water, he overhauled Thornton. When he felt him grasp his tail, Buck headed for the bank, swimming with all his splendid strength. But the progress shoreward was slow; the progress down-stream amazingly rapid. From below came the fatal roaring where the wild current went wilder and was rent in shreds and spray by the rocks which thrust through like the teeth of an enormous comb. The suck of the water as it took the beginning of the last steep pitch was frightful, and Thornton knew that the shore was impossible. He scraped furiously over a rock, bruised across a second, and struck a third with crushing force. He clutched its slippery top with both hands, releasing Buck, and above the roar of the churning water shouted: "Go, Buck! Go!"

Buck could not hold his own, and swept on down-stream, struggling desperately, but unable to win back. When he heard Thornton's command repeated, he partly reared out of the water, throwing his head high, as though for a last look, then turned obediently toward the bank. He swam powerfully and was dragged ashore by Pete and Hans at the very point where swimming ceased to be possible and destruction began.

They knew that the time a man could cling to a slippery rock in the face of that driving current was a matter of minutes, and they ran as fast as they could up the bank to a point far above where Thornton was hanging on. They attached the line with which they had been snubbing the boat to Buck's neck and shoulders, being careful that it should neither strangle him nor impede his swimming, and launched him into the stream. He struck out boldly, but not straight enough into the stream. He discovered the mistake too late, when Thornton was abreast of him and a bare half-dozen strokes away while he was being carried helplessly past.

Hans promptly snubbed with the rope, as though Buck were a boat. The rope thus tightening on him in the sweep of the current, he was jerked under the surface, and under the surface he remained till his body struck against the bank and he was hauled out. He was half-drowned, and Hans and Pete threw themselves upon him, pounding the breath into him and the water out of him. He staggered to his feet and fell down. The faint sound of Thornton's voice came to them, and though they could not make out the words of it, they knew that he was in his extremity. His master's voice acted on Buck like an electric shock. He sprang to his feet and ran up the bank ahead of the men to the point of his previous departure.

Again the rope was attached and he was launched, and again he struck out, but this time straight into the stream. He had miscalculated once, but he would not be guilty of it a second time. Hans paid out the rope, permitting no slack, while Pete kept it clear of coils. Buck held on till he was on a line straight above Thornton; then he turned, and with the speed of an express train headed down upon him. Thornton saw him coming, and, as Buck struck him like a battering ram, with the whole force of the current behind him, he reached up and closed with both arms around the shaggy neck. Hans snubbed the rope around the tree, and Buck and Thornton were jerked under the water. Strangling, suffocating, sometimes one uppermost and sometimes the other, dragging over the jagged bottom, smashing against rocks and snags, they veered in to the bank.

Thornton came to, belly downward and being violently propelled back and forth across a drift log by Hans and Pete. His first glance was for Buck, over whose limp and apparently lifeless body Nig was setting up a howl, while Skeet was licking the wet face and closed eyes. Thornton was himself bruised and battered, and he went carefully over Buck's body, when he had been brought around, finding three broken ribs.

"That settles it," he announced. "We camp right here." And camp they did, till Buck's ribs

knitted and he was able to travel.

That winter, at Dawson, Buck performed another exploit, not so heroic, perhaps, but one that puts his name many notches higher on the totem pole of Alaskan fame. This exploit was particularly gratifying to the three men; for they stood in need of the outfit which it furnished, and were enabled to make a long-desired trip into the virgin East, where miners had not yet appeared. It was brought about by a conversation in the Eldorado Saloon, in which men waxed boastful of their favorite dogs. Buck, because of his record, was the target for these men, and Thornton was driven stoutly to defend him. At the end of half an hour one man stated that his dog could start a sled with five hundred pounds and walk off with it; a second bragged six hundred for his dog; and a third, seven hundred.

"Pooh! Pooh!" said John Thornton. "Buck can start a thousand pounds."

"And break it out, and walk off with it for a hundred yards?" demanded Matthewson, a Bonanza king, he of the seven hundred vaunt.

"And break it out, and walk off with it for a hundred yards," John Thornton said coolly.

"Well," Matthewson said, slowly and deliberately, so that all could hear, "I've got a thousand dollars that says he can't. And there it is." So saying, he slammed a sack of gold dust of the size of a bologna sausage down upon the bar.

Nobody spoke. Thornton's bluff, if bluff it was, had been called. He could feel a flush of warm blood creeping up his face. His tongue had tricked him. He did not know whether Buck could start a thousand pounds. Half a ton! The enormousness of it appalled him. He had great faith in Buck's strength and had often thought him capable of starting such a load; but never, as now, had he faced the possibility of it, the eyes of a dozen men fixed upon him, silent and waiting. Further, he had no thousand dollars; nor had Hans or Pete.

"I've got a sled standing outside now, with twenty fifty-pound sacks of flour on it," Matthewson went on with brutal directness; "so don't let that hinder you."

Thornton did not reply. He did not know what to say. He glanced from face to face in the absent way of a man who has lost the power of thought and is seeking somewhere to find the thing that will start it going again. The face of Jim O'Brien, a Mastodon king and old-time comrade, caught his eyes. It was as a cue to him, seeming to rouse him to do what he would never have dreamed of doing.

"Can you lend me a thousand?" he asked, almost in a whisper.

"Sure," answered O'Brien, thumping down a plethoric sack by the side of Matthewson's. "Though it's little faith I'm having, John, that the beast can do the trick."

The Eldorado emptied its occupants into the street to see the test. The tables were deserted, and the dealers and gamekeepers came forth to see the outcome of the wager and to lay odds. Several hundred men, furred and mittened, banked around the sled within easy distance. Matthewson's sled, loaded with a thousand pounds of flour, had been standing for a couple of hours, and in the intense cold (it was sixty below zero) the runners had frozen fast to the hard-packed snow. Men offered odds of two to one that Buck could not budge the sled. A quibble arose concerning the phrase "break out." O'Brien contended it was Thornton's privilege to knock the runners loose, leaving Buck to "break it out" from a dead standstill. Matthewson insisted that the phrase included breaking the runners from the frozen grip of the snow. A majority of the men who had witnessed the making of the bet decided in his favor, whereat the odds went up to three to one against Buck.

There were no takers. Not a man believed him capable of the feat. Thornton had been hurried into the wager, heavy with doubt; and now that he looked at the sled itself, the concrete fact, with the regular team of ten dogs curled up in the snow before it, the more impossible the task appeared. Matthewson waxed jubilant.

"Three to one!" he proclaimed. "I'll lay you another thousand at that figure, Thornton. What d'ye say?"

Thornton's doubt was strong in his face, but his fighting spirit was aroused—the fighting spirit that soars above odds, fails to recognize the impossible, and is deaf to all save the clamor for battle. He called Hans and Pete to him. Their sacks were slim, and with his own the three partners could rake together only two hundred

dollars. In the ebb of their fortunes, this sum was their total capital; yet they laid it unhesitatingly against Matthewson's six hundred.

The team of ten dogs was unhitched, and Buck, with his own harness, was put into the sled. He had caught the contagion of the excitement, and he felt that in some way he must do a great thing for John Thornton. Murmurs of admiration at his splendid appearance went up. He was in perfect condition, without an ounce of superfluous flesh, and the one hundred and fifty pounds that he weighed were so many pounds of grit and virility. His furry coat shone with the sheen of silk. Down the neck and across the shoulders, his mane, in repose as it was, half bristled and seemed to lift with every movement, as though excess of vigor made each particular hair alive and active. The great breast and heavy fore legs were no more than in proportion with the rest of the body, where the muscles showed in tight rolls underneath the skin. Men felt these muscles and proclaimed them hard as iron, and the odds went down to two to one.

"Gad, sir! Gad, sir!" stuttered a member of the latest dynasty, a king of the Skookum Benches. "I offer you eight hundred for him, sir, before the test, sir; eight hundred just as he stands."

Thornton shook his head and stepped over to Buck's side.

"You must stand off from him," Matthewson protested. "Free play and plenty of room."

The crowd fell silent; only could be heard the voices of the gamblers vainly offering two to one. Everybody acknowledged Buck a magnificent animal, but twenty fifty-pound sacks of flour bulked too large in their eyes for them to loosen their pouch-strings.

Thornton knelt down by Buck's side. He took his head in his two hands and rested cheek on cheek. He did not playfully shake him, as was his wont, or murmur soft love curses; but he whispered in his ear, "As you love me, Buck. As you love me," was what he whispered. Buck whined with suppressed eagerness.

The crowd was watching curiously. The affair was growing mysterious. It seemed like a conjuration. As Thornton got to his feet, Buck seized his mittened hand between his jaws, pressing in with his teeth and releasing slowly, half-reluctantly. It was the answer, in terms, not of speech, but of love. Thornton stepped well back.

"Now, Buck," he said.

Buck tightened the traces, then slacked them for a matter of several inches. It was the way he had learned.

"Gee!" Thornton's voice rang out, sharp in the tense silence.

Buck swung to the right, ending the movement in a plunge that took up the slack and with a sudden jerk arrested his one hundred and fifty pounds. The load quivered, and from under the runners arose a crisp crackling.

"Haw!" Thornton commanded.

Buck duplicated the maneuver, this time to the left. The crackling turned into a snapping, the sled pivoting and the runners slipping and grating several inches to the side. The sled was broken out. Men were holding their breaths, intensely unconscious of the fact.

"Now, MUSH!"

Thornton's command cracked out like a pistol-shot. Buck threw himself forward, tightening the traces with a jarring lunge. His whole body was gathered compactly together in the tremendous effort, the muscles writhing and knotting like live things under the silky fur. His great chest was low to the ground, his head forward and down, while his feet were flying like mad, the claws scarring the hard-packed snow in parallel grooves. The sled swayed and trembled, half-started forward. One of his feet slipped, and one man groaned aloud. Then the sled lurched ahead in what appeared a rapid succession of jerks, though it never really came to a dead stop again . . . half an inch . . . an inch . . . two inches. . . . The jerks perceptibly diminished; as the sled gained momentum, he caught them up, till it was moving steadily along.

Men gasped and began to breathe again, unaware that for a moment they had ceased to breathe. Thornton was running behind, encouraging Buck with short, cheery words. The distance had been measured off, and as he neared the pile of firewood which marked the end of the hundred yards, a cheer began to grow and grow, which burst into a roar as he passed the firewood and halted at command. Every man was tearing himself loose, even Matthewson. Hats and mittens were flying in the air. Men were shaking hands, it did not matter with whom, and bubbling over in a general incoherent babel.

But Thornton fell on his knees beside Buck. Head was against head, and he was shaking him back and forth. Those who hurried up heard him cursing Buck, and he cursed him long and fervently, and softly and lovingly.

"Gad, sir! Gad, sir!" spluttered the Skookum Bench king. "I'll give you a thousand for him, sir, a thousand, sir—twelve hundred, sir."

Thornton rose to his feet. His eyes were wet. The tears were streaming frankly down his cheeks. "Sir," he said to the Skookum Bench king, "no, sir. You can go to hell, sir. It's the best I can do for you, sir."

Buck seized Thornton's hand in his teeth. Thornton shook him back and forth. As though animated by a common impulse, the onlookers drew back to a respectful distance; nor were they again indiscreet enough to interrupt.

The Last Will And Testament of Silverdene Emblem O'Neill

Eugene O'Neill

I, Silverdene Emblem O'Neill (familiarly known to my family, friends and acquaintances as Blemie), because the burden of my years and infirmities is heavy upon me, and I realize the end of my life is near, do hereby bury my last will and testament in the mind of my Master. He will not know it is there until after I am dead. Then, remembering me in his loneliness, he will suddenly know of this testament, and I ask him then to inscribe it as a memorial to me.

I have little in the way of material things to leave. Dogs are wiser than men. They do not set great store upon things. They do not waste their days hoarding property. They do not ruin their sleep worrying about how to keep the objects they have, and to obtain the objects they have not. There is nothing of value I have to bequeath except my love and my faith. These I leave to all those who have loved me, to my Master and Mistress, who I know will mourn me most, to Freeman who has been so good to me, to Cyn and Roy and Willie and Naomi and—But if I should list all those who have loved me it would force my Master to write a book. Perhaps it is vain of me to boast when I am so near death, which returns all beasts and vanities to dust, but I have always been an extremely lovable dog.

I ask my Master and Mistress to remember me always, but not to grieve for me too long. In my life I have tried to be a comfort to them in time of sorrow, and a reason for added joy in their happiness. It is painful for me to think that even in death I should cause them pain. Let them remember that while no dog has ever had a happier life (and this I owe to their love and care for me), now that I have grown blind and deaf and lame, and even my sense of smell fails me so that a rabbit could be right under my nose and I might not know, my pride has sunk to a sick, bewildered humiliation. I feel life is taunting me with having over-lingered my welcome. It is time I said goodbye, before I become too sick a burden on myself and on those who love me. It will be sorrow to leave them, but not a sorrow to die. Dogs do not fear death as men do. We accept it as part of life, not as something alien and terrible which destroys life. What may come after death, who knows? I would like to believe with those of my fellow Dalmatians who are devout Mohammedans, that there is a Paradise where one is always young and full-bladdered; where all the day one dillies and dallies with an amorous multitude of houris, beautifully spotted; where jack rabbits that run fast but not too fast (like the houris) are as the sands of the desert; where each blissful hour is mealtime; where in long evenings there are a million fireplaces with logs forever burning, and one curls oneself up and blinks into the flames and nods and dreams, remembering the old brave days on earth, and the love of one's Master and Mistress.

I am afraid this is too much for even such a dog as I am to expect. But peace, at least, is certain. Peace and long rest for weary old heart and head and limbs, and eternal sleep in the earth I have loved so well. Perhaps, after all, this is best.

One last request I earnestly make. I have heard my Mistress say, "When Blemie dies we must never have another dog. I love him so much I could never love another one." Now I would ask her, for love of me, to have another. It would be a poor tribute to my memory never to have a dog again. What I would like to feel is that, having once had me in the family, now she cannot live without a dog! I have never had a narrow jealous spirit. I have always held that most dogs are good (and one cat, the black one I have permitted to share the living room rug during the evenings, whose affection I have tolerated in a kindly spirit, and in rare sentimental moods, even reciprocated a trifle). Some dogs, of course, are better than others. Dalmatians, naturally, as everyone knows, are best. So

I suggest a Dalmatian as my successor. He can hardly be as well bred or as well mannered or as distinguished and handsome as I was in my prime. My Master and Mistress must not ask the impossible. But he will do his best, I am sure, and even his inevitable defects will help by comparison to keep my memory green. To him I bequeath my collar and leash and my overcoat and raincoat, made to order in 1929 at Hermes in Paris. He can never wear them with the distinction I did, walking around the Place Vendôme, or later along Park Avenue, all eyes fixed on me in admiration; but again I am sure he will do his utmost not to appear a mere gauche provincial dog. Here on the ranch, he may prove himself quite worthy of comparison, in some respects. He will, I presume, come closer to jack rabbits than I have been able to in recent years. And, for all his faults, I hereby wish him the happiness I know will be his in my old home.

One last word of farewell, Dear Master and Mistress. Whenever you visit my grave, say to yourselves with regret but also with happiness in your hearts at the remembrance of my long happy life with you: "Here lies one who loved us and whom we loved." No matter how deep my sleep I shall hear you, and not all the power of death can keep my spirit from wagging a grateful tail.

Every Dog Should Own A Man

Corey Ford

Every dog should have a man of his own. There is nothing like a well-behaved person around the house to spread the dog's blanket for him, or bring him his supper when he comes home man-tired at night.

For example, I happen to belong to an English setter who acquired me when he was about six months old and has been training me quite successfully ever since. He has taught me to shake hands with him and fetch his ball. I've learned not to tug at the leash when he takes me for a walk. I am completely housebroken, and I make him a devoted companion.

The first problem a dog faces is to pick out the right man—a gay and affectionate disposition is more important than an expensive pedigree. I do not happen to be registered but my setter is just as fond of me as though I came from a long line of blue bloods. Also, since a dog is judged by the man he leads, it is a good idea to walk the man up and down a couple of times to make sure his action is free and he has springy hindquarters.

The next question is whether the dog and man should share the house together. Some dogs prefer a kennel because it is more sanitary, but my setter decided at the start that he'd move right in the house with me. I can get into any of the chairs I want except the big overstuffed chair in the living room, which is his.

Training a man takes time. Some men are a little slow to respond, but a dog who makes allowances and tries to put himself in the man's place will be rewarded with a loyal pal. Men are apt to be highstrung and sensitive, and a dog who loses his temper will only break the man's spirit.

Punishment should be meted out sparingly—more can be accomplished by a reproachful look than by flying off the handle. My setter has never raised a paw to me, but he has cured me almost entirely of the habit of running away. When he sees me start to pack my suitcase he just lies down on the floor with his chin on his forepaws and gazes at me sadly. Usually I wind up by canceling my train reservations.

The first thing to teach a man is to stay at heel. For this lesson the dog should hook one end of a leash to his collar and loop the other end around the man's wrist so he cannot get away. Start down the street slowly, pausing at each telephone pole until the man realizes that he's under control. He may tug and yank at first, but this can be discouraged by slipping deftly between his legs and winding the leash around his ankles. If the man tries to run ahead, brace all four feet and halt suddenly, thus jerking him flat on his back. After a few such experiences the man will follow his dog with docility. Remember, however, that all such efforts at discipline must be treated as sport, and after a man has sprawled on the sidewalk the dog should lick his face to show him it was all in fun.

Every man should learn to retrieve a rubber ball. The way my setter taught me this trick was simple. He would lie in the center of the floor while I carried the ball to the far side of the room and rolled it toward him, uttering the word "Fetch!" He would watch the ball carefully as it rolled past him and under the sofa. I would then get the ball from under the sofa and roll it past him again, giving the same command, "Fetch!"

This lesson would be repeated until the setter was asleep. After I got so I would retrieve the ball every time I said "Fetch!" my dog substituted other articles for me to pick up, such as an old marrow bone or a piece of paper he found in the wastebasket.

The matter of physical conditioning is important. A man whose carriage is faulty, and who slouches and droops his tail, is a reflection on the dog who owns him. The best way to keep him in shape is to work him constantly and never give him a chance to relax. Racing him up and down the street at the end of a leash is a great conditioner. If he attempts to slump into an easy chair when he gets back, the dog should leap into it ahead of him and force him to sit in a straight-backed chair to improve his posture. And be sure to get him up several times a night to go out for a walk, especially if it is raining.

Equally important is diet. Certain liquids such as beer have a tendency to bloat a man, and a dog should teach him restraint by jumping up at him and spilling his drink, or tactfully knocking the glass off the table with a sweep of his tail.

Not every dog who tries to bring up a man is as successful as my setter. The answer lies in understanding. The dog must be patient and not work himself into a tantrum if his man can't learn to chase rabbits or wriggle under fences as well as the dog does. After all, as my setter says, it's hard to teach an old man new tricks.

Fred

Gene Hill

Fred arrived late in the Spring as if he had had a long standing appointment with us. Or like an old and tired fellow looking for a friend to take him in and tide him over for a bit until he was back on his feet again. Nothing permanent, you understand, just a little while until the expected letter arrived or a distant, but well-to-do, relative came to collect him and return him to the standard of living he was obviously accustomed to.

He was pathetically tired and listless for the first week or so; no doubt the journey had been long and arduous, beset with perils he had somehow, with pluck and wit, survived—no easy task for a rather small beagle more than a little done in by age and its accompanying nuisances.

At first the other dogs more or less ignored

him, and he seemed to prefer it that way. But as his condition improved and most of the aches and pains went away he would join them in a few minutes of rolling around, then retire to his spot under the front porch and watch them with a distant look in his eyes as if remembering other days and other pleasures.

Nor did he pay very much attention to me or anyone else in the family. He had the typical beagle disdain for coming when he was called—or perhaps he just didn't care for our calling him Fred. Now and then he would want to be scratched or petted and would come over to me and put his head against my foot and look away into some secret vision of his own for a few minutes. Then having done his duty or satisfied some canine itch, he would wander off and stretch out by himself. I was surrounded by a mixed group of indifferent bird dogs—a couple of setters and a pointer—so in deference to Fred's age, his refusal to come when called unless it was convenient, and my lack of interest in rabbit hunting, I left him alone to do as he pleased. I had, at one point, put him in a wire run to force him to rest and because, for some sentimental reason or other, I had become rather attached to him and didn't want him taking off and starting another journey of indefinite end and purpose. But after a couple of weeks I set him free to wander around the house and yard since he seemed content to do just that; besides, he had a habit of digging holes in his area that were about 10 inches wide and 2 feet deep, and I was beginning to be afraid I'd step in one in the dark and snap an ankle.

After he'd been with us a couple of months Fred actually began to act rather spry every so often. He had a little game he liked to play, and I can see him yet with his pet toy—an old leather gardening glove of mine—running and barking and throwing the glove up in the air and catching it, hoping that one of the other dogs would come and try to play catch with him. Sadly, they never seemed to express more than the most fleeting interest in Fred's glove, and after a minute or two of barking and throwing he would give up and take his glove with him back under the porch.

Once a week or so Fred would disappear on some personal errand in the morning and be gone until almost dark; typical beagle goings-on. But when, on one occasion, he didn't come home for a couple of days, I began to worry and started asking around the neighborhood for sightings of the old man. I was very much relieved to come home from work one night and see his gray muzzle poking out from near the front step. I called him, but he wouldn't move; he just lay there and banged his tail against the ground as if he was glad to be home but needed a couple of more hours to compose himself before any formal greetings. I brought him some food and water, and when I got down on my knees to slide it under the porch, I could hear him whimpering. I reached in and pulled him out, and saw instantly that he had been shot in his right rear leg with what looked like a .22. Our vet agreed that's what it was, but the bullet had passed rather

harmlessly through the flesh, and we felt he would be all right in just a couple of days.

Fred seemed more mystified than anything else, and it put him in a rather depressed mood that lasted quite a while after the slight wound had healed. He would sulk around, shaking his head at the unsolvable situation, and he spent more and more time under the porch with his old glove as his only companion. It would be a long time before he would trust anyone again, was his attitude—and I can't say that I blamed him in the least.

Any of us who has owned a dog that has taken a particular hold on our heart has dwelt on the unfairness of allotted time. It seems but an instant—or at best a couple of good gunning seasons—and the puppy we so carefully carried home and placed on the rug by our bed has suddenly become a little dim of eye, a touch slow to get up in the morning, and more and more content to lay in some sunny spot and salute our passings-by with a turning of the head and a wagging of the tail. Somehow even through the dozen dogs I've owned I've never ceased to be surprised and a little hurt to discover that today Tippy or Ben or Judy doesn't race me to the door to go out but stands in the warmth of the kitchen and merely follows me with eyes and heart.

You'd think, as I should have, but didn't, that having Fred move in in his declining years would have made this understanding of the impermanence of things a little easier, but somehow it never did. I knew Fred was old, but like some people, he seemed to be the type that might have been born old and would keep the kind of curious dignity and charming wisdom for quite a time to come. It was the fact that he'd been shot that brought the truth home to me.

When I carried him to the vet, stroking and trying to soothe his hurts—trying to show him that I cared and was truly sorry that this disastrous, monstrous thing had happened to him—it was then that I really noticed how gray he was, how brittle his coat, how worn out he seemed, how pathetic, how fragile and brave. I felt the thumping of his little heart against my arm, his head, as usual, turned slightly away as if in some sort of apology for causing me all this trouble. The tiny hole in his leg encrusted with a dime-sized spot of blood made me think of the Calvary, and as much as I tried to think of something else, I could hear who ever it was that held the sights of a rifle on this poor little dog saying over and over again "I nailed him . . . I nailed him."

Toward the end of that summer Fred finally formed some sort of obvious attachment to me. Needless to say, I had made every effort to spoil him. The best of the table scraps were delivered to the cavern under the porch, and I found that some of the work I usually did somewhere else could be done as easily on the front step where I could reach down and scratch his head for whatever comfort that might have been. At least it comforted me, and ever since then I am often consumed with the belief that one of the selfish reasons we get so attached to our dogs is the fact that they give us something to love and care for which is different and irreplaceable in our lives. A quiet, understanding, grateful being that is there when we feel the need to hold and love something warm, mute, and grateful. I would think of my teasing Patty or Jennifer about a room full of stuffed animals as I rolled on the lawn and played with old Fred and have to laugh at myself.

One of Fred's habits had been to come out from under the porch when I drove up to the house and then bark once or twice. Just enough to let me know he cared. He would never bark at anyone else; I was special.

Fred continued to have his restless side. His habit of stopping whatever he was doing and sort of staring beyond whatever my normal eyes could see was always slightly unnerving, as if the dog were seeing ghosts or hearing sounds or musing on thoughts that were beyond sharing with me. He never let me really, deep down inside, believe that our relationship was anything more than a transient one; that he was in the course of a journey that was constantly tempting him to be on with it. Often I watched him pace slowly to the edge of the driveway and stare down the road, consider all the alternatives, and slowly shaking his head, turn around and make his way back under the porch as if saying under his breath, "Not today, but perhaps tomorrow."

And that "tomorrow" finally came. I pulled into the driveway burdened by some large and small worries and needed someone to sit with and sort them out into piles of "not today, but perhaps tomorrow." Fred was always the perfect companion with whom to discuss this sort of thing. He would let me go on and on, knowing as any close friend would, that this was the best way—to say nothing and let me work things out for myself. I went into the house and made myself a drink and came out and sat on the front step. The emptiness of the little dusty hole was cavernous; no, it was more than that. By the time I had finished my glass of whiskey I realized that it was final. Even the old glove was gone, and I could easily imagine Fred inching along at his ancient pace, carrying his glove both as a reminder of where he'd been and as a symbol of total commitment to going on . . . all of his worldly possessions were with him; there was no need ever to turn back.

After a week of teasing myself, I rummaged around in the barn and found the old lattice that I had taken out from the porch to paint and put it back as if to erase the sight of Fred's room; closing a door to a place I would rather not have anyone else see or use.

That particular hunting season turned out to be an especially good one, and the one bird dog that had begun to show some promise finally came into her own. I spent almost all of my free time on some finishing touches with a check cord and getting her to retrieve. It was pleasant work and rewarding to see it all come together, finally, to where I had what might pass for a "gentleman's shooting dog" if you could overlook the odd point on a field mouse and try not to notice the occasional, but rare, breaking and chasing at flush.

Fred had gone from my mind for the most part, and I could sit on the porch with an evening glass and think about him more in terms of pleasure than remorse. In the overall of how these things usually go, he had left on good terms, and the loss I felt was, in all fairness, rather selfish on my part, and I'd come to see it just like that. So I was not prepared for Fred's return in spirit or name when a man who worked for the county road crew stopped by one afternoon when I was doing some outside chores and asked me if I hadn't had a beagle fairly recently who had disappeared. I said I did have one—in a way. He asked me if I knew what had become of him, and I said that I didn't. He then told me that he had found him, shot, lying along the edge of the road and had buried him, not knowing at the time that he was my dog. I couldn't think of anything to say. I never could and still can't. Death has a way of affecting my mind for a while and I seem forever falling short of finding any way to take it all in and make sense of it. But after a minute or so I thanked him for his kindness toward the dog and his courtesy of coming by. He asked me if I wanted to know who did it and I thought about that and remembering a red rage I had felt once during a long ago war, I said I'd rather not know. He seemed a little surprised at that, but I didn't feel I wanted to explain; I didn't feel I could—since I didn't understand it myself—it just sort of came out. He said "Okay" in a way that embarrassed me and got back in his truck. He started the motor and rolled the window down and held out an old leather glove. "This yours?" he asked.

I took it, wordlessly, and he put the truck in gear and drove off.

I went back and sat on the front step, trying not to think and not having much luck. My wife came out and asked who had stopped by in the truck. I couldn't say anything to her but I held up the glove. "I'm glad to have that," she said and took it from me and pushed it under the lattice and went back into the house. She came back in a minute or two and handed me a glass and went away again. I sat there and watched the sun go down, and off in the shallow part of the sky where the weakening yellow was being pushed back by the dark I saw the evening star and I made a wish. It had been a long time since I had done a thing like that, since I was a kid, I guess, and the difference is that I was wishing, now, for something I really didn't want, since it wasn't really right to wish for things like that, but I did anyway. And I think you know exactly what it was.

The Dog That Bit People

James Thurber

Probably no one man should have as many dogs in his life as I have had, but there was more pleasure than distress in them for me except in the case of an Airedale named Muggs. He gave me more trouble than all the other fifty-four or -five put together, although my moment of keenest embarrassment was the time a Scotch terrier named Jeannie, who had just had four puppies in the shoe closet of a fourth-floor apartment in New York, had the fifth and last at the corner of—but we shall get around to that later on. Then, too, there was the prize-winning French poodle, a great big black poodle—none of your little, untroublesome white miniatures—who got sick riding in the rumble seat of a car with me on her way to the Greenwich Dog Show. She had a red rubber bib tucked around her throat and, since a rain-storm came up when we were halfway through the Bronx, I had to hold over her a small green umbrella, really more of a parasol. The rain beat down fearfully, and sud-

denly the driver of the car drove into a big garage, filled with mechanics. It happened so quickly that I forgot to put the umbrella down, and I shall always remember the look of incredulity that came over the face of the garageman who came over to see what we wanted. "Get a load of this, Mac," he called to someone behind him.

But the Airedale, as I have said, was the worst of all my dogs. He really wasn't my dog, as a matter of fact; I came home from a vacation one summer to find that my brother Robert had bought him while I was away. A big, burly, choleric dog, he always acted as if he thought I wasn't one of the family. There was a slight advantage in being one of the family, for he didn't bite the family as often as he bit strangers. Still, in the years that we had him he bit everybody but Mother, and he made a pass at her once but missed. That was during the month when we suddenly had mice, and Muggs refused to do anything about them. Nobody ever had mice exactly like the mice we had that month. They acted like pet mice, almost like mice somebody had trained. They were so friendly that one night when Mother entertained at dinner the Friraliras, a club she and my father had belonged to for twenty years, she put down a lot of little dishes with food in them on the pantry floor so that the mice would be satisfied with that and wouldn't come into the dining room. Muggs stayed out in the pantry with the mice, lying on the floor, growling to himself—not at the mice, but about all the people in the next room that he would have liked to get at. Mother slipped out into the pantry once to see how everything was going. Everything was going fine. It made her so mad to see Muggs lying there, oblivious of the mice—they came running up to her—that she slapped him and he slashed at her, but didn't make it. He was sorry immediately, Mother said. He was always sorry, she said, after he bit someone, but we could not understand how she figured this out. He didn't act sorry.

Mother used to send a box of candy every Christmas to the people the Airedale bit. The list finally contained forty or more names. Nobody could understand why we didn't get rid of the dog. I didn't understand it very well myself, but we didn't get rid of him. I think that one or two people tried to poison Muggs—he acted poisoned once in a while—and old Major Moberly fired at him once with his service revolver near the Seneca Hotel in Easy Broad Street—but Muggs lived to be almost eleven years old, and even when he could hardly get around, he bit a congressman who had called to see my father on business. My mother had never liked the congressman—she said the signs of his horoscope showed he couldn't be trusted (he was Saturn with the moon in Virgo)—but she sent him a box of candy that Christmas. He sent it right back, probably because he suspected it was trick candy. Mother persuaded herself it was all for the best that the dog had bitten him, even though father lost an important business association because of it. "I wouldn't be associated with such a man," Mother said. "Muggs could read him like a book."

We used to take turns feeding Muggs to be on his good side, but that didn't always work. He was never in a very good humor, even after a meal. Nobody knew exactly what was the matter with him, but whatever it was it made him irascible, especially in the mornings. Robert never felt very well in the morning, either, especially before breakfast, and once when he came downstairs and found that Muggs had moodily chewed up the morning paper he hit him in the face with a grapefruit and then jumped on the dining-room table, scattering dishes and silverware and spilling the coffee. Muggs' first leap carried him all the way across the table and into a brass fire screen in front of the gas grate, but he was back on his feet in a moment, and in the end he got Robert and gave him a pretty vicious bite in the leg. Then he was all over it; he never bit anyone more than once at a time. Mother always mentioned that as an argument in his favor; she said he had a quick temper but that he didn't hold a grudge. She was forever defending him. I think she liked him because he wasn't well. "He's not strong," she would say, pityingly, but that was inaccurate; he may not have been well but he was terribly strong.

One time my mother went to the Chittenden Hotel to call on a woman mental healer who was lecturing in Columbus on the subject of "Harmonious Vibrations." She wanted to find out if it was possible to get harmonious vibrations into a dog. "He's a large tan-colored Airedale," Mother explained. The woman said she had never treated a dog, but she advised my mother to hold the thought that he did not bite and would not bite. Mother was holding the thought the very next morning when Muggs got the iceman, but she blamed that slip-up on the iceman. "If you didn't think he would bite you, he wouldn't," Mother told him. He stomped out of the house in a terrible jangle of vibrations.

One morning when Muggs bit me slightly, more or less in passing, I reached down and grabbed his short stumpy tail and hoisted him into the air. It was a foolhardy thing to do and the last time I saw my mother, about six months ago, she said she didn't know what possessed me. I don't either, except that I was pretty mad. As long as I held the dog off the floor by his tail he couldn't get at me, but he twisted and jerked so, snarling all the time, that I realized I couldn't hold him that way very long. I carried him to the kitchen and flung him onto the floor and shut the door on him just as he crashed against it. But I forgot about the back stairs. Muggs went up the back stairs and down the front stairs and had me cornered in the living room. I managed to get up onto the mantelpiece above the fireplace, but it gave way and came down with a tremendous crash, throwing a large marble clock, several vases, and myself heavily to the floor. Muggs was so alarmed by the racket that when I picked myself up he had disappeared. We couldn't find him anywhere, although we whistled and shouted, until old Mrs. Detweiler called after dinner that night. Muggs had bitten her once, in the leg, and she came into the living room only after we assured her that Muggs had run away. She had just seated herself when, with a great growling and scratching of claws, Muggs emerged from under a davenport where he had been quietly hiding all the time, and bit her again. Mother examined the bite and put arnica on it and told Mrs. Detweiler that it was only a bruise. "He just bumped you," she said. But Mrs. Detweiler left the house in a nasty state of mind.

Lots of people reported our Airedale to the police, but my father held a municipal office at the time and was on friendly terms with the police. Even so, the cops had been out a couple of times—once when Muggs bit Mrs. Rufus Sturtevant and again when he bit Lieutenant-Governor Malloy—but Mother told them that it hadn't been Muggs' fault but the fault of the people who were bitten. "When he starts for them, they scream," she explained, "and that excites him." The cops suggested that it might be a good idea to tie the dog up, but Mother said that it mortified him to be tied up and that he wouldn't eat when he was tied up.

Muggs at his meals was an unusual sight. Because of the fact that if you reached toward the floor he would bite you, we usually put his food plate on top of an old kitchen table with a bench alongside the table. Muggs would stand on the bench and eat. I remember that my mother's Uncle Horatio, who boasted that he was the third man up Missionary Ridge, was splutteringly indignant when he found out that we fed the dog on a table because we were afraid to put his plate on the floor. He said he wasn't afraid of any dog that ever lived and that he would put the

dog's plate on the floor if we would give it to him. Robert said that if Uncle Horatio had fed Muggs on the ground just before the battle he would have been the first man up Missionary Ridge. Uncle Horatio was furious. "Bring him in! Bring him in now!" he shouted. "I'll feed the ———on the floor!" Robert was all for giving him a chance, but my father wouldn't hear of it. He said that Muggs had already been fed. "I'll feed him again!" bawled Uncle Horatio. We had quite a time quieting him.

In his last year Muggs used to spend practically all of his time outdoors. He didn't like to stay in the house for some reason or other—perhaps it held too many unpleasant memories for him. Anyway, it was hard to get him to come in, and as a result the garbage man, the iceman, and the laundryman wouldn't come near the house. We had to haul the garbage down to the corner, take the laundry out and bring it back, and meet the iceman a block from home. After this had gone on for some time, we hit on an ingenious arrangement for getting the dog in the house so that we could lock him up while the gas meter was read, and so on. Muggs was afraid of only one thing, an electrical storm. Thunder and lightning frightened him out of his senses (I think he thought a storm had broken the day the mantelpiece fell). He would rush into the house and hide under a bed or in a clothes closet. So we fixed up a thunder machine out of a long narrow piece of sheet iron with a wooden handle on one end. Mother would shake this vigorously when she wanted to get Muggs into the house. It made an excellent imitation of thunder, but I suppose it was the most roundabout system for running a household that was ever devised. It took a lot out of Mother.

A few months before Muggs died, he got to "seeing things." He would rise slowly from the floor, growling low, and stalk stiff-legged and menacing toward nothing at all. Sometimes the Thing would be just a little to the right or left of a visitor. Once a Fuller Brush salesman got hysterics. Muggs came wandering into the room like Hamlet following his father's ghost. His eyes were fixed on a spot just to the left of the Fuller Brush man, who stood it until Muggs was about three slow, creeping paces from him. Then he shouted. Muggs wavered on past him into the hallway, grumbling to himself, but the Fuller

Brush man went on shouting. I think Mother had to throw a pan of cold water on him before he stopped. That was the way she used to stop us boys when we got into fights.

Muggs died quite suddenly one night. Mother wanted to bury him in the family plot under a marble stone with some such inscription as "Flights of angels sing thee to thy rest" but we persuaded her it was against the law. In the end we just put up a smooth board above his grave along a lonely road. On the board I wrote with an indelible pencil *"Cave Canem."* Mother was quite pleased with the simple, classic dignity of the old Latin epitaph.

Charley and the Bear
(*from* Travels With Charley)

John Steinbeck

I must confess to a laxness in the matter of National Parks. I haven't visited many of them. Perhaps this is because they enclose the unique, the spectacular, the astounding—the greatest waterfall, the deepest canyon, the highest cliff, the most stupendous works of man or nature. And I would rather see a good Brady photograph than Mount Rushmore. For it is my opinion that we enclose and celebrate the freaks of our nation and of our civilization. Yellowstone National Park is no more representative of America than is Disneyland.

This being my natural attitude, I don't know what made me turn sharply south and cross a state line to take a look at Yellowstone. Perhaps it was a fear of my neighbors. I could hear them say, "You mean you were that near to Yellowstone and didn't go? You must be crazy." Again it might have been the American tendency in travel. One goes, not so much to see but to tell afterward. Whatever my purpose in going to Yellowstone, I'm glad I went because I discovered something about Charley I might never have known.

A pleasant-looking National Park man checked me in and then he said, "How about that dog? They aren't permitted in except on leash."

"Why?" I asked.

"Because of the bears."

"Sir," I said, "this is an unique dog. He does not live by tooth or fang. He respects the rights of cats to be cats although he doesn't admire them. He turns his steps rather than disturb an earnest caterpillar. His greatest fear is that someone will point out a rabbit and suggest that he chase it. This is a dog of peace and tranquility. I suggest that the greatest danger to your bears will be pique at being ignored by Charley."

The young man laughed. "I wasn't so much worried about the bears," he said. "But our bears have developed an intolerance for dogs. One of them might demonstrate his prejudice with a clip on the chin, and then—no dog."

"I'll lock him in the back, sir. I promise you Charley will cause no ripple in the bear world, and as an old bear-looker, neither will I."

"I just have to warn you," he said. "I have no doubt your dog has the best of intentions. On the other hand, our bears have the worst. Don't leave food about. Not only do they steal but they are critical of anyone who tries to reform them. In a word, don't believe their sweet faces or you might get clobbered. And don't let the dog wander. Bears don't argue."

We went on our way into the wonderland of nature gone nuts, and you will have to believe what happened. The only way I can prove it would be to get a bear.

Less than a mile from the entrance I saw a bear beside the road, and it ambled out as though to flag me down. Instantly a change came over Charley. He shrieked with rage. His lips flared, showing wicked teeth that have some trouble with a dog biscuit. He screeched insults at the bear, which hearing, the bear reared up and seemed to me to overtop Rocinante. Frantically I rolled the windows shut and, swinging quickly to the left, grazed the animal, then scuttled on while Charley raved and ranted beside me, describing in detail what he would do to that bear if he could get at him. I was never so astonished in my life. To the best of my knowledge Charley had never seen a bear, and in his whole history had showed great tolerance for every living thing. Besides all this, Charley is a coward, so deep-seated a coward that he has developed a technique for concealing it. And yet he showed every evidence of wanting to get out and murder a bear that outweighed him a thousand to one. I don't understand it.

A little farther along two bears showed up, and the effect was doubled. Charley became a maniac. He leaped all over me, he cursed and growled, snarled and screamed. I didn't know he had the ability to snarl. Where did he learn it? Bears were in good supply, and the road became a nightmare. For the first time in his life Charley resisted reason, even resisted a cuff on the ear. He became a primitive killer lusting for the blood of his enemy, and up to this moment he had had no enemies. In a bearless stretch, I opened the cab, took Charley by the collar, and locked him in the house. But that did no good. When we passed other bears he leaped on the table and scratched at the windows trying to get out at them. I could hear canned goods crashing as he struggled in his mania. Bears simply brought out the Hyde in my Jekyll-headed dog. What could have caused it? Was it a pre-breed memory of a time when the wolf was in him? I know him well. Once in a while he tries a bluff, but it is a palpable lie. I swear that this was no lie. I am certain that if he were released he would have charged every bear we passed and found victory or death.

It was too nerve-wracking, a shocking spectacle, like seeing an old, calm friend go insane. No amount of natural wonders, of rigid cliffs and belching waters, of smoking springs could even engage my attention while that pandemonium went on. After about the fifth encounter I gave up, turned Rocinante about, and retraced my way. If I had stopped the night and bears had gathered to my cooking, I dare not think what would have happened.

At the gate the park guard checked me out. "You didn't stay long. Where's the dog?"

"Locked up back there. And I owe you an apology. That dog has the heart and soul of a bear-killer and I didn't know it. Heretofore he has been a little tender-hearted toward an underdone steak."

"Yeah!" he said. "That happens sometimes. That's why I warned you. A bear dog would know his chances, but I've seen a Pomeranian go up like a puff of smoke. You know, a well-favored bear can bat a dog like a tennis ball."

I moved fast, back the way I had come, and I was reluctant to camp for fear there might be some unofficial non-government bears about. That night I spent in a pretty auto court near Livingston. I had my dinner in a restaurant, and when I had settled in with a drink and a comfortable chair and my bathed bare feet on a carpet with red roses, I inspected Charley. He was dazed. His eyes held a faraway look and he was totally exhausted, emotionally no doubt. Mostly he reminded me of a man coming out of a long, hard drunk—worn out, depleted, collapsed. He couldn't eat his dinner, he refused the evening walk, and once we were in he collapsed on the floor and went to sleep. In the night I heard him whining and yapping, and when I turned on the light his feet were making running gestures and his body jerked and his eyes were wide open, but it was only a night bear. I awakened him and gave him some water. This time he went to sleep and didn't stir all night. In the morning he was still tired. I wonder why we think the thoughts and emotions of animals are simple.

Blue and Some Other Dogs

John Graves

One cool still night last March, when the bitterest winter in decades was starting to slack its grip and the first few chuckwill's-widows were whistling tentative claims to nest territories, the best dog I ever owned simply disappeared. Dogs do disappear, of course. But not usually dogs like Blue or under conditions like ours here in the cedar hills.

A crossbred sheep dog, he had spent his whole ten years of life on two North Texas country places and had not left the vicinity of the house at either of them without human company since the age of two or less, when his mother was still alive and we also had an aging and lame and anarchic dachshund who liked to tempt the two of them out roaming after armadillos and feral cats and raccoons and other varmints. This happened usually at night when we'd neglected to bring the dachshund into the house, or he had tricked his way outside by faking a call of nature or pushing open an unlatched screen door. The dachshund, named Watty (it started as Cacahuate or Peanut), had a very good nose and the two sheep dogs didn't, and having located quarry for them he would scream loud sycophantic applause as they pursued it and attacked, sometimes mustering the courage to run in and bite an exposed hind leg while the deadly mother and son kept the front part occupied.

It was fairly gory at times, and I'm not all that much at war with varmints except periodically with individual specimens that have developed a taste for chickens or kid goats or garden corn. In fact, I rather like having them around. But the main problem was the roaming itself, which sometimes took the dogs a mile or so from home and onto other property. In the country wandering dogs are an abomination, usually in time shifting their attention from wild prey to poultry and sheep and goats and calves, and nearly always dying sooner or later from a rifle bullet or buckshot or poison bait, well enough deserved. Few people have lived functionally on the land without having to worry sooner or later about such raiders, and the experience makes them jumpy about their own dogs' habits. Thus they find much irony in city visitors' standard observation that country dogs are very lucky to have so much space for roving and playing.

To cope, you can chain or pen your dogs when they aren't with you, or you can teach them to stay at home. While I favor the latter approach, with three dogs on hand and one of them a perverse and uncontrollable old house pet too entwined with my own past and with the family to get rid of, it was often hard to make training stick. At least it was until the dachshund perished under the wheels of a pickup truck, his presence beneath it unsuspected by the driver and his cranky senile arrogance too great to let him scuttle out of the way when the engine started.

Blue's mother was a brindle-and-white Basque sheep dog from Idaho, of a breed said to be called Pannish, though you can't prove that by me since I've never seen another specimen. Taut and compact and aggressive, she was quick to learn but also quick to spot ways to nudge rules aside or to get out of work she didn't savor. She came to us mature and a bit over-disciplined, and if you tried to teach her a task too roughly she would refuse permanently to have anything to do with it. I ruined her for cow work by whipping her for running a heifer through a net fence for the hell of it, and ever afterward if I started dealing with cattle when she was with me, she would go to heel or disappear. Once while chousing a neighbor's Herefords out of an oat patch toward the spate-ripped fence watergap through which they had invaded it, I looked around for Pan and glimpsed her peeking at me slyly from a shin oak thicket just beyond the field's fringe, hiding there till the risk of being called on for help was past.

Not that she feared cows or anything else that walked—or crawled or flew or swam or for that matter rolled on wheels. She attacked strange dogs like a male and had a contemptuous hatred of snakes that made her bore straight in to grab them and shake them dead, even after she had been bitten twice by rattlers, once badly. After such a bout I've seen her with drops of amber venom rolling down her shoulder where fangs had struck the thick fine hair but had failed to reach her skin. Occasionally she bit people too, always men, though she was nervous enough around unfamiliar children that we never trusted her alone with them. Women, for her own secret reasons, she liked more or less indiscriminately.

She was a sort of loaded weapon, Pan, and in town there would have been no sense in keeping such a dog around, except maybe to patrol fenced grounds at night. But we were living then on a leased place just beyond the western honky-tonk fringe of Fort Worth, where drunken irrationals roved the byways after midnight, and I was often away. There, what might otherwise have been her worst traits were reassuring. She worshiped my wife and slept beside the bed when I was gone, and would I am certain have died in defense of the household with the same driven ferocity she showed in combat with wild things.

A big boar coon nearly got her one January night, before she had Blue to help her out. The old dachshund sicked her on it by the barn, where it had come for a bantam supper, and by the time I had waked to the noise and pulled on pants and located a flashlight, the fight had rolled down to the creek and Pan's chopping yap had suddenly stilled, though Watty was still squalling hard. When I got there and shone the light on a commotion in the water, all that showed was the coon's solemn face and his shoulders. Astraddle Pan's neck with an ear clutched in each hand, he was quite competently holding her down despite her mightiest struggles; big bubbles rolled up as I watched with dachshund Watty dancing yet uproarious beside me on good firm land. Grabbing up a stick I waded into the frigid chest-deep pool, whacked the coon out of his saddle, declined his offer to climb me in retaliation, and sent him swimming somewhat groggily for the other bank. But by then Pan was unconscious, and on shore I shook and pumped the better part of a gallon of water out of her before she started to wheeze and cough. Which didn't keep her from tearing into the very next coon her brave, small, black friend sniffed out, though I don't recall her ever following another one into water.

She was not too rash to learn what an impossibility was.

We had a plague of feral housecats at that place, strayed outward from the city or dumped along the roads by the kind of people who do that sort of thing, and a huge tom one time gave the dachshund his comeuppance. After a notable scrap with Pan the tom decided to leave as I arrived, but she grabbed him by the tail as he went. At this point old Watty, thinking in dim light that the customary face-to-face encounter was still in progress and gaining from my arrival the courage the cat had lost, dashed in for a furtive chomp and was received in a loving, tight, clawed embrace with sharp teeth in its middle. His dismay was piercingly loud and he bore those scars for life. . . . The tomcat got away, wiser too I suspect.

If my less than objective interest in these violent matters is evident, I have the grace to be a bit ashamed of it, but not much. I have friends among the hound-dog men whose main pleasure in life lies in fomenting such pursuits and brawls, and some of them are very gentle people—i.e., I am not of the school that believes hunting per se makes worse brutes of men than they already are, or ever did or ever will. Though I still hunt a little myself, I don't hunt in that way, and these home-ground uproars I seldom encouraged except occasionally much later, when Blue had become our only dog and had constituted himself our Protector of Garden and Poultry. The toll of wildlife actually killed over the years was light, reaching a mild peak during the brief period after Blue was full grown and before Pan died, when they hunted and fought as a skillful team. Most chases would end with a treeing and I would go and call the dogs home with no blood spilled on either side. But Man the Hunter's association with dogs is very very long-standing, and anyone who can watch a slashing battle between his own dogs and something wild and tough, when it does occur, without feeling a flow of the old visceral reckless joy, is either quite skilled at suppressing his emotions or more different from me than I think most men are.

There being of course the additional, more primary and cogent fact that in the country varmints around the house and barn and chicken yard are bad news, and the best help in keeping them away, if you dislike poison and traps and such things, is aggressive dogs. They can give you a bad turn on occasion, though, as Pan did one evening when she assailed something in a tight V-mesh fence corner and, hearing high shrill yipes, I thought she was murdering a friend and neighbor's treasured tiny poodle, a wide wanderer named Pierre. I ran out and yanked her away, and out came not Pierre but a quite rumpled little gray fox, who did not give his name but streaked off to safety.

Unable to find any males of Pan's breed in this region, we mated her with one of those more numerous sheep dogs, similar in build and coat but colored white and black-speckled gray, known as Queensland Blue Heelers or more commonly just as Australians. Three of the resultant pups had her hue and the fourth was Blue, marked like his sire but with less speckling and no trace of the blue "glass" or "china" tinge that many, perhaps most Australians have in one or both eyes, sometimes as only a queer pale blaze on an iris. When the time came to choose, we picked him to keep, and as a result he turned out to be a far different sort of grown dog than he would have if we had given him away.

For Pan was an impossibly capricious, domineering mother, neurotic in her protectiveness but punitive toward the pups to the point of drawing blood when they annoyed her, which was often. The others got out from under at six or eight weeks of age, but Blue had to stay and take it, and kept on taking it until Pan died—run over too, while nudging at the rule against chasing cars. Even after he had reached full size, at seventy-five pounds half again bigger than either Pan or his sire, he had to be always on the watch for her unforeseeable snarling fits of displeasure.

I used to wish he would round on her and whip her hard once and for all, but he never did. Instead he developed the knack of turning clownish at a moment's notice, reverting to ingratiating puppy tricks to deflect the edge of her wrath. He would run around in senseless circles yapping, would roll on his back with his feet wiggling in the air, and above all would grin— crinkle his eyes and turn up the corners of his mouth and loll his tongue out over genially bared teeth. It was a travesty of all mashed-down human beings who have had to clown to survive, like certain black barbershop shoeshine "boys,"

some of them sixty years old, whom I remember from my youth.

These antics worked well enough with Pan that they became a permanent part of the way Blue was, and he brought them to his relationship with people, mainly me, where they worked also. It was quite hard to stay angry at a large strong dog, no matter what he had just done, who had his bobtailed butt in the air and his head along his forelegs on the ground and his eyes skewed sidewise at you as he smiled a wide, mad, minstrel-show smile. If I did manage to stay angry despite all, he would most often panic and flee to his hideout beneath the pickup's greasy differential, which may have been another effect of Pan's gentle motherliness or may just have been Australian; they are sensitive dogs, easily cowed, and require light handling. For the most part, all that Blue did require was light handling, for he wanted immensely to please and was the easiest dog to train in standard matters of behavior that I have ever had to deal with. Hating cats, for instance, he listened to one short lecture concerning a kitten just purchased by my small daughters for twenty-five cents at a church benefit sale, and not only let her alone thereafter but became her staunchest friend, except perhaps in the matter of tomcats she might have favored, which he kept on chasing off. And he learned things like heeling in two hours of casual coaching.

Which harks back to my description of him as the best dog I ever owned. He was. But it is needful at this point to confess that that is not really saying much. Nearly all the dogs I owned before Blue and Pan and Watty were pets I had as a boy in Fort Worth, a succession of fox terriers and curs and whatnot that I babied, teased, cajoled, overfed, and generally spoiled in the anthropomorphic manner of kids everywhere. Most perished young, crushed by cars, and were mourned with tears and replaced quite soon by others very much like them in undisciplined worthlessness. In those years I consumed with enthusiasm Jack London's dog books and other less sinewy stuff like the works of Albert Payson Terhune, with their tales of noble and useful canines, but somehow I was never vouchsafed the ownership of anything that faintly resembled Lad or Buck or White Fang.

The best of the lot was a brown-and-white

mongrel stray that showed up already old and gray-chopped, with beautiful manners and training, but he liked grownups better than children and stayed with my father when he could. The worst but most beloved was an oversized Scotty named Roderick Dhu, or Roddy, who when I was twelve or thirteen or so used to accompany me and a friend on cumbersome hunting and camping expeditions to the Trinity West Fork bottom beyond the edge of town, our wilderness. He had huge negative will power and when tired or hot would often sit down and refuse to move another inch. Hence from more than one of those forays I came hiking back out of the valley burdened not only with a Confederate bedroll, a canteen, a twenty-two rifle, a bowie knife, an ax, a frying pan, and other such impedimenta, but with thirty-five deadweight pounds of warm dog as well.

The friend's dog in contrast was a quick bright feist called Buckshot, destined to survive not only our childhood but our college years and the period when we were away at the war and nearly a decade longer, dying ultimately, my friend swears, at the age of twenty-two. A canine wraith, nearly blind and grayed all over and shrunken, he would lie in corners and dream twitching of old possums and rabbits we had harried through the ferns and poison ivy, thumping his tail on the floor when human movement was near if he chanced to be awake.

With this background, even though I knew about useful dogs from having had uncles and friends who kept them for hunting and from having seen good herd dogs at work during country work in adolescence, as well as from reading, I arrived at my adult years with a fairly intact urban, middle-class, sentimental ideal of the Nice Dog, a cleancut fellow who obeyed a few selected commands, was loyal and gentle with his masters, and refrained conscientiously from "bad" behavior as delineated by the same said masters. I had never had one and knew it, and the first dog I owned after years of unsettled existence was the dachshund Watty, who was emphatically not one either.

He started out all right, intelligent and affectionate and as willing to learn as dachshunds ever are, and with the nose he had he made a fair retriever, albeit hardmouthed with shot birds and inclined to mangle them a bit before reluc-

tantly giving them up. He was fine company too, afield or in a boat or a car, and we had some good times together, even collaborating on a book about a float trip we made down the Brazos River. But his temper started souring when I married, and grew vile when children came, and the job was finished by a paralyzing back injury with a long painful recovery, never complete, and by much sympathetic spoiling along the way. As an old lame creature, a stage that lasted at least five years, he snarled, bit, disobeyed, stank more or less constantly and from time to time broke wind to compound it, yowled and barked for his supper in the kitchen for two hours before feeding time, subverted the good sheep dogs' training, and was in general the horrid though small-scale antithesis of a Nice Dog. And yet in replication of my childhood self I loved him, and buried him wrapped in a feed sack beneath a flat piece of limestone with his name scratched deep upon it.

(While for Blue, than whom I will never have a Nicer Dog even if perhaps one more useful, there is no marker at all because there is no grave on which to put one . . .)

I do think Watty knocked out of me most of my residual kid sentimentality about dogs in general—he along with living in the country where realism is forced on you by things like having to cope with goat-killing packs of sterling canines, and the experience of having the sheep dogs with their strong thrust and potential, never fully attained—to the point that I'm certain I will never put up with an unmanageable dog again. I remember one time of sharp realization during the second summer after we had bought this cedar-hill place, long before we lived here any part of the year or even used it for grazing. That spring after the dachshund had been thrown from the pickup's seat when I jammed on the brakes in traffic, I had carried him partly paralyzed to the vet, a friend, who advised me frankly that the smart thing would be a lethal painless shot of pentothal. But he added that he had always wanted to try to cure one of those tricky dachshund spines, and that if I would go along with him he'd charge me only his actual costs. Though by that time Watty was already grumpy and snappish and very little pleasure to have around, sentimentality of course triumphed over smart. The trouble was that with intensive therapy still going strong after several weeks, "actual costs" were mounting absurdly, to the point that even now in far costlier times I can grunt when I think of them.

Engaged that summer in some of the endless construction that has marked our ownership of the place, I was in and out every day or so with loads of lumber and cement and things, and paused sometimes to talk with a pleasant man who lived on the road I used. He had a heterogeneous troop of dogs around the yard, some useful and some just there, their ringleader a small white cur with pricked ears and redrimmed eyes who ran cars and was very noisy, but was prized by the man's children and had the redeeming trait of being, quote, hell at finding rattlesnakes.

One morning as I drove in, this dog was sitting upright under a liveoak fifty yards short of the house, with his head oddly high and askew. He had found one snake too many. His eyes were nearly shut and on the side of his neck was a lump about the size of his head. Nor did he acknowledge my passage with as much as a stifled yip. Thinking perhaps they didn't know, I stopped by the house.

"Yes," said my friend. "He run onto a big one up by the tank yesterday evening and by the time I got there with a hoe it had done popped him good."

"Did you do anything for him?"

"Well, we put some coal oil on it," he said. "I was going to cut it open but there's all those veins and things. You know they say if a snake hits a dog in the body he's a goner, but if it's the head he'll get all right. You reckon the neck's the head?"

I said I hoped so, and for days as I passed in and out I watched the little dog under his oak, from which he did not stir, and checked with the family about him. They were not at all indifferent; he was a main focus of interest and they kept fresh food and water by him. The neck swelled up still fatter and broke open, purging terrible fluids. After this happened he seemed to feel better and even ate a little, but then one morning he was dead. Everyone including me was sad that he had lost his fight to live, and the children held a funeral for him, with bouquets of wild prairie pinks.

And such was my changing view that it seemed somehow to make more healthy sense than all that cash I was ramming into a spoiled irascible dachshund's problematic cure. . . .

"Good" country dogs are something else, and are often treated like members of the family and worried over as much when sick. This is not sentimentality but hard realism, because they're worth worrying over in pragmatic terms. There aren't very many of them. As good dogs always have, they come mainly from ruthless culling of promising litters and from close careful training, and most belong to genuine stockmen with lots of herding work to do. These owners routinely turn down offers of a thousand or more dollars for them, if you believe the stories, as you well may after watching a pair of scroungy border collies, in response to a lowwhistle or a word, run a half-mile up a brush-thick pasture and bring back seventy-nine Angora wethers and pack them into a fence corner or a pen for shearing, doctoring, or loading into a trailer, all while their master whittles a mesquite twig to a point and picks his teeth with it.

Blue wasn't that kind of dog or anywhere near it, nor was there much chance to develop such talent on a place like ours, where the resident cows and goats are fairly placid and few problems in handling them emerge that can't be solved with a little patience and a rattling bucket of feed. For that matter, I don't know nearly enough about the training of such dogs to have helped him get to be one, though a livestock buyer I know, who has superb dogs himself and handles thousands of sheep and goats each year on their way from one owner to another, did tell me after watching Blue try to help us one morning that if I'd let him have him for six months, he might be able to "make a dog out of him." I was grateful and thought it over but in the end declined, partly because I mistrusted what six months of training by a stranger might do to that queer, one-man, nervous Australian streak in Blue, but mainly because I didn't know what I'd do with such a dog if I had him, in these rather miniature and unstrenuous livestock operations. His skills would rust unused, and the fact I had to face was that I didn't deserve a dog like that.

What Blue amounted to, I guess, was a country Nice Dog, which in terms of utility is a notable cut above the same thing in the city. These dogs stay strictly at home without being tied or penned, announce visitors, keep varmints and marauding dogs and unidentified nocturnal boogers away, cope with snakes (Blue, after one bad fanging that nearly killed him, abandoned his dam's tactics of headlong assault and would circle a snake raising hell till I came to kill it, or to call him off if it was harmless), watch over one's younger children, and are middling to good help at shoving stock through a loading chute or from one pen to another, though less help in pastures where the aiming point may be a single gate in a long stretch of fence and judgment is required. Some learn simple daily herding tasks like bringing in milk cows at evening, though I've observed that much of the time these tasks involve an illusion on the part of the dog and perhaps his owner that he is making cows or goats or sheep do something, when actually they have full intention of doing it on their own, unforced. Or the whole thing may be for fun, as it was with one old cowman I knew, who had an ancient collie named Babe. When visitors came to sit with the old man on his porch, he would at some point level a puzzled blue glare across the pasture and say in conversational tones, "I declare, Babe, it looks like that old mare has busted out of the corral again. Maybe you better bring her in." And Babe would rise and go do as he had been bidden and the visitors would be much impressed, unless they happened to be aware that it was the one sole thing he could do and that the mare was in on it too.

On the whole, to be honest, Blue was pretty poor at herding even by such lax standards—too eager and exuberant and only occasionally certain of what it was we were trying to do. But he was controllable by single words and gestures and like his mother unafraid, and in his later years when I knew his every tendency, such as nipping goats, I could correct mistakes before he made them, so that he was often of some help. He was even more often comic relief, as when a chuted cow turned fighty and loaded him into the trailer instead of he her, or when a young bull, too closely pressed, kicked him into a thick clump of scrub elm, where he landed upside down and lay stuck with his legs still running in the air. When I went over and saw that he wasn't hurt and started laughing at the way he looked, he started laughing too, at least in his own way.

For a sense of humor and of joy was the other side of that puppyish clowning streak which he always retained but which turned less defensive with time. The nervousness that went with it never left him either, but grew separate from the clowning, ritualizing itself most often in a weird habit he had of grinning and slobbering and clicking his teeth together when frustrated or perplexed. He regularly did this, for instance, when friends showed up for visits and brought their own dogs along. Knowing he wasn't supposed to attack these dogs as he did strays, Blue was uncertain what else to do with them. So he would circle them stiff-legged, wagging his stub and usually trying to mount them, male or female, small or large, and after being indignantly rebuffed would walk about popping his jaws and dribbling copious saliva. I expect some of those visiting friends thought him a very strange dog, and maybe in truth he was.

He was a bouncing, bristling, loudmouthed watchdog, bulkily impressive enough that arriving strangers would most often stay in their cars until I came out to call him off. Unlike Pan, he bore them no real hostility and never bit anyone, though I believe that if any person or thing had threatened one of us those big white teeth would have been put to good use. Mainly, unfamiliar people disconcerted him and he wanted nothing to do with them unless I was around and showed myself receptive, at which point he was wont to start nuzzling their legs and hands like a great overgrown pup, demanding caresses. Once when the pickup was ailing I left it at a garage in town and mooched a ride home with a friend whose car Blue did not know. No one in the family was there, and when we drove up to the house there was no sign of Blue, but then I saw him peering furtively around a corner of the porch, much as his mother had eyed me from those shin oak bushes long before.

With his size, clean markings, silky thick coat, broad head, alert eyes, and usual mien of grave dignity, he was quite a noble-looking fellow. Having him along was often a social asset with strangers, even if it could turn out to be the opposite if something disturbed him and he went into his jaw-popping, drooling phase. One day when he was young and we were still living outside Fort Worth, I was apprehended in that city for running a red light, though I had thought I'd seen no light on at all when I drove through the intersection. I explained this to the arresting officer, a decent type, and together we went back and watched the damned thing run through six or eight perfectly sequenced changes from red to yellow to green and back again. Blue watched with us and, attuned to the situation, accepted a pat from the cop with an austere but friendly smile. Against pregnant silence I said with embarrassment that I guessed my eyes were failing faster than I'd thought, accepted the appropriate summons, and went my disgruntled way.

When I got home that afternoon my wife said the officer had telephoned. More decent even than I'd known, he had watched the light for a while longer by himself and had finally caught it malfunctioning, and he told Jane I could get the ticket canceled.

She thought me off in the cedar hills and believed there was some mistake. "Did he have a sheep dog in the back of the pickup?" she asked.

"No, ma'am," said Blue's till-then secret admirer. "That great big beautiful animal was sitting right up on the front seat with him."

We spent a tremendous lot of time together over the years, Blue and I—around the house and barn and pens, wandering on the place, batting about in a pickup (his pickup more than mine, for he spent much of each day inside it or beneath, even when it was parked by the house), or at farm work in the fields. When young he would follow the tractor around and around as I plowed or harrowed or sowed, but later he learned to sit under a tree and watch the work's progress in comfort, certain I was not escaping from him, though sometimes when he got bored he would bounce out to meet the tractor as it neared him and would try to lead it home. Fond of the whole family and loved by all, he would go along with the girls to swim at the creek or when they went horseback across the hills, good protection for them and good company. But he needed a single main focus and I was it, so completely that at times I felt myself under surveillance. No imperfectly latched door missed his notice if I was indoors and he was out, and he could open one either by shoving or by pulling it with his teeth, as permanent marks on some of them still testify. Failing to get in, he would

ascertain as best he could, by peering in windows or otherwise, just where I was located inside and then would lie down by the exterior wall closest to that spot, even if it put him in the full blast of a January norther.

At one friend's house in town that he and I used to visit often, he would if left outside go through the attached garage to a kitchen door at odds with its jamb and seldom completely shut. Easing through it, he would traverse the breakfast room and a hall, putting one foot before another in tense slow motion, would slink behind a sofa into the living room, and using concealment as craftily as any old infantryman, would sometimes be lying beside my chair before I even knew he was in. More usually we would watch his creeping progress while pretending not to notice, and after he got where he was headed I would give him a loud mock scolding and he would roll on his back and clown, knowing he was home free and wouldn't be booted back out, as sometimes happened when he was shedding fat ticks or stinking from a recent battle with some polecat.

But there were places he wouldn't go with me, most notable among them the bee yard, his first apicultural experience having been his definite last. It happened one early spring day when I was helping a friend check through a neglected hive someone had given him and Blue had tagged along with us. The hive body and supers were badly gummed up with the tree-sap propolis bees use for glue and chinking, the combs in the frames were crooked and connected by bridge wax and tore when we took them out, and on that cool day all thirty or forty thousand workers were at home and ready to fight. They got under our veils and into all cracks in our attire, and those that didn't achieve entry just rammed their stings home through two or three layers of cloth. They also found Blue, a prime target for apian rage since they hate all hairy things, probably out of ancestral memory of hive-raiding bears. With maybe a hundred of them hung whining in his coat and stinging when they found skin, he tried to squeeze between my legs for protection and caused me to drop a frame covered with bees, which augmented the assault. Shortly thereafter, torn between mirth and pain, we gave up and slapped the hive back together and lit out at a hard run, with Blue thirty yards in front and clouds of bees flying escort. And after that whenever he saw me donning the veil and firing up my smoker, he would head in the other direction.

He did work out a method of revenge, though, which he used for the rest of his life despite scoldings and other discouragements. Finding a place where small numbers of bees were coming for some reason—a spot on the lawn where something sweet had been spilled, perhaps, or a lime-crusted dripping faucet whose flavor in their queer way they liked—he would stalk it with his special tiptoeing slink and then loudly snap bees from the air one by one as they flew, apparently not much minding the occasional stings he got on his lips and tongue. I suppose my scoldings were less severe than they ought to have been; it was a comical thing to watch and for that matter he got few bees in relation to their huge numbers, unlike another beekeeper friend's Dalmatian, afflicted with similar feelings, who used to sit all day directly in front of a hive chomping everything that flew out, and had to be given away.

Maybe Blue considered bees varmints. He took his guardianship of the home premises dead seriously and missed few creatures that came around; along with clowning, I guess this was the thing he did best. Except for the unfortunate armadillos, which he had learned to crunch, the mortality inflicted was low after Pan's death, as I've said, for most could escape through the net yard fence that momentarily blocked Blue's pursuit and few of them cared to stay and dispute matters except an occasional big squalling coon. With these we did have some rousing fine midnight fights, though I'd better not further sully my humanitarian aura, if any remains, by going into details. During the time when cantaloupes and roasting ears were coming ripe and most attractive to coons, I would leave the garden gate open at dark and Blue would go down during the night on patrol. There was sometimes a question as to whether a goodly squad of coons given full license could have done half as much damage to garden crops as the ensuing battles did, but there was no question at all about whether the procedure worked. After only two or three brawls each year, word would spread around

canny coondom that large hairy danger lurked in the Graves corn patch and they would come no more, much to Blue's disappointment.

I talked to him quite a bit, for the most part childishly or joshingly as one does talk to beasts, and while I'm not idiot enough to think he "understood" any of it beyond a few key words and phrases, he knew my voice's inflections and tones, and by listening took meaning from them if meaning was there to be had, responding with a grin, a sober stare, melting affection, or some communicative panting, according to what seemed to be right. Like most dogs that converse with humans he was a thorough yes type, honoring my every point with agreement. Nice Dogs are ego boosters, and have been so since the dim red dawn of things.

I could leave him alone and untethered at the place for three or more days at a time, with dry food in a bucket under shelter and water to be had at the cattle troughs. Neighbors half a mile away have told me that sometimes when the wind was right they could hear him crooning softly wolflike, lonely, but he never left. When I came back he would be at the yard gate waiting, and as I walked toward the house he would go beside me leaping five and six feet straight up in the air in pure and utter celebration, whining and grunting maybe but seldom more; he saved loud barks for strangers and snakes and threatening varmints and such.

Last winter I slept inside the house instead of on the screen porch we shared as night quarters during much of each year unless, as often, he wanted to be outside on guard, and I hadn't moved back out by that March night when he disappeared. He had been sleeping on a horse-blanket on a small open side porch facing south, and I'd begun to notice that sometimes he would be still abed and pleasantly groggy when I came out at daybreak. He was fattening a bit also, and those eyes were dimmer that once had been able to pick me out of a jostling sidewalk crowd in town and track me as I came toward the car. Because, like mine, his years were piling up. It was a sort of further bond between us.

He ate a full supper that evening and barked with authority at some coyotes singing across the creek, and in the morning was gone. I had to drive two counties north that day to pick up some grapevines and had planned to take him along. When he didn't answer my calling I decided he must have a squirrel in the elms and cedars across the house branch, where he would often sit silent and taut for hours staring up at a chattering treed rodent, oblivious to summonings and to everything else. It was a small sin that I permitted him at his age; if I wanted him I could go and search him out and bring him in, for he was never far. But that morning it didn't seem to matter and I took off without him, certain he'd be at the yard gate when I drove in after lunch, as he had invariably been over the years that had mounted so swiftly for both of us.

Except that he wasn't. Nor did a tour of his usual squirrel grounds yield any trace, or careful trudges up and down the branch, or a widening week-long search by myself and my wife and kids (whose spring vacation it used up and thoroughly ruined) that involved every brush pile and crevice we could find within half a mile or more of home, where he might have followed some coon or ringtail and then gotten stuck or been bitten in a vein by a rattler just out of its long winter's doze and full of rage and venom. Or watching for the tight downspiral of feeding buzzards. Or driving every road in the county twice or more and talking with people who, no, had not seen any dogs like that or even any bitches in heat that might have passed through recruiting. Or ads run in the paper and notices taped to the doors of groceries and feed mills, though these did produce some false hopes that led me up to thirty miles away in vain.

Even his friend the two-bit cat, at intervals for weeks, would sit and meow toward the woods in queer and futile lament. . . .

I ended fairly certain of what I'd surmised from the start, that Blue lay dead, from whatever cause, beneath some thick heap of bulldozed brush or in one of those deep holes, sometimes almost caves, that groundwater eats out under the limestone ledges of our hills. For in country as brushy and wrinkled and secret as this we can't have found all of such places roundabout, even fairly close.

Or maybe I want to believe this because it has finality.

And maybe he will still turn up, like those long-lost animals you read about in children's books and sometimes in newspaper stories.

He won't.

And dogs are nothing but dogs and I know it better than most, and all this was for a queer and nervous old crossbreed that couldn't even herd stock right. Nor was there anything humanly unique about the loss, or about the emptiness that came in the searching's wake, which comes sooner or later to all people foolish enough to give an animal space in their lives. But if you are built to be such a fool, you are, and if the animal is to you what Blue was to me the space he leaves empty is big.

It is partly filled for us now by a successor, an Old English pup with much promise—sharp and alert, wildly vigorous but responsive and honest, puppy-absurd but with an underlying gravity that will in time I think prevail. There is nothing nervous about him; he has a sensitivity that could warp in that direction if mishandled, but won't if I can help it. Nor does he show any fear beyond healthy puppy caution, and in the way he looks at cows and goats and listens to people's words I see clearly that he may make a hell of a dog, quite possibly better than Blue. Which is not, as I said, saying much . . .

But he isn't Blue. In the domed shape of his head under my hand as I sit reading in the evenings I can still feel that broader, silkier head, and through his half-boisterous, half-bashful, glad morning hello I still glimpse Blue's clown grin and crazy leaps. I expect such intimate remembrance will last a good long while, for I waited the better part of a lifetime to own a decent dog, and finally had him, and now don't have him any more. And I resolve that when this new one is grown and more or less shaped in his ways, I am going to get another pup to raise beside him, and later maybe a third. Because I don't believe I want to face so big a dose of that sort of emptiness again.

The Watermen
(from Chesapeake)

James Michener

The Golden Age of the Eastern Shore came in that four-decade span from 1880 to 1920 when the rest of the nation allowed the marshy counties to sleep undisturbed. True, in these years the world experienced panics and wars, and revolutions and contested elections, but these had almost no impact on the somnolent estuaries and secluded coves. Roads now connected the important towns situated at the heads of rivers, but they were narrow and dusty, and it took wagons days to cover what a speedy boat could negotiate in an hour. When roads paved with white oyster shells did arrive, at the end of this happy age, they were usually one car-width only and formed not a reasonable means of transportation but a lively invitation to suicide.

There was, of course, excitement, but it rarely arrived from the outside world. A black male servant was accused of assaulting a white woman, and a lynching party composed mainly of Turlocks and Cavenys broke down the jail to string the accused from an oak tree, but Judge Hathaway Steed proposed to have no such blot on his jurisdiction; armed only with a family pistol, he confronted the mob and ordered it to disperse. The terrified black man was then transported to a neighboring county, where he was properly hanged.

The Eastern Shore baseball league, composed of six natural rivals, including Easton, Crisfield, Chestertown and Patamoke, flourished and became notorious for having produced Home Run Baker, who would hit in one year the unheard-of total of twelve round-trippers. A luxurious ferryboat left Baltimore every Saturday and Sunday at seven-thirty in the morning to transport day-trippers to a slip at Claiborne, where the throngs would leave the ship and crowd into the cars of the Baltimore, Chesapeake and Atlantic Railroad for a two-hour race across the peninsula to Ocean City on the Atlantic. At four forty-five in the afternoon the railroad cars would refill, the train would chug its way back to Claiborne, passengers would reboard the ferry

and arrive back at Baltimore at ten-thirty at night—all for one dollar and fifty cents.

One of the adventures which caused most excitement came in 1887 when a ship commanded by Captain Thomas Lightfoot, a troublemaker if there ever was one, docked at Patamoke with its cargo of ice sawed from the freshwater ponds of Labrador. When the sawdust had been washed away, and the blue-green cakes were stored in ice-houses along the riverfront, Captain Lightfoot produced an object which was to cause as much long-lasting trouble as the golden apple that Paris was required to award to the most beautiful goddess.

"I've somethin' extra for you," Lightfoot announced as he directed one of his black stevedores to fetch the item from below. "Before it appears I wish to inform you that it is for sale, ten dollars cash."

A moment later the stevedore appeared on deck leading by a leash one of the most handsome dogs ever seen in Maryland. He was jet-black, sturdy in his front quarters, sleek and powerful in his hind, with a face so intelligent that it seemed he might speak at any moment. His movements were quick, his dark eyes following every development nearby, yet his disposition appeared so equable that he seemed always about to smile.

"He's called a Labrador," Lightfoot said. "Finest huntin' dog ever developed."

"He's what?" Jake Turlock snapped.

"Best huntin' dog known."

"Can't touch a Chesapeake retriever," Turlock said, referring to the husky red dog bred especially for bay purposes.

"This dog," said Lightfoot, "will take your Chesapeake and teach him his ABC's."

"That dog ain't worth a damn," Turlock said. "Too stocky up front."

But there was something about this new animal that captivated Tim Caveny, whose red Chesapeake had just died without ever fulfilling the promise he had shown as a pup—"Fine in the water and persistent in trackin' downed birds, but not too bright. Downright stupid, if you ask me." This new black dog displayed a visible intelligence which gave every sign of further development, and Caveny announced, "I'd like to see him."

Captain Lightfoot, suspecting that in Caveny he had found his pigeon, turned the Labrador loose, and with an almost psychic understanding that his future lay with this Irishman, the dog ran to Caveny, leaned against his leg and nuzzled his hand.

It was an omen. Tim's heart was lost, and he said, "I'll take him."

"Mr. Caveny, you just bought the best Labrador ever bred." With grandiloquent gestures he turned the animal over to his new owner, and the dog, sensing that he had found a permanent master, stayed close to Tim, and licked his hand and rubbed against him and looked up with dark eyes overflowing with affection.

Tim paid the ten dollars, then reached down and patted his new hunting companion. "Come on, Lucifer," he said.

"That's a hell of a name for a dog," Turlock growled.

"He's black, ain't he?"

"If he's black, call him Nigger."

"He's Old Testament black," Tim said. And to Captain Lightfoot's surprise, he recited, " 'How art thou fallen from heaven, O Lucifer, son of the morning!' " Turning his back on the others he stooped over the dog, roughed his head and said in a low voice, "You'll be up in the morning, Lucifer, early, early."

Lightfoot then startled the crowd by producing three other dogs of this new breed, one male and two females, and these, too, he sold to the hunters of Patamoke, assuring each purchaser, "They can smell ducks, and they've never been known to lose a cripple."

"To me they look like horse manure," Jake Turlock said.

"They what?" Caveny demanded.

"I said," Turlock repeated, "that your black dog looks like a horse turd."

Slowly Tim handed the leash he had been holding to a bystander. Then, with a mighty swipe, he knocked Turlock to the wet and salty boards of the wharf. The waterman stumbled in trying to regain his feet, and while he was off balance Caveny saw a chance to deliver an uppercut which almost knocked him into the water. Never one to allow a fallen foe an even chance, Caveny leaped across the planking and kicked the waterman in his left armpit, lifting him well into the air, but this was a mistake, because when Turlock landed, his hand fell upon some lumber stacked for loading onto Captain Lightfoot's ship, and after he had quickly tested three or four clubs he found one to his liking, and with it delivered such a blow to the Irishman's head that the new owner of the Labrador staggered back, tried to control his disorganized feet, and fell into the Choptank.

In this way the feud between Tim Caveny, owner of a black Labrador, and Jake Turlock, owner of a red Chesapeake, began.

The first test of the two dogs came in the autumn of 1888 at the dove shoot on the farm of old Lyman Steed, who had spent his long life running one of the Refuge plantations and had now retired to a stretch of land near Patamoke.

Nineteen first-class hunters of the area convened at regular intervals during the dove season to shoot this most interesting of the small game birds: gentlemen like Lyman Steed, middle-class shopkeepers and rough watermen like Jake Turlock and Tim Caveny. For a dove shoot was one of the most republican forms of sport so far devised. Here a man's worth was determined by two criteria: the way he fired his gun and how he managed his dog.

Each hunter was allowed to bring one dog to the shoot, and the animal had to be well trained, because the birds came charging in at low altitude, swerved and dodged in unbelievable confusion and, on the lucky occasions when they were hit, fell maliciously in unpredictable spots. If there was a swamp nearby, as on the Steed farm, the doves would fall there. If there were brambles, the dying doves seemed to seek them out, and the only practical way for the hunter to retrieve his dove, if he hit one, was to have a dog trained to leap forward when he saw a dove fall from the sky and find it no matter where it dropped. The dog must also lift the fallen bird gently in its teeth, carry it without bruising it against thorns, and drop it at the feet of his master. A dove hunt was more a test of dog than of master.

Jake Turlock had a well-trained beast, a

large, surly red-haired Chesapeake, specially bred to work the icy waters of the bay in fall and winter. These dogs were unusual in that they grew a double matting of hair and produced an extra supply of oil to lubricate it. They could swim all day, loved to dive into the water for a fallen goose and were particularly skilled in breaking their way through ice. Like most of this breed, Jake's Chesapeake had a vile temper and would allow himself to be worked only by his master. Every other gunner in the field was his enemy and their dogs were beneath his contempt, but he was kept obedient by Jake's stern cry: "Hey-You, hee!"

His name was Hey-You. Jake had started calling him that when he first arrived at the Turlock shack, a fractious, bounding pup giving no evidence that he could ever be trained. In fact, Jake had thought so little of him that he delayed giving him a proper name. "Hey-You! Get the dove!" The pup would look quizzical, wait, consider whether he wanted to obey or not, then leap off when Jake kicked him.

So during his useless youth he was plain "Hey-You, into the water for the goose!" But at the age of three, after many kicks and buffetings, he suddenly developed into a marvelous hunting dog, a raider like his master, a rough-and-tumble, uncivilized beast who seemed made for the Chesapeake. "Hey-You! Go way down and fetch the dove." So when this red-haired dog swaggered onto the dove field this October day, he was recognized as one of the best ever trained in the Patamoke area.

Lucifer, Tim Caveny's Labrador, was un-known quantity, for he had never before partici-pated in a dove shoot; furthermore, he had been trained in a manner quite different from Hey-You. "My children were raised with love," the Irishman said, "and my dog is trained the same way." From the moment Lucifer came down off Captain Lightfoot's ice ship, he had known noth-ing but love.

His glossy coat was kept nourished by a daily supply of fat from the Caveny table, and his nails were trimmed. In return he gave the Caveny family his complete affection. "I believe that dog would lay down his life for me," Mrs. Caveny told her neighbors, for when she fed him he always looked up at her with his great black eyes and rubbed against her hand. A peddler came to the door one day, unexpectedly and in a frightening manner; Lucifer's hackles rose, and he leaned forward tensely, waiting for a sign. Startled at seeing the man, Mrs. Caveny emitted a short gasp, whereupon Lucifer shot like a thun-derbolt for the man's throat.

"Down, Lucifer!" she cried, and he stopped almost in midair.

But whether he could discipline himself to retrieve doves was another matter. Jake Turlock predicted widely, "The stupid Irishman has spoiled his dog, if'n he was any good to begin with." Other hunters who had trained their beasts more in the Turlock tradition agreed, adding, "He ain't gonna get much out of that what-you-call-it—Labrador."

But Caveny persisted, talking to Lucifer in sweet Irish phrases, trying to convince the dumb animal that great success awaited him on the dove field. "Luke, you and me will get more doves than this town ever seen. Luke, when I say, 'Fetch the dove!' you're to go direct to the spot you think it fell. Then run out in wide and wider circles." Whether the dog would do this was uncertain, but Tim had tried with all his guile to get the animal in a frame of mind condu-cive to success. Now, as he led him to Lyman Steed's farm, he prayed that his lessons had been in the right direction, but when he turned the last corner and saw the other eighteen men with their Chesapeakes awaiting him, eager to see what he had accomplished with this strange animal, his heart fluttered and he felt dizzy.

Pulling gently on the rope attached to the dog's collar, he brought him back, kneeled be-side him and whispered in his lilting brogue, "Lucifer, you and me is on trial. They're all watchin' us." He stroked the dog's glistening neck and said, "At my heel constantly, little fel-low. You don't move till I fire. And when I do, Luke, for the love of a merciful God, find that dove. Soft mouth, Luke, soft mouth and drop him at my toes, like you did with the rag dolls."

As if he knew what his master was saying, Luke turned and looked at Tim impatiently, as if to say, "I know my job. I'm a Labrador."

The field contained about twenty acres and had recently been harvested, so that it provided a large, flat, completely open area, but it was surrounded by a marsh on one side, a large blackberry bramble on another, and a grove of loblollies covering a thicket of underbrush on a third. The doves would sweep in over the loblollies, drop low, hear gunfire and veer back toward the brambles. Placement of gunners was an art reserved for Judge Hathaway Steed, who hunted in an expensive Harris tweed imported from London.

The judge had been a hunter all his life, raised Chesapeakes and sold them to his friends. He had acquired a much better intuition concerning doves than he had of the law, and he now proposed to place his eighteen subordinates strategically, about sixty yards apart and in a pattern which pretty well covered the perimeter of the field. Toward the end of his assignments he came to Tim Caveny. "You there, with the what-you-call-it dog."

"Labrador," Caveny said, tipping his hat respectfully, as his father had done in the old country when the laird spoke.

"Since we can't be sure a dog like that can hunt . . ."

"He can hunt."

The judge ignored this. "Take that corner," he said, and Tim wanted to complain that doves rarely came to that corner, but since he was on trial he kept his mouth shut, but he was most unhappy when he saw Jake Turlock receive one of the best positions.

Then everyone stopped talking, for down the road edging the field came a carriage driven by a black man. On the seat beside him sat a very old gentleman with a shotgun across his knees. This was Lyman Steed, owner of the field. He was eighty-seven years old and so frail that a stranger would have wondered how he could lift a gun, let alone shoot it. Behind him, eyes and ears alert, rode a large red Chesapeake.

The carriage came to a halt close to where Hathaway Steed was allocating the spots, and the black driver descended, unfolded a canvas chair and lifted the old man down into it. "Where do we sit today?" Steed asked in a high, quavering voice.

"Take him over by the big tree," Hathaway said, and the black man carried the chair and its contents to the spot indicated. There he scraped the ground with his foot, making a level platform, and on it he placed the owner of the farm and one of the best shots in this meet. "We's ready," the black man cried, and the judge gave

his last instructions: "If you see a dove that the men near you don't, call 'Mark!' Keep your dogs under control. And if the dove flies low, absolutely no shooting in the direction of the man left or right."

The men took their positions. It was half after one in the afternoon. The sun was high and warm; insects droned. The dogs were restless, but each stayed close to his master, and the men wondered whether there would be any doves, because on some days they failed to show.

But not today. From the woods came six doves, flying low in their wonderfully staggered pattern, now in this direction, now swooping in that. Jake Turlock, taken by surprise, fired and hit nothing. "Mark!" he shouted at the top of his voice. Tim Caveny fired and hit nothing. "Mark!" he bellowed. In swift, darting patterns the doves dived and swirled and twisted, and three other hunters fired at them, to no avail, but as the birds tried to leave the field old Lyman Steed had his gun waiting. With a splendid shot he hit his target, and his big Chesapeake leaped out before the bird hit the ground and retrieved it before the dove could even flutter. Bearing it proudly in his mouth, but not touching its flesh with his teeth, he trotted back, head high, to his master and laid the bird at the old man's feet.

"That's how it's done," Tim Caveny whispered to his Labrador.

There was a long wait and the hunters began to wonder if they would see any more doves, but Hathaway Steed, walking the rounds to police the action, assured each man as he passed, "We're going to see flocks."

He was right. At about two-thirty they started coming in. "Mark!" one hunter shouted as they passed him before he could fire. Jake Turlock was waiting and knocked one down, whereupon Hey-You leaped out into the open field, pounced on the fallen bird and brought it proudly back. Jake looked at Tim, but the Irishman kept his eyes on the sky. He did whisper to Lucifer, "Any dog can retrieve in an open field. Wait till one falls in the brambles."

On the next flight Tim got no chance to shoot, but Turlock did, and this time he hit a bird that had come over the field, heard the shooting and doubled back. This dove fell into brambles. "Fetch the dove!" Jake told his

THE AKC'S WORLD OF THE PURE-BRED DOG

Chesapeake, but the bushes were too thick. That bird was lost.

But now another dove flew into Tim's range, and when he fired, this one also fell into brambles. "Fetch the dove!" Tim said calmly, his heart aching for a good retrieve.

Lucifer plunged directly for the fallen bird but could not penetrate the thick and thorny briars. Unlike Turlock's Chesapeake, he did not quit, for he heard his master calling softly, "Circle, Luke! Circle!" And he ran in wide circles until he found a back path to the brambles. But again he was stopped, and again his master cried, "Circle, Luke!" And this time he found an entrance which allowed him to roam freely, but with so much ranging he had lost an accurate guide to the fallen bird. Still he heard his master's voice imploring, "Circle, Luke!" and he knew that this meant he still had a chance.

So in the depth of the bramble patch, but below the reach of the thorns, he ran and scrambled and clawed and finally came upon Caveny's bird. He gave a quiet *yup*, and when Tim heard this his heart expanded. Lucifer had passed his first big test, but on the way out of the patch the dog smelled another fallen bird, Turlock's, and he brought this one too.

When he laid the two doves at Tim's feet, the Irishman wanted to kneel and kiss his rough black head, but he knew that all the hunters in his area were watching, so in a manly way he patted the dog, then prepared for his moment of triumph.

It was a custom in dove shooting that if a hunter downed a bird which his dog could not retrieve and another man's dog did fetch it, the second hunter was obligated to deliver the dove to the man who had downed it. It was a nice tradition, for it allowed the second man to make a show of carrying the dove to its rightful owner while all the other hunters observed his act of sportsmanship. Implied in the gesture was the challenge: "My dog can retrieve and yours can't."

Proudly Tim Caveny walked the hundred-odd yards to where Jake Turlock was standing. Lucifer started to follow, but Tim cried sharply, "Stay!" and the dog obeyed. The other hunters took note of this, then watched as Tim gravely delivered the bird, but at this moment another hunter shouted, "Mark!" and a whole covey flew over.

Automatically Jake and Tim fired, and two birds fell. Jake's Hey-You was on the spot, of course, and proudly ran out to recover the dove his master had knocked down, but Lucifer was far distant from where his master had shot, yet he was so obedient to the earlier command, "Stay," that he did not move. But when Tim yelled, "Fetch the dove," he leaped off his spot, rushed directly to the fallen bird, and carried it not to where Tim was standing, but back to his assigned location.

The hunter next to Tim on the down side of the field called, "You got yourself a dog, Tim."

When Caveny returned to his location and saw the dove neatly laid beside his pouch, he desperately wanted to smother the dark beast with his affection; instead he said merely, "Good dog, Luke."

"Mark!" came the call and up went the guns.

The day was a triumph. Luke hunted in marshland as well as he had in brambles. He proved he had a soft mouth. He circled well in woods, and on the open field he was superb. And with it all he displayed the bland, sweet disposition of the Labradors and the Cavenys.

It was the tradition on these dove shoots for one member at the end of the day to provide refreshments. At quarter to five, religiously, the hunting ceased. The dogs were put back on leashes, and if the owners had come by wagon, were stowed in back while their masters ate cold duck and drank Baltimore beer. Turlock and Caveny, having come on foot, tied their dogs to trees, and as they did so the former muttered, "Doves ain't nothin', Caveny. It's what a dog does in ice that counts."

"Lucifer will handle ice," Tim said confidently.

"On the bay proper, my Chesapeake is gonna eat 'im up. Out there they got waves."

"Your Labrador looks like a breed to be proud of," old Lyman Steed said as the black servant carried him into position to share the duck.

"Possibilities," Judge Hathaway Steed said. "But we won't know till we see him after geese."

Each man complimented Tim on what he had accomplished with this strange dog, but each also predicted, "Probably won't be much on the bay. Hair's not thick enough."

Tim did not argue, but when he got Lucifer home he hugged him and gave him chicken livers, and whispered, "Lucifer, geese is just doves, grown bigger. You'll love the water, cold or not." During the whole dove season, during which this fine black dog excelled, Tim repeated his assurances: "You're gonna do the same with geese."

The test came in November. As the four men and their dogs holed up in a blind at the Turlock marshes, Jake reminded them, "Geese ain't so plentiful now. Can't afford any mistakes, man or dog." He was right. Once the Choptank and its sister rivers had been home for a million geese; now the population had diminished to less than four hundred thousand, and bagging them became more difficult. Jake, a master of the goose call, tried from dawn till ten in the morning to lure the big birds down, but failed. The hunters had a meager lunch, and toward dusk, when it seemed that the day was a failure, nine geese wheeled in, lowered the pitch of their wings, spread their feet and came right at the blind. Guns blazed, and before the smoke had cleared, Jake's Chesapeake had leaped out of the blind and with powerful swimming motions had retrieved the goose that his master had appeared to kill. Lucifer went into the water, too, but many seconds after Hey-You, and he was both splashy and noisy in making his retrieve of Tim's goose.

"Sure doesn't like cold water," Jake said contemptuously.

"Neither did yours, when he started," Tim said.

"A Chesapeake is born lovin' water, colder the better."

It became obvious to the hunters, after eight mornings in the blind, that while Tim Caveny's new dog was exceptional with doves on warm days, he left much to be desired as a real hunter in the only form of the sport that mattered—goose on water. He displayed a discernible reluctance to plunge into cold waves, and they began to wonder whether he would go into ice at all.

Talk at the store centered on his deficiencies: "This here Labrador is too soft. Can't hold a candle to a Chesapeake for hard work when it matters. You ask me, I think Caveny bought

hisse'f a loser." Some hunters told him this to his face.

Tim listened and said nothing. In his lifetime he had had four major dogs, all of them Chesapeakes, and he understood the breed almost as well as Jake Turlock did, but he had never owned a dog with the charm of Lucifer, the warmth, the love, and that meant something—"I come home, the room's bigger when that dog's in it."

"Point is," the men argued, "a huntin' dog oughtn't to be in a room in the first place. His job is outside."

"You don't know Lucifer. Besides, he's sired the best lot of pups in the region. This breed is bound to catch on."

The Patamoke hunters were a suspicious clan. The most important thing in their lives, more important than wife or church or political party, was the totality of the hunting season: "You got to have the right gun, the right mates, the right spot, the right eye for the target and, above all, the right dog. And frankly, I doubt the Labrador." The pups did not sell.

Tim had faith. He talked with Lucifer constantly, encouraging him to leap more quickly into the cold water. He showed what ice was like, and how the dog must break it with his forepaws to make a path for himself to the downed goose. Using every training trick the Choptank had ever heard of, he tried to bring this handsome dog along step by step.

He failed. In January, when real ice formed along the edges of the river, the men went hunting along the banks of the bay itself, and when Jake Turlock knocked down a beautiful goose, it fell on ice about two hundred yards from the blind—"Hey-You, get the bird!"

And the big Chesapeake showed what a marvelous breed he was by leaping into the free water, swimming swiftly to the edge of the ice, then breaking a way for himself right to the goose. Clutching the big bird proudly in his jaws, he plunged back into the icy water, pushed aside the frozen chunks and returned to the blind, entering it with a mighty, water-spraying leap.

"That's what I call a dog," Jake said proudly, and the men agreed.

17

Inside AKC

John Mandeville

The American Kennel Club is the largest animal registry in the world. Its two main functions are to register pure-bred dogs and to act as governing body for the sport of pure-bred dogs in the United States. A third large area of responsibility is educational—Communications and Special Services.

Registration

Registering pure-bred dogs—the maintenance of a Stud Book and the services associated with it—occupies 60 percent of AKC's 400 employees. Today AKC registers 125 different breeds—a section at the end of this chapter lists the first registered dog of each recognized breed. Each year more than one million new dogs are registered in the Stud Book, and more than 375,000 litters and 250,000 transfers of ownership are recorded.

In 1945 there were 147,707 dogs registered with the American Kennel Club and a combined total of 394 events—licensed and member all-breed and specialty Dog Shows, Obedience Trials, and Field Trials. The following table shows the dramatic growth since the end of World War II, necessitating the move, in 1964, from the American Woolen Building at 221 Fourth Avenue to the current handsome offices at 51 Madison Avenue in New York City.

YEAR	TOTAL REGISTRATIONS	TOTAL EVENTS
1950	251,812	2,878
1960	442,875	5,264
1970	1,056,225	7,063
1980	1,011,799	8,885

Reception room of the AKC's second headquarters at 55 Liberty Street, New York City. *A. C. Wilmerding*

Stud Book files at 221 Fourth Avenue, the AKC's fourth address.

The AKC's modern computer has taken over the Stud Book files.

Computer terminals provide instant Stud Book information to callers.

This growth also necessitated a change in 1973, from a manual system of registration using 3 x 5 file cards to a sophisticated computer system. The records of more than 10 million individual dogs and litters are now stored and maintained in AKC's master computer file. Computer equipment is also used by Show Operations for the approval of Show and Obedience Trial dates and judging panels, by the Certified Pedigree Department, by the *Gazette* for setting type for virtually all of the copy that appears in the magazine, and by the *Gazette* Circulation Department.

Award Medals for the U.S. Ses-
quicentennial Dog Show, Philadelphia, 1926 *(left)*, and from the AKC
Centennial Show, Philadelphia, 1984
(right).

The Certified Pedigree Department prepares three- and four-generation pedigrees of AKC registered dogs. Every dog on every pedigree is checked against AKC's master title file, so that the pedigree will show every Championship, Obedience, and Field Trial title earned by any dog on the pedigree as of the date of issue. This department issues over 100,000 pedigrees a year to serious breeders and owners interested in the ancestry of their dogs.

Communications and Special Services

The American Kennel Club provides many services to anyone interested in dogs, whether they are would-be new owners trying to decide on the best breed to buy or long-time students of pure-bred dogs doing historical research. Each year, AKC responds to more than 250,000 inquiries about pure-bred dogs.

Many of these inquiries are handled by AKC's Library, which contains more than 13,000 books and magazines and adds all new titles on *Canis familiaris* as they are published. The library has the largest collection of books and periodicals on dogs available to the public in the country.

AKC's official magazine, *Pure-Bred Dogs—American Kennel Gazette*, has appeared every month since January 1889 and is intended to serve both the newcomer to the world of pure-bred dogs and the long-established breeder and exhibitor as well. AKC's other two monthly publications are the *Stud Book Register*, which lists the names of all registered dogs and bitches that produce a litter for the first time, and *Show and Trial Awards* which carries the official results of all licensed Dog Shows, Obedience Trials, and Field Trials. AKC also publishes *The Complete Dog Book*, which has sold more than 1,250,000 copies since its first publication in 1929, and which includes the official breed standards by which all of the various breeds are judged, a brief history of each breed, and an extensive section on how to keep a dog healthy, happy, and well-behaved. It also carries a section on things to consider before buying a dog, AKC's advice being to think before buying, know your source, don't buy on impulse, *buy from a reputable breeder*.

From time to time, AKC produces films, primarily as educational and informational tools for dog clubs. The first two films were produced in the mid 1950s—*221* (AKC's address in New York at the time was 221 Fourth Avenue) and *Dog Shows and You*. Since 1973, some ten films have been produced, including *Gait: Observing Dogs in Motion*, which won the second highest award at the United States Industrial Film Festival.

AKC's support of basic scientific research for the benefit of dogs is one of the organization's most significant yet least known undertakings. Funding of such research was initiated by John C. Neff, who was a Board member and Executive Vice-President, in 1952, with a donation to Cornell's University's Research Laboratory for Diseases of Dogs. In more than thirty years since then, AKC has donated nearly a million dollars to research, including primary support of the breakthrough research into artificial insemination using frozen canine semen.

Charles A. T. O'Neill

The AKC's first library
at 221 Fourth Avenue.

The AKC's current library at 51 Madison Avenue, New York City.

EX LIBRIS

The AMERICAN
KENNEL CLUB

The AKC's bookplate, designed by Edwin Megargee.

P. B. EVERETT

Phyllis B. Everett was Secretary of the American Kennel Club from 1945 until her retirement in 1965 following an AKC career that spanned some 36 years.

It would be impossible to calculate the number of official AKC letters and documents that went out from her superbly efficient office bearing, as each did, the shortened signature of "P. B. Everett."

It can be said with certainty that thousands of dog breeders and participants in all phases of the sport of pure-bred dogs in the United States have Championship Certificates bearing her signature.

Interest in dogs is worldwide, and there are national kennel clubs comparable to the American Kennel Club in countries around the world. AKC's Foreign Department examines the registration papers issued by these other agencies for dogs imported to the United States to see whether they meet the requirements for registration in AKC's Stud Book. While the bulk of this activity involves dogs from Canada and Great Britain, the Foreign Department handles correspondence from every continent and more than thirty countries every year.

While the sport of dogs has shown substantial growth over the years, it is important to remember that the majority of AKC-registered dogs are not show dogs. They are for the most part household companions, and the business of breeding and selling dogs for the commercial pet market to meet the public demand has become a matter of considerable concern to serious breeders and to the American Kennel Club. John A. Lafore, Jr., former AKC President, recognized AKC's responsibility in this area and in 1973, set up AKC's Registration Inspection and Investigations Unit, which expends a continuing effort to combat abuses generated by the proliferation of the commercial pet industry.

Shows, Field Trials, Obedience Trials

From its inception, the principal role of the American Kennel Club has been to serve as governing body for the sport of dogs. Originally this meant only Dog Shows. Field Trials were not included until 1890. Obedience Trials were first approved in 1936.

The dog club is the basic unit of the sport in the United States. Thousands of clubs, recognized by the American Kennel Club, hold events under AKC rules. There are all-breed clubs, specialty clubs devoted to interests of a single breed, Obedience clubs with activities devoted to the training of dogs as companions to man, and Field Trial clubs. New clubs in all of these categories are constantly coming into existence. Before a new club is permitted to hold events in which credit toward AKC titles can be earned, it must go through a step-by-step accreditation process. A club must represent a reasonable concentration of dog

John C. Neff, an Irish Setter breeder, for over thirty-five years variously served the AKC as Delegate, Director, Executive Secretary, and Executive Vice President.

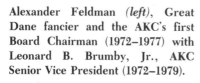

Alfred M. Dick, Dachshund fancier and AKC's first full-time President (1964–1968).

Alexander Feldman (left), Great Dane fancier and the AKC's first Board Chairman (1972–1977) with Leonard B. Brumby, Jr., AKC Senior Vice President (1972–1979).

John S. Ward, AKC Treasurer and Judge of all Obedience Classes.

LEONARD BRUMBY, SR.

Leonard Brumby, Sr., holds an important place in the history of the AKC, having become its first Field Representative in 1946. Prior to that time, clubs throughout the country held shows without the benefit of a hands-on AKC representative, and confusion and rancor over Rule interpretations was both common and inevitable. Len Brumby's fine example changed all that. His presence at shows across the nation, answering countless questions and settling disputes, brought a stability to the world of dog shows that remains the expected norm. Len Brumby was also founder and president of the Professional Handlers' Association and was executive secretary for Dogs for Defense during World War II.

interest in a given community. It must be democratically organized, holding regular meetings and regular elections of officers. Only after it has held a series of sanctioned events, events that do not give credit toward AKC titles, may it be considered for approval to hold licensed events.

The Show Plans Department assists clubs with all requirements that must be met prior to the holding of events. The dates for competitions and the names of persons submitted as judges for those events must be checked and approved. The sites must be cleared as adequate for the type and size of the event. In addition, Show Plans publishes and updates on an annual basis a 150-page *Dog Show Manual* containing suggestions, checklists, and other material to better enable clubs to cope with the numerous details that go into holding a quality Show or Obedience Trial.

After a Show or Obedience Trial is held, the results are forwarded to AKC's Show Records Department, where individual dog records are updated and where the records for each event as a whole are prepared for publication. When a dog's record indicates that it has met the requirements for a championship or other title, the appropriate certificate is issued. Each year more than 12,000 dogs earn Show Championships, more than 10,000 earn Obedience titles, and some 400 earn Tracking titles.

The Field Trial Plans and Field Trial Records Departments, smaller than Show Plans and Show Records, handle comparable details for field events in which dogs are tested under circumstances approximating hunting conditions. Field Trial Records issues more than 600 certificates to those dogs that have completed the requirements for a Field Championship or an Amateur Field Championship.

An AKC Field Representative attends virtually every all-breed Show in the country and a large percentage of the specialty shows, Obedience Trials, and Field Trials. These representatives serve both as observers and, when necessary, as advisors on Rules and Regulations. Their general aim is to facilitate the smooth running of these events.

Hon. William H. Timbers, a senior judge of the U.S. Court of Appeals and long-time Norwegian Elkhound enthusiast, was elected AKC Board Chairman in 1982.

Haworth Hoch, AKC Board Chairman (1979–1982) and respected Dog Show Judge.

Left to right: John A. Lafore, Jr., AKC President, 1968–1978, Alexander Feldman, and William F. Stifel, AKC President (1978–).

PRESIDENTS OF THE AKC

Major James M. Taylor	1884–1885	Charles T. Inglee	1932–1933
Elliot Smith	1885–1887	Russell H. Johnson, Jr.	1933–1940
William H. Child	1887–1888	Dudley P. Rogers	1940–1951
August Belmont, Jr.	1888–1916	William E. Buckley	1951–1968
Hollis H. Hunnewell	1916–1921	Alfred M. Dick	1968–1971
Howard Willets	1921–1923	John A. Lafore, Jr.	1971–1978
John E. de Mund	1923–1932	William F. Stifel	1978–

EXECUTIVE VICE-PRESIDENTS OF THE AKC

Charles T. Inglee	1933–1941	John A. Lafore, Jr.	1968–1971
Henry D. Bixby	1942–1951	William F. Stifel	1976–1978
John C. Neff	1951–1964	Charles A. T. O'Neill	1978–
Alfred M. Dick	1964–1968		

CHAIRMEN OF THE BOARD OF THE AKC

Alexander Feldman	1972–1977	Haworth F. Hoch	1979–1982
August Belmont	1977–1979	William H. Timbers	1982–

The judges at Shows and Obedience Trials held under AKC Rules are licensed by AKC's Board of Directors. Judging is at the very heart of any competitive sport, and obtaining approval to judge Dog Shows or Obedience Trials is no casual proposition. Applicants are required to fill out a comprehensive form, outlining their background in dogs. They must take a procedural test, and be interviewed, and must also have notice of their applications published in the *Gazette* for the purpose of eliciting comment from the dog public. The Judges Department processes these applications and maintains the files of almost 3,000 active Dog Show and Obedience Trial judges.

Field Trial competition is always judged by at least two judges, and a club may submit for approval as judges the names of any persons in good standing with the American Kennel Club. However, for the majority of Field Trials there is a requirement that the two judges between them have a combined total of past judging experience that meets a specified minimum. In other words, a relatively new judge will always officiate at a Trial with a judge who has more extensive experience in judging that particular kind of Trial.

The Dog Museum of America

The tradition of the dog in art (as Shirlee Kalstone chronicles in an earlier section of this book) dates back thousands of years; there is now a substantial and distinguished body of books and art on canine themes. In order to broaden public appreciation of these treasures, the American Kennel Club in June 1980 established the American Kennel Club Foundation, the primary goal of which was to set up a national repository for books and art objects relating to the dog.

The Foundation moved quickly toward the establishment of The Dog Museum of America, the first public repository for the display and study of canine art. The Museum formally opened, in space provided for it on the main floor of AKC headquarters at 51 Madison Avenue, in September 1982.

What brought urgency to the establishment of The Dog Museum of America was the realization that over and over again important works of canine art were lost to the public and the world of dog lovers when the long-established collections were dispersed through auctions and dealers. A number of substantial collections have been broken up and sold in this way. The most vital challenge facing The Dog Museum of America is to preserve a sense of heritage and continuity in the dog world. The activities of the Museum will serve to introduce coming generations to all aspects of the sport.

It is fitting that The Dog Museum of America—a major undertaking to preserve for all time the history of man and dog—should mark the closing of AKC's first hundred years. As The American Kennel Club enters its second hundred years, it strives to preserve and promote in all ways the best interests of pure-bred dogs.

At preview opening of The Dog Museum of America, Director William Secord (*left*) admires a promised gift painting along with donor Nancy Lindsay and Dog Museum of America President William F. Stifel.

AKC Registrable Breeds

For each breed, the country of origin is listed first, then the date that the first dog was registered with the AKC, its name, and its registration number. Note that "Adonis," the English Setter, is Number 1.

Group 1—Sporting Dogs

BRITTANYS (breed name changed from Brittany Spaniels on September 1, 1982)
France   1934   Edir Du Mesnil   949896

POINTERS
Spain and England   1878   Ace of Spades   1187

POINTERS (GERMAN SHORTHAIRED)
Germany   1930   Greif V.D. Fliegerhalde   723642

POINTERS (GERMAN WIREHAIRED)
Germany   1959   Eiko Vom Schultenhof   S-963376

RETRIEVERS (CHESAPEAKE BAY)
United States   1878   Sunday   1408

RETRIEVERS (CURLY-COATED)
England   1924   Knysna Conjurer   398399

RETRIEVERS (FLAT-COATED)
England   1915   Sand Bridge Jester   190223

RETRIEVERS (GOLDEN)
England   1925   Lomberdale Blondin   492685

RETRIEVERS (LABRADOR)
Newfoundland   1917   Brocklehirst Floss   223339

SETTERS (ENGLISH)
England   1878   Adonis   1

SETTERS (GORDON)
Scotland   1878   Bank   793

SETTERS (IRISH)
Ireland   1878   Admiral   534

SPANIELS (AMERICAN WATER)
United States   1940   Tidewater Teddy   A-426838

SPANIELS (BRITTANY) See BRITTANYS

SPANIELS (CLUMBER)
Probably England   1878   Bustler   1353

SPANIELS (COCKER)
England   1878   Capt   1354

SPANIELS (ENGLISH COCKER)
England   (Separated from Cocker Spaniel in 1946)

SPANIELS (ENGLISH SPRINGER)
England   1910   Denne Lucy   142641

SPANIELS (FIELD)
England   1894   Colehill Rufus   33395

SPANIELS (IRISH WATER)
Ireland   1878   Bob   1352

SPANIELS (SUSSEX)
England   1878   Jack (Alias Toby)   1363

SPANIELS (WELSH SPRINGER)
Wales   1914   Faircroft Bob   185938

VIZSLAS
Hungary   1960   Rex Z. Arpadvar   SA-63201

WEIMARANERS
Germany   1943   Adda v. Schwarzen Kamp   646165

WIREHAIRED POINTING GRIFFONS (originally registered as Russian Setters)
Holland   1887   Zolette   6773

Group 2—Hounds

AFGHAN HOUNDS
Afghanistan   1926   Tezin   544928

BASENJIS
Africa   1944   Phemister's Bois   A-738970

BASSET HOUNDS
France   1885   Bouncer   3234

BEAGLES
England   1885   Blunder   3188

BLACK AND TAN COONHOUNDS
England   1945   Grand Mere Big Rock Molly   A-898800

BLOODHOUNDS
Constantinople   1885   Carsdoc   3237

BORZOIS (originally registered as Russian Wolfhounds)
Russia   1891   Princess Irma   20716

DACHSHUNDS
Germany   1885 Dash   3223

FOXHOUNDS (AMERICAN)
England/United States   1886 Lady Stewart   4320

FOXHOUNDS (ENGLISH)
England   1909 Auditor   129533

GREYHOUNDS
Egypt   1885 Baron Walkeen   3241

HARRIERS
England   1885 Jolly   3236

IBIZAN HOUNDS
Egypt   1978 Asuncion   HC-522350

IRISH WOLFHOUNDS
Ireland   1897 Ailbe   45994

NORWEGIAN ELKHOUNDS
Norway   1913 Koik   170389

OTTER HOUNDS
England   1910 Hartland Statesman   135334

RHODESIAN RIDGEBACKS
South Africa   1955 Tchaika of Redhouse   H-520551

SALUKIS
Egypt   1929 Jinniyat of Grevel   674570

SCOTTISH DEERHOUNDS
Scotland   1886 Bonnie Robin   4345

WHIPPETS
England   1888 Jack Dempsey   9804

Group 3—Working Dogs

AKITAS
Japan   1972 Akita Tani's Terukoshi   WC-292650

ALASKAN MALAMUTES
Alaska   1935 Rowdy of Nome   998426

BERNESE MOUNTAIN DOGS
Switzerland   1937 Quell v. Tiergarten   A-156752

BOXERS
Germany   1904 Arnulf Grandenz   78043

BULLMASTIFFS
England   1934   Fascination of Felons Fear   914895

DOBERMAN PINSCHERS
Germany   1908   Doberman Intelectus   122650

GIANT SCHNAUZERS
Germany   1930   Bella v. Fuchspark Potzhauss   721736

GREAT DANES
Germany   1887   Don Caesar   6046

GREAT PYRENEES
*Central Asia
   or Siberia*   1933   Blanchette   866751

KOMONDOROK
Hungary   1937   Andrashazi Dorka   A-199838

KUVASZOK
Hungary   1931   Tamar v. Wuermtal   791292

MASTIFFS
England   1885   Bayard   3271

NEWFOUNDLANDS
Newfoundland   1886   Fly   4447

ROTTWEILERS
Italy (Roman era) 1931   Stina v. Felsenmeer   805867

ST. BERNARDS
Swiss Alps   1885   Chief   3280

SAMOYEDS
Arctic   1906   Moustan of Argenteau   102896

SIBERIAN HUSKIES
Northeastern Asia 1930   Fairbanks Princess Chena   758529

STANDARD SCHNAUZERS
Germany   1904   Norwood Victor   77886

Group 4—Terriers

AIREDALE TERRIERS
England   1888   Pin   9087

AMERICAN STAFFORDSHIRE TERRIERS (until 1972 registered as Staffordshire Terriers)
England   1936   Wheeler's Black Dinah   A-86066

AUSTRALIAN TERRIERS
Australia   1960 Canberra Kookaburra C.D.X.   R-258126

BEDLINGTON TERRIERS
England   1886 Ananian   4475

BORDER TERRIERS
Scotland and England   1930 Netherbyers Ricky   719372

BULL TERRIERS
England   1885 Nellie II   3308

CAIRN TERRIERS
Scotland   1913 Sandy Peter Out of the West   173555

DANDIE DINMONT TERRIERS
Scotland   1886 Bonnie Britton   4472

FOX TERRIERS
England   1885 Cricket   3289

IRISH TERRIERS
Ireland   1885 Aileen   3306

KERRY BLUE TERRIERS
Ireland   1922 Brian of Muchia   349159

LAKELAND TERRIERS
England   1934 Egton What a Lad of Howtown   938424

MANCHESTER TERRIERS
England   1886 Gypsy   4485

MINIATURE SCHNAUZERS
Germany   1926 Schnapp v. Dornbusch of Hitofa   551063

NORFOLK TERRIERS (in 1979, the AKC recognized the "Drop Ear" Norwich
                      Terrier as the Norfolk Terrier, a separate breed)
England   1979 Bar Sinister Little Ruffian   RA-47550

NORWICH TERRIERS
England   1936 Witherslack Sport   A-58858

SCOTTISH TERRIERS
Scotland   1885 Prince Charlie   3310

SEALYHAM TERRIERS
Wales   1911 Harfats Pride   151623

SKYE TERRIERS
Scotland   1887 Romach   6184

SOFT-COATED WHEATEN TERRIERS
Ireland   1973   Holmenocks Gramachree C.D.   RA-44600

STAFFORDSHIRE BULL TERRIERS
England   1974   Tinkinswood Imperial   RA-161150

WELSH TERRIERS
Wales   1888   T'Other   9171

WEST HIGHLAND WHITE TERRIERS
Scotland   1908   Talloch   116076

Group 5—Toys

AFFENPINSCHERS
Germany   1936   Nollie v. Anwander   A-107711

BRUSSELS GRIFFONS
Belgium   1910   Dolley's Biddy   137219

CHIHUAHUAS
Mexico   1904   Midget   82291

ENGLISH TOY SPANIELS
England   1886   Mildmay Park Beauty   4456

ITALIAN GREYHOUNDS
Italy   1886   Lilly   4346

JAPANESE CHIN (until 1977 registered as Japanese Spaniels)
China   1888   Jap   9216

MALTESE
Malta   1888   Topsy   12056

MINIATURE PINSCHERS
Germany   1925   Asta von Sandreuth   454601

PAPILLONS
Spain and Italy   1915   Joujou   192539

PEKINGESE
China   1906   Rascal   95459

POMERANIANS
Iceland   1888   Dick   10776

PUGS
China   1885   George   3286

SHIH TZU
China   1969   Choo Lang of Telota   TA-573228

SILKY TERRIERS
Australia   1959   Winsome Beau Ideal   T-610051

YORKSHIRE TERRIERS
England   1885   Belle   3307

Group 6—Non-Sporting Dogs

BICHON FRISES
Canary Islands   1972   Sha-Bob's Nice Girl Missy   NS-077900

BOSTON TERRIERS
United States   1893   Hector   28814

BULLDOGS
England   1886   Bob   4982

CHOW CHOWS
China   1903   Yen How   74111

DALMATIANS
Austria   1888   Bessie   10519

FRENCH BULLDOGS
France   1898   Guguss II   49705

KEESHONDEN
Holland   1930   Bella v. Trennfeld   751187

LHASA APSOS
Tibet   1935   Empress of Kokonor   987979

POODLES
Germany and France   1887   Czar   7597

SCHIPPERKES
Belgium   1904   Snowball   83461

TIBETAN TERRIERS
Tibet   1973   Amanda Lamleh of Kalai   NS-107000

Group 7—Herding Dogs

AUSTRALIAN CATTLE DOGS
Australia   1980   Glen Iris Boomerang C.D.X.   WE-507650

BEARDED COLLIES
Central Europe/England   1976   Cannamoor Cartinka   WD-439250

BELGIAN MALINOIS (registered as Belgian Sheepdogs until 1959)
Belgium

BELGIAN SHEEPDOGS
Belgium   1912 Rumford Dax   160405

BELGIAN TERVUREN (registered as Belgian Sheepdogs until 1959)
Belgium

BOUVIERS DES FLANDRES
France   1931 Hardix   780160

BRIARDS
France   1928 Dauphine de Montjoye   635613

COLLIES
Scotland   1885 Black Shep   3249

GERMAN SHEPHERD DOGS
Germany   1908 Queen of Switzerland   115006

OLD ENGLISH SHEEPDOGS
England   1888 Champion of Winkleigh   9252

PULIK
Hungary   1936 Torokvesz Sarika   A-107734

SHETLAND SHEEPDOGS
Shetland Islands   1911 Lord Scott   148760

WELSH CORGIS (CARDIGAN)
England   1935 Blodwen of Robinscroft   965012

WELSH CORGIS (PEMBROKE)
Flemish Belgium/England   1934 Little Madam   939536

Italicized numbers indicate illustrations